The Bridge of Deaths

(Revised Edition)

M.C.V. Egan

The Bridge of Deaths

(Revised Edition)

M.C.V. Egan

© M.C.V. Egan 2014

Copyright 2014 M. C. V. Egan

Published by Introspective Press

ISBN-13: 978-0692267738

ISBN-10: 0692267735

The Author is M. C. V. Egan and is the copyright holder.

Cover Design by Daz Smith

DEDICATION

WITH GRATITUDE TO ARCHIVISTS EVERYWHERE;

THE MEN AND WOMEN WHO SO CAREFULLY

GUARD, FILE, AND STORE INFORMATION FOR US ALL.

ESPECIALLY TO THE FIRST AMONG THEM TO HELP ME,

WHO SADLY DID NOT LIVE TO SEE THE FINISHED STORY.

MR. FRED HUNTLEY, MBE 1923–2000

CONSULTANT ARCHIVIST BRITISH AIRWAYS

M. C. V. Egan

INDEX

The Bridge of Deaths...ii

DEDICATION 3

Acknowledgements...7

INTRODUCTION 10

CHAPTER ONE - BILL..15

CHAPTER TWO – MAGGIE 21

CHAPTER THREE – BILL & MAGGIE...29

CHAPTER FOUR – THE MUNICH PACT 43

CHAPTER FIVE – CATALINA 52

CHAPTER SIX – WETTING THE BED...58

CHAPTER SEVEN – MEANWHILE in FLORIDA 64

CHAPTER EIGHT – FACING THE FACTS 71

CHAPTER NINE – CONNECTING ACROSS THE POND 79

CHAPTER TEN – PARENTS & FRIENDS 83

CHAPTER ELEVEN – PSYCHICS 88

CHAPTER TWELVE – TRUST 92

CHAPTER THIRTEEN – MORE PSYCHICS 97

CHAPTER FOURTEEN – WHAT IS IN A NUMBER? 103

CHAPTER FIFTEEN – REACHING OUT...114

CHAPTER SIXTEEN – APART..120

CHAPTER SEVENTEEN – CONTAGIOUS OBSSESION 131

CHAPTER EIGHTEEN – CAREFUL COMPARISSONS....................................138

CHAPTER NINETEEN – LIGHTING WICKS or THE WILD GOOSE CHASE 146

CHAPTER TWENTY – SKYPE & WINE..159

CHAPTER TWENTY-ONE – THE PLANE..169

CHAPTER TWENTY-TWO –THE FIRE 182

CHAPTER TWENTY- THREE – JACK SINCLAIR'S OBSERVATIONS & THE AUTOPSY DISSECTED 187

CHAPTER TWENTY-FOUR – UNTAGLING WHO IS WHO 194

CHAPTER TWENTY-FIVE – TEQUILA..205

CHAPTER TWENTY-SIX – HOMECOMING 211

CHAPTER TWENTY-SEVEN – PRIVATE HYPNOTHERAPY 220

CHAPTER TWENTY-EIGHT –CONTAGIOUS ENERGY.................................236

CHAPTER TWENTY-NINE – BODY NUMBER ONE......................................252

CHAPTER THIRTY – THE DEVIL IS IN THE DETAILS 268

CHAPTER THIRTY-ONE – SYNDIKUS..276

CHAPTER THIRTY-TWO – MORE QUESTIONS THAN ANSWERS................283

CHAPTER THIRTY-THREE– THE BRITISH MP 286

CHAPTER THIRTY-FOUR – *THE LONDON TIMES* 297

CHAPTER THIRTY-FIVE – SECOND REGRESSION 307

CHAPTER THIRTY-SIX – VIDEO TAPE..315

CHAPTER THIRTY-SEVEN – CAN OF WORMS?..321

CHAPTER THIRTY-EIGHT – BODIES FOUR AND FIVE................................333

CHAPTER THIRTY-NINE – THE TRUTH IS LIBERATING............................354

CHAPTER FORTY – THE FINAL CALL...370

EPILOUGUE LONDON ~ SUMMER 2012 386

APPENDIX A ~ Store, keep or sell? 394

APPENDIX B ~ *THE LONDON TIMES* ANTHONY CROSSLEY 402

Acknowledgements

In the original book, I had several pages of acknowledgements; in this one, I want to spare the reader but will add my huge list of acknowledgements on my website www.thebridgeofdeaths.com. Every archive I used is credited in the bibliography. I also included the books of anyone who helped me.

To all at the British Airways Heritage Collection, in Harmondsworth, Middlesex. (020) 8562 5777 or (202) 8562 5737. Special thanks to Keith Hayward, Jim Davies, Jack Ligertwood, and Fred Huntley; the latter for making me copy by hand all of the documents in the AW1-1869 file and for saying, "Remember, Catalina, it was 1939, and sabotage was not a word used lightly, as it is today."

The staff that was so helpful at the Danish National Archives in Copenhagen.

Torben Jessen, Chief of Police, Nykoøbing F. (2002), as well as all of the staff at Nykøbing F. police station.

Henning Neerup Rasmussen, Sheriff of Praesto, Denmark (2000), for his interest in history and for his help finding the diver's daughters.

Mr. Bill Taylor and the New England Air Museum in Windsor Locks, Connecticut, who built a Lockheed Electra 10A, piece by piece. I am grateful to you and your "crew" for allowing me to measure and look at every detail of the Lockheed Electra

10A, for answering all my questions, and for telling me not to quit. I would also like to thank the staff at the New England Air Museum in Windsor Locks, Connecticut, for helping me with follow-up questions.

The staff at Wimberly Library at Florida Atlantic University in Boca Raton, Florida during 1995, 2003 and 2001 for all their help.

Mr. Tim Sherwood, author of Coming in to Land: The Steamboat Revolution, for the various days at the British Airways Archives together, where you so generously shared your opinions on the G-AESY. Thank you for the list of newspapers to search at Colindale, for the nice correspondence through the years, but most of all, for not laughing when I explained my use of unconventional sources and for saying, "I do suppose it is important to keep an open mind."

In this new edition, I must thank author Christoph Fischer for his invaluable input on how to simplify, as well as Ally Bishop of Upgrade Your Story for her magic at proofreading.

Cover designer Daz Smith, in Bath, UK, created not only a book cover I absolutely love, but offered his guidance in other resources and was most generous with his time and knowledge. The photographer Matt Sturgess of 4th Avenue Photography in Delray Beach, Florida, carefully took the time to photograph the two watches in a way I could have never imagined.

I also want to thank every reader and reviewer of the previous edition. Their support and input has been so valuable to me; amongst those, Wanda Hartzenberg and her amazing group. Some reviewers not affiliated with review groups have amazed me with their support, including Terry Tipton and Mary Anthony.

Worldwide, the support of other authors and bloggers has been such a special experience for me. I wish to thank them all, but the list would also be absurdly long. It is easy to find them, however, as guests on my blogs, where I enjoy helping other authors promote their own work.

'Somewhere, something incredible is waiting to be known.'

Carl Sagan

1934–1996

American astronomer, writer, and scientist

INTRODUCTION

From The New York Times, August 16th 1939

Two Standard Oil Men Killed in Plane Crash; British M.P. Also Is a Victim in Denmark.

Special Cable to THE NEW YORK TIMES. August 16, 1939

COPENHAGEN, Denmark, Aug. 15.--Samuel J. Simonton of Allentown, Pa., and C.A. Casteillo, a Mexican, both representatives of the Standard Oil Company of New Jersey, and Anthony C. Crossley, a member of the British Parliament, were among five persons killed in a plane crash in Denmark today.

The British Airways Ltd. airplane in the above article was the G-AESY, a Lockheed Electra 10A from British Airways Ltd. It is one of several airlines that merged to create British Airways (BOAC) that we know today. British Airways Ltd. (BAL) ceased to exist shortly after that plane crash. Of the two Standard Oil men killed, Cesar Agustin Castillo (his name was misspelled by The New York Times) was my maternal grandfather.

My journey began when, for the first time, I was able to see the 1939 file for the G-AESY. It was stored in the British Airways archives near Heathrow (the archives have since moved).

In January of 1993, the archivist in charge was Mr. Fred Huntley, who, when he found the file, was very surprised, as it was his opinion that BAL was not their "direct ancestry."

"Our direct ancestry lies with Imperial Airways, and in 1939, British Airways Ltd. was to a great extent, a competitor. Although Imperial and British Airways Ltd. came together when BOAC was formed, we inherited very little archive material from British Airways Ltd." On that very cold day outside London, 1993, after asking me a few questions about my interest in the file and understanding my curiosity about my grandfather's death, and especially why it had been called "a mystery that would probably never be solved," he handed me the file and said, "Can of worms you are about to open, young lady."

Several stumbling blocks, not the least of which was my absolute lack of knowledge about world history in 1939 (today, it is only slightly better), I published the first edition of The Bridge of Deaths. I used a combination of conventional and unconventional sources, ranging from archives, newspapers, history books, as well as psychics and past life regressions.

Before the disappearance of the Malaysian Air 370 flight I was often asked how someone devotes two decades in research. In my case the bodies and plane were of course recovered but the world events in 1939 left family members with damaged belongings, in our case an urn full of ashes and many questions with no real answers.

The only entirely fictional characters in this book are Maggie, her parents, and her friends. Maggie came to me after a group past-life regression last September, when a pretty young woman, who looked a little like the newspaper photos of the pilot's wife, shared what she had "seen" in her past-life regression. What she described was similar to a regression I had experienced many years before. This made me think that by creating a fictional character out of the pilot's wife, I could further detach my private life from the story. In addition, a gentleman who experienced the past life regressions – very similar to Bill's – has asked to remain anonymous, so while Bill is a fictional character, he is inspired by a real person.

In the last few years, I have found people related to the story; some are very open, while others are not. In this 75th anniversary of the crash, I simplified the story while keeping all of the information intact by adding appendices and summarizing the information in the narrative, as well as by doing away with my numerous footnotes. The original version might still be a favorite for history buffs; whereas, this edition should be an easier read.

In February of 2011, I wrote: "Today, we as a world hold our breath while we hope and wait to see if the changes in the Middle East will be less violent than the changes other countries have experienced in the past." So, sadly, today in 2014, we are well aware that the changes have included so much violence and instability affecting the world at large.

When I said good-bye to Maggie, the wonderful young woman who believes war, all war, to be inexcusable, I felt like I was losing that piece of myself that could see all things as possible. I have even more hope in people all over the world who identify with Maggie--a pacifist who is willing to search and eager to learn about war and history. My hope stems from the reactions of readers that through social media I have gotten to know. Inasmuch as my hope for peace and harmony in the world has increased since February 2011, I feel I am no longer able to write about peace through a character as full of light a Maggie. I can only imagine that if I wrote her today, I would give her life more conflict and perhaps, pain. I think that is because since I wrote this story, we have all seen so much suffering through natural and man-made situations.

M.C.V. Egan

August 15, 2014

CHAPTER ONE - BILL

He perceived himself to be a sensible man. He surrounded himself with facts and numbers. Those who worked and interacted with him saw him as a levelheaded, reasonable, and credible individual. He was a man of logic and common sense. And aside from a handful of therapists, no one knew him, not wholly.

At this point in time, he had exhausted all sensible, reasonable, credible, traditional, levelheaded, common sense-based, and rational options to solve his problem. He now found himself open to the possibility of the unreasonable, incredible, irrational, implausible, and illogical. It could even be said that he was open to the possibility of the absurd and the ridiculous.

He functioned and lived well enough. To be sure, he functioned and lived better than most. And until now, this had been acceptable, a reasonable way of living. But now this was no longer the case, and at least in part, this was due to his age. He was now past the age of thirty, and he began to have a strong desire for a family of his own. The stress of such desires could also be a contributing factor that was aggravating his problem.

His logical mind made him fully aware of one thing, and that was the type of woman he wanted to share his life with: she was not going to settle for "enough." It is also probably important to note here that although he did not realize it, he was by all accounts a hopeless romantic.

Now that he was an accomplished success in his chosen field and in a financially stable situation, he felt a need to fulfill other aspects of his life. As was mentioned before, like so many men past the age of thirty, he sought to find a partner in life. It was not a particular physical type he imagined, for he found (as most men do) all pretty women attractive. The list of requirements for the perfect woman was more along the lines of an educational and socioeconomic nature. And, of course, he required that she have mental stability.

His problems seemed, as so many things in life, not to be fair. Fortunately, he was not one to wallow in self-pity. He knew that enough effort and resources had been spent on various traditional medicines and therapies to try to solve his problem. He had also indulged in the untraditional recreational drug and alcohol escapism cure, as some do in youth. None of the aforementioned had worked, not in the long term.

He had originally sought hypnosis to learn relaxation and control techniques. The first hypnosis session taught him how to apply relaxation techniques. In that session, he learned that while under hypnosis he was always ultimately in control. He quickly learned that he could choose to stop the session at any time. He could do this by simply opening his eyes.

The second session was quite a different story; it brought back his worst nightmare with such clarity that he had a strong physical reaction. He started moving his arms and legs in such a way that he unfortunately somehow hit the psychologist and gave the poor man a rather nasty black eye. The session was interrupted before he tasted the salty water of the cold sea and saw the bridge (that part was always in his nightmare).

With an icepack held to his face, the therapist warned him that a certain door to his subconscious had been opened, and that he might start having the dream more vividly than he had experienced in the past. He could not imagine that his dream would feel any more real than it already did. The therapist also stated that a problem existing for seventeen years could hardly be solved overnight.

Inasmuch as he accepted that the therapy might work, he had begun to develop a level of distrust of his doctor. Frankly, he had a strong dislike for the man and felt that the therapist made him feel inferior. The doctor was pushing, trying to take him to places in his mind that he was not ready to visit. And with regard to what he saw in his dreams, the therapist had discussed certain beliefs he might consider as a possibility for his problems. These beliefs were such that most in a world of facts and numbers would find hard to digest.

He did realize that his first trip to Europe as a teenager with his school had been the beginning of his unpleasant dreams. The therapist called that the trigger. The trouble had begun with nightmares, but those had grown into other problems. Aside from the trigger, the doctor also spoke of layers of trauma acquired afterwards. These problems had created obstacles in his life.

At first, the transfer to London had been a feather in his cap, a desired jump up the ladder to reach his career goals. As the weeks passed, he felt more and more uncomfortable. Here in London, he felt this "problem" was interrupting the way he liked to function in his life and in his work.

This trigger, according to the therapist, bridged who he had been (in a past life) with who he was now. This principle of past lives was not a tangible idea that he could relate to. If he needed to believe in reincarnation at all, he needed facts that made it seem plausible.

The dreams continued to haunt him. They started out in different ways but always ended the same: the same lettering on the wings and on the side of the aircraft; the taste of salty, cold water in his mouth; the anxious feeling of loneliness and apprehension; and, these days, the inevitability of awakening to a wet bed, and the frustrating and unpleasant feeling that he had no control over this.

It was his dislike for the therapist that had introduced him to past-life regression, coupled with the embarrassment about the black eye he had given him, that made Bill seek elsewhere for answers on his own. He had to tackle the problem, as he had a fear of losing all that he had accomplished: the steady climb up a corporate ladder—although, in his case, it was more of a fancy marble staircase. This had been accomplished through hard work and an extensive and expensive Ivy League education.

Seeking to understand past lives was the very reason he found himself in one of London's finest (if not, the finest) bookstores that had survived the bad economy and competition from Amazon and other online sources. It was there at Foyles bookstore that he held a book from an impressive source, which explained why such an unlikely and illogical type of therapy might actually work.

CHAPTER TWO – MAGGIE

It was the excuse of searching for the perfect birthday gift for her mother that placed her at the same book section at Foyles on Charing Cross Road. From the moment she saw the tall, slender man walking down the street, she felt that she needed to follow him. Maggie liked the store and shopped there often. She had been raised with all that is unlikely, unconventional, and supernatural (perhaps even magical). When she was a child, her world was that of fairies, ghosts, wishes, and the power of crystals and planets. She was taught that answers were to be found in round circles called astrology charts, and that there were many people in the world who were psychic and could foretell the future. Although that world was an appealing world, it was inevitable that Maggie, as so many teenagers do, would rebel against the beliefs she was raised with and seek other philosophies.

She experimented with various traditional religions and belief systems that existed to fill in the voids felt by those lacking any sort of faith. She found that although she liked many traditional religions and appreciated what they stood for, it was indeed Buddhism that made her feel the most complete. Maggie was, for all intents and purposes, an illogical, whimsical, adventuresome, and happy young woman. She slept soundly and lived a very complete life.

The philosophies of acceptance by which she lived her life made her compatible with most people. She had a nice relationship with her mother, a Danish astrologer, and her father, a successful English businessman who was content to receive a little guidance from the planets. (If anyone objected to this, he happily pointed out that it had worked for Ronald Reagan.) Maggie often read the books her mother spoke about, and every once in a while, she even joined her mother in some new age ritual or other.

She was pretty, and more often than not, men approached her. Experience had taught her that many men worth talking to could be shy and sometimes needed to be approached, though she couldn't remember having done it before. With the confidence that is often exhibited by very pretty women, she was not deterred in the least by his surprised reaction to her smile as she discovered him in the bookstore.

"So, which of the women in your life recommended that book to you? Was it your mum or your girlfriend?"

She was indeed pretty, and inasmuch as he was instantly attracted to her, it was not in a purely physical way. Someday, as their love story flourished, she would explain to him that when two souls from the past meet, they recognize each other. This happens in love stories, to parents when they first encounter the eyes of their newborn, and to friends as well as enemies.

As so many lovers do, when they first met, neither one of them spoke the absolute truth. If they had known where this would lead, both of them might have run out of the bookstore. But they both chose to stay, and so on a cold winter day in January of 2010, when the world was mourning the passing of so many souls in Haiti, their love story began.

He smiled back and answered her question. "Why would it have to be a woman? Why couldn't a man recommend it?"

"Oh, I see. You are an American."

"No, Canadian, actually."

"Same difference. Perhaps in America or Canada, a man other than the author would recommend Many Lives, Many Masters. But here in England, well, it would have to be a girlfriend, probably on her grand quest as to how you are soul mates eternally destined to be together. Or maybe it would be a middle-aged mum who just discovered Dr. Brian Weiss." She gestured to the author's name."So, it is that, or you have some sort of existential crisis that led you to find the book on your own. So, mum or girlfriend?"

"Hmmm, let me see. My mother prefers to pray and attend church. I don't have a girlfriend, and it was the medical background of the guy who wrote the book that impressed me. So, maybe I do fall into the existential crisis category."

Her beautiful eyes widened."Existential crisis it is then, but if you seek impressive credentials in past-life therapy, you might want to read this book, Other Lives, Other Selves. Tell me, what triggered your belief in past lives?"

"Belief! I would not call it belief. Rather, possibility. I've come to realize that strange things happen."

"You know, once you read that book, you will believe. In life, there are certain doorways that once you cross them, they will forever change you. And you might also resolve your existential crisis. What you will definitely find is that women love to sleep with men who search for depth through such beliefs."

So in that cold European winter when some in the world denied global warming, he lay in bed, holding her.

He could not imagine a less likely place to have encountered the perfect girl – in the self-help section at a bookstore. Her laughter and smiling eyes were contagious. He was ready to settle down, and she might be the one, even if that involved accepting some very unlikely ideas that she held. There was the most extraordinary feeling of comfort in simply being with her.

Maggie had to laugh; she thought he'd be a quick and fun adventure, one that she would soon get out of her system. But this yuppie geek, as it turned out, was surprisingly special from the very first moment. This could be far more than a casual adventure.

Bill had not spoken to anyone about his problems. Not anyone other than doctors or therapists. Maggie worked as a counselor to young children. She was trained to ask just the right questions to make people talk. Bill was used to carefully giving only the information he wanted to offer in business and in his private life. He sometimes caught himself telling Maggie much more than what he thought was safe.

She thought that she knew just how to pry and could tell he was holding back. This, of course, made him all the more interesting.

Their love story grew and expanded. Maggie usually led, and Bill followed. They enjoyed the typical things new couples enjoy, such as going to restaurants, the cinema, shops, and museums. Sometimes, if the winter weather allowed, they went for long walks. Before Bill met Maggie, he had spent all his time in London buried in his work, with his colleagues at the gym, or finding ways to run away from the dreams and thoughts that haunted him. He did this by playing any distracting "brain game" that helped him to forget the letters, the same five letters, on the wings and on the side of the aircraft in his nightmares.

He liked to remember how it had been the day they met while he had been holding a book that seemed sensible enough to explain past lives. (He had also noticed one discussing future lives. That seemed ridiculous, and he was wondering if, in spite of Dr. Weiss's credentials, this was the right way to learn more about past-life regression therapy?) It was right at that moment that she had smiled and spoken. He liked the thought of how later that day, before they left the bookstore together, they each had purchased a book; he bought Many Lives, Many Masters, and Maggie chose the one about future lives, Same Soul, Many Bodies, the irrational one. They often visited Foyles on rainy days.

Maggie loved that bookstore, so it could not exactly be said that she had followed him inside. That would have been completely out of character for her. She had not only felt attracted to his physique, but also the way he moved as he walked seemed so familiar; there was a very strong force there, and there had been something she recognized.

Then he absolutely surprised her; he went to the section she had least expected "his type"—the cute, yuppie geek type—to choose: he went to her mother's favorite section, the self-help and new age philosophies section, and in his hand was one of the new age beliefs' basic books.

This was good; it could only mean that he was new to such ideas. It was from the 1980s. Maybe even older. It had to be that old; she remembered a copy or two in her parents' house for as long as she could remember. This guy, this conquest—Maggie, as many pretty young women do, conquered the hearts of men for sport—would be a breeze. It was then that he felt different; when he spoke, and she heard his accent, an accent so familiar to her from the cinema and the telly, the accent of all the handsome men of her fantasies, an accent that made him even more appealing. Unlike the man she had just met, Maggie was very aware that she was a hopeless romantic.

CHAPTER THREE – BILL & MAGGIE

In a few weeks, Maggie and Bill's relationship became exclusive and was growing steadily, developing into a durable strong force in each of their lives. Maggie had willingly accepted that Bill was far more than a conquest. He was the type of man she could fall in love with, and perhaps she already had. He was almost perfect. He had a very nice career and the potential for great choices in the future. He was good company and loads of fun. Their physical relationship left nothing to be desired.

In Maggie's imaginary list of requirements for the perfect man, he only failed on two counts—his existential crisis and that he did not smoke. She was a very casual smoker and did not like the feeling of imposing her smoke on others, but after sex or having a drink, it was nice to smoke and was always nice to have smoking company.

At this stage in life, he was not likely to start smoking. She assumed that if this continued, it would eventually be up to her to quit. The other problem was one she needed to help him overcome. That was a bit more complicated.

So he had been right when they met; he fell into the existential crisis category. His was the worst kind of existential crisis: the kind which one cannot find enough to blame in this lifetime, so one seeks out other lifetimes to blame. This was a very middle-aged, new age woman thing to do. This was something her mother would do.

It was seemingly fated that Maggie led and Bill followed. In an attempt to solve Bill's problem, Maggie had led them to this place, the type of location that Bill would have never even bothered to imagine existed, before he met Maggie. They were there to participate in the sort of thing that Maggie avoided when her mother asked her to join. Maggie would respectfully find a good excuse to explain she was busy.

The place was a spiritual "new age" center, full of crystals and stones in heart shapes, crystal spheres, Buddha in many colors and poses, pyramids, angels, fairies, statues of elephants, scarabs, owls, turtles, and any other possible type of good luck shape made of energy-giving materials. Sandalwood incense scented the air, and baskets full of all types of incense were available to buy.

The irony that just a few weeks before Bill would have, at the very least, avoided such a place did not escape him. By the same token, the feeling of familiarity he felt when he touched certain stones was too tangible to ignore.

There were thirteen people in the room, including the hypnotist. Someone in the group explained that this was a powerful and fortuitous number; that contrary to the common reputation of the number thirteen, it was in fact a number full of "good energy." The group held a wide array of individuals varying in age and style of attire; some seemed serious and fancy, while others seemed to be hippie–like bohemians. There were only three men in all, including the hypnotist.

The hypnotist was a clean-cut man in his sixties, the kind of man one would not be able to describe; a man that could blend in any crowd – an average man. The hypnotist spoke about his hypnotherapy background and his vast experience acquired over many years. This was apparently something he did as a side job. His other work was at some government office or other. He had clearly explained that he was trained in hypnosis but had not called himself a psychologist or therapist of any kind. Somehow this made Bill feel safe. The knowledge that he was only a hypnotist and not a therapist made Bill feel that he could easily dismiss anything he found uncomfortable or perhaps absurd.

The hypnotist described the process by which the group would go under hypnosis and experience a past-life experience. He asked the group if anyone present did not believe in reincarnation. A man in his thirties said that he was not at all certain what he believed in (the very attractive woman sitting next to him was obviously not impressed), and this helped Bill, a man of numbers, facts and logic—as he still perceived himself—feel more at ease. He liked the fact that he was not the only one there with a certain or complete degree of skepticism. A very young woman, the youngest in the group, said that she had recently had a series of very odd experiences that had led her to question the possibility, but that she too did not really know what to think about past lives or about any other philosophy. There were some who believed unquestionably. A number of them were very experienced in past-life regression. Bill was grateful to Maggie that she just smiled and listened to the group with him.

In spite of, or perhaps because of, how Maggie was raised, this was the first time she had participated in a past-life regression. This was partly because when she did something wrong as a child, her mother would roll her eyes and claim to be paying past-life karma. This had led Maggie to imagine that perhaps in a past life, she had not been very nice. As she got older, her mother informed her that due to the nature of the retrograde planets in her astrology chart, Maggie had some past-life issues to resolve that were of a difficult nature. Here, doing this to help Bill, Maggie felt very comfortable that only good could come out of it for her.

The past few weeks had been amazing, as the beginning of love often is, the best time Bill could ever remember. The incredible sex, the wonderful meals, and every minute they shared. Maggie was so easy to talk to if he wanted to talk; she filled in the blanks when words failed him. She somehow knew how and when to be around. Bill hoped that he would see the images and clearly release them out into the universe, as Maggie had explained one could. Just like a quick surgery, it would all be resolved with minimal recovery time.

Bill was so busy in his thoughts that he did not follow the explanations given by the hypnotist, especially the most important one: raise your left hand if anything made you uncomfortable or scared during the hypnosis process. He had not given much thought to listening to the directions, as he had already been hypnotized twice. He was also unaware that he was far likelier to go in deeper and quicker.

Once the hypnotist started to use a melodious and special tone of voice, it was impossible for Bill not to listen.

"We are first going to take four very deep breaths; as you inhale, let this breath enter as deeply as possible into your body." This was familiar enough.

"Exhale and slowly release all tension from your body. Deep breath.... Focus on that little spot between your eyebrows and release the tension there and the breath...again, inhale and slowly exhale. Release every bit of tension...Release and leave your body feeling soft...good. Now, another deep inhalation...deeper and more relaxed...as you exhale, release...the light of relaxation is now entering your right toe. As you exhale, your toe feels very heavy."

The hypnotist spoke slowly, and each word seeped into the minds of the subjects being hypnotized. The voice continued to move from one body part to the next. The process was to relax each element of the right side of the body. Once the head was relaxed, the process started with the left shoulder and relaxed every part of the left side of the body until, finally, the left toe. At that point, the feeling of relaxation was full of comfort, and somewhere in the background the sound of snoring could be heard.

Bill felt like he was floating and clearly understood he was not the one snoring as the hypnotist guided the group down a staircase and into a tunnel. Bill could hear a thought at the back of his mind, that this was different from his previous experiences.

Bill's tunnel was full of color and light. It was made of something that seemed organic and alive. Bill felt very safe in this tunnel. He had never created such a clear image of anything he had tried to visualize; the images had always guided Bill in the past, whether through hypnosis or in his dreams. He was not alone in his tunnel; as he walked slowly down the tunnel, many others were present, and their arms and hands were all raised. The hands were passing a large ball of light. Bill raised his hands and touched the ball; he could feel the energy flowing from his hands into every cell in his body, and as odd as this would have been to him a few weeks ago, today it made him feel very comfortable. It gave him the knowledge that he was not alone.

"Remember, you are in control. Your body is asleep, but your mind is awake. You are protected, and you are going to visit a good life, a happy life."

A good life, a happy life...he was going to visit a good and happy life; he was protected, and he was in control. His hand turned the doorknob that the hypnotist told the group to find. The door was locked. He carefully retrieved a key from his pocket, placed the key in the keyhole, and opened the door. He stepped in; the wooden floor under his feet was supportive and creaked invitingly. He felt safe. What an odd feeling. It was as if simultaneously he was observing, detached as if watching a movie, but he was also there as if in the movie. There was an extraordinary comfort in that. As he looked up, he could see the smile of the pretty face that had become so familiar to him these past few weeks. Maggie's hair was much shorter and not in her current style. Her clothes were strange, as if she were in some black-and-white movie, and she sat in a chair, sewing. He knew he loved her. The surroundings were plain and austere. Suddenly, something caught their attention, and they both looked toward a closed door. An envelope had been slipped under the door. He reached for it and nervously opened it. He did not like what he saw; he opened the door and ran after the sound of the footsteps down the stairwell. He could almost see the man's back, and he wanted to catch up.

"Now you are going to move to another important event in that same lifetime...you are that same person, but you are somewhere else...look at your surroundings, if you can just be an observer. Are you indoors or outdoors? Are you alone, or is anyone with you?"

There he was, just like in his nightmares. Those were the very nightmares that were the root of his problems. There he was, in the cockpit, flying the plane. He was uncomfortable, and he could hear shouting in the back. Where was the mechanic? He should have returned from the toilet. Where was he? There was some contraption he could pull that allowed him to stand up and look at the passenger cabin. He got up, and the shouting grew stronger. What language was that? As he looked in, someone told him to get back in the cockpit, and one of the men...was that blood?

Bill's breathing got very heavy, and he began to feel very uncomfortable.

"You are in control. Lift your left hand if you need to leave. You are safe. You are in control. You are safe."

He had to obey the voice. He lifted his left hand, and the moment remained as if suspended in time. He did not like what he saw, and he knew he saw blood.

"You are now ready to move to another important and happy event in the same lifetime. Remember, you are in control, and nothing can hurt you. Now you are there."

He was at ease in a very clean bed. The smells of rubbing alcohol and disinfectant were as powerful as the images. His left arm was bandaged, and it hurt. As long as he made the right choices, he was safe. Her beautiful face lit the room, and he could hardly believe she was there right when he needed her the most. She lit his cigarette and laughed at the same time as she cried.

"You are now much older," the hypnotist said.

No, please, Bill thought. I know I am safe; I love to look at her face.

"You are much older, and you are ready to leave this life. Let your spirit float out of your body, and as you float into the light, remember what was the most important lesson you took from that life."

This was not so pleasant. He did not want to hear the most important lesson. In a life full of love and accomplishments, he knew there was a dark cloud. There was something he had never found a way to resolve or accept.

"You will now visit your guides and your higher self. Let them tell you why you are here, in this life.

What is your most important mission in this life? At this place in time and during this life."

His guides spoke clearly: "Tell her your story." He could see an unclear picture of who it was that needed his story.

"You will now feel your body. You will feel refreshed and relaxed, and you will remember everything that transpired here today to help you in your mission in this life. As I count to three, you will feel the need to move around and wake up feeling relaxed."

He opened his eyes and looked to his left. There she was, her eyes happy and sad at the same time. She reached her hand to his face and knowingly smiled. He knew one thing for certain; she was not the one the guide had told him to tell his story to. This made him feel deeply sad and afraid, because he wanted Maggie to be the one, the only one he needed to talk to. He knew she was the love of his life.

The group sat up. It was obvious who had been sleeping, and those who had slept blushed with embarrassment at their public snoring. Some in the group got up quickly to use the loo. At first, Bill just wanted a nice drink of water, so he took the thermos Maggie had brought. She smiled, winked, and told him she understood so much more.

As the group began to share their experiences, some said they saw nothing at all, and two people claimed to have jumped from one era to another. The hypnotist explained that such a jumping around from life to life was most common on a first regression.

The young woman, who at the beginning of the session had stated she was not sure what she believed, excitedly described her past life as a man; it was now completely obvious that she was now a firm believer in past lives.

"I was drinking and smoking, and then I went into the woods to pee; it was such a real feeling to undo my pants and pull out..."

She was so dainty and feminine that it was comical to hear her describe her masculinity with such pleasure, excitement, and detail.

Bill and Maggie did not share their experiences; they just listened. Bill found that he was craving a cigarette. Funny, he had never smoked before. The hypnotist thanked them for participating and explained that the spiritual center sponsored a group regression every month. He also offered, for a substantially higher fee, private sessions in which one could go far more in depth.

Bill's need to smoke was so strong that he just wanted to say goodnight and leave. As the group began to leave, he followed the first one out who was going to smoke and asked for a cigarette. The feel of dragging the hot fire into his lungs was so comforting and familiar; he could not understand why he had never smoked before.

Maggie came out and seemed surprised but happy to see him smoking. She touched his face again and sighed.

"So it was you! It was you that I lit the cigarette for! I knew it looked like you, and in a hospital bed, nonetheless."

"You saw the same thing?"

"I don't know that I saw the same thing, but I saw you with a little less hair and, judging by the furniture, not in today's world, but I thought it was you, and I lit your cigarette. I was crying, but happy."

The man who had given Bill the cigarette was not at all pleased to overhear the conversation. *The only bloke who seemed normal in that whole group*, the man thought to himself, *is just as loopy as the rest.* He knew that if his date were less pleasing in bed, he would never have agreed to this ridiculous thing.

Maggie and the attractive girl informed them both that they had already signed them up for the next month's session. The man who had perceived himself as one of logic knew he would continue to follow Maggie anywhere she led. The other man doubted he would still be seeing the attractive girl in a month's time.

CHAPTER FOUR – THE MUNICH PACT

Maggie and Bill were essentially living together as soon as they met. The level of ease and comfort they felt with each other was beyond anything either had experienced, even with their immediate families. They were both very busy with their jobs and enjoyed going to the gym and exploring London, as newly dating couples do. After the regression, Maggie wanted to find the era they had both visited in their regression.

"I knew we were soul mates from the moment I saw you."

Maggie often started the conversations, even the everyday conversations. Bill was happy that she took charge. "I know that I felt very comfortable with you."

"How romantic: comfortable."

"Not boring comfortable; exciting comfortable."

"Exciting comfortable as in recognizing a soul mate?"

"Anything you say, Maggie."

Her smile could have lit the city. Something had deeply touched him that night, and now he even enjoyed smoking. And that was good: one down on the perfect man list.

Drinking strong black coffee in the mornings was another new habit he had picked up after the regression. Maggie, however, had not changed at all.

One evening as they lay in bed after making love, enjoying their Marlboros, Bill turned on the flat screen. Maggie was about to protest at the interruption of their romantic moment, but Bill's expression stopped her. It was a black and-white documentary with Neville Chamberlain walking toward an airplane to great cheers, and he started to speak: "Out of this nettle, danger, we pluck this flower, safety..."

Maggie did not know why Shakespeare was of any relevance, but Bill was clutching the remote control, pale as a ghost. He started to shake and perspire. As she reached for him, he passed out. His eyes rolled back. She noticed he was breathing normally, so it was a shock. She found rubbing alcohol, and with the smell, got him to react and awaken. It took a few moments, but he was fine. Once he was well enough to light a cigarette, she decided to ask.

"I need to know what made you react that way."

"The airplane."

"I saw Neville Chamberlain was off to see Hitler..."

He interrupted her. "No, not that airplane; the one he walked past, the lettering on the wings."

"I didn't notice any other airplane."

"He walked past an airplane, and I saw the letters that haunt my dreams."

"Okay, let's look it up."

She got out of bed, took the laptop off the desk, and switched it on. Perhaps there was some truth to her mother's astrological warnings; how her chart said that delving into the past might open doors she needed to be strong to face. Her mother had always warned Maggie that in past lives, we might not have been as nice or kind. So here it was, in a documentary that presented a doorway to World War II. Maybe she wasn't going to like what she found.

Maggie started to search for Neville Chamberlain and Hitler in Yahoo UK and Ireland. When she found Critical Past and that the choice of videos of Neville Chamberlain was all related to the Munich Pact, she began to click.

In one of the video clips, she heard the voice from the newsreel in the background describing Neville chamberlain as a "gray haired knight" and explaining how Prime Minister Chamberlain had the "fate of millions." The voice and any other sound faded, as there was something far more important to Maggie in that black-and-white screen. For the first time, she saw the airplane that haunted the man she loved.

British Prime Minister Neville Chamberlain at Heston Aerodrome in

London, England. September 9, 1938.

www.CriticalPast.com

As the newsreel continued, she heard Prime Minister Neville Chamberlain ask if he could speak, presumably as he waited to be recorded. He quoted Shakespeare's Henry the IV, and spoke of plucking a flower safety.

She remembered that in 2003, those who opposed or who opposed opposition to Mr. Bush and Mr. Blair's invasion of Iraq often quoted the Munich Pact. Now, so many years after, the war in Iraq still continued. Maybe "plucking the flower, safety" would not have been a bad idea at all. She had gladly participated in any and all protests that she could. The red ink flowing in the Trafalgar Square fountain to show the unnecessary blood being spilled had nearly gotten her arrested. Maggie opposed war, all war. She was always ready and very happy to voice her opinion to anyone she encountered.

While Maggie pondered the uselessness of war, Bill simply absorbed the plane he continuously dreamt about, and which he always saw sinking into the ocean. It was there, in 1938, whole and on land. That unmistakable Griffin and the lightning bolt which formed the logo. The letters on the wings that he had tried hopelessly to forget—he could not see the side from this angle, but he knew they were there too--those five letters of his nightmares.

The airline was British Airways Ltd., and the airplane looked very familiar. Not just because of Bill's nightmares. The airplane also looked familiar to Maggie. The next logical step was to search for the letters on the wings of the plane. They searched for the G and dash that showed it to be a British plane. They typed the G dash and the four letters, and there it was, at an online Aviation Safety Network--the facts that matched nightmares. There was the airplane that looked so familiar because of all the movie posters showing Hillary Swank as Amelia Earhart, standing in front of one just like it, a Lockheed Electra.

There it was, reality matching Bill's nightmares. The G-AESY had crashed into the Storstrøm waters on its way to Stockholm on August 15, 1939. The online source said that five men had died and the pilot had survived.

There it was.

"What is Storstrøm?"

"It's a place in Denmark, between Vordingborg and Nykøbing, where I can assure you, even in August, you will find the water is cold and salty just like in your nightmares."

"How could you possibly know that?"

"I'm half Danish, remember? My grandparents live in that area, in a place called the

Moon!"

"You know those waters? Is there a bridge?"

"Oh yes, Storstrøm has a very famous bridge that was built in the 1930s. My grandfather loves to tell stories about how the Germans had all of these antiaircraft guns set up on that bridge to shoot down allied planes. It was some sort of marker for the allied planes on their way to bomb Berlin. In that era, Storstrøm bridge was probably the longest bridge in Europe. It was built by an English engineering firm called Dorman Long.

"My grandfather was opposed to the outsourcing even then. 'Danes should have been perfectly capable to create their own Bridge.' If he said that once after a drink or two, he said it a hundred times! It cost something like two million pounds sterling to build. Can you imagine what that would be today? You can still see holes in the bridge from the aircraft guns; Grandfather says that the water is a sort of graveyard, full of dead airplanes, each with a story to tell. My brother and I nicknamed it the 'Bridge of Deaths.'

"According to this, your plane was pulled out and written off as damaged beyond repair," Maggie continued. "So your plane is not in that graveyard."

"It sounds funny for you to call it 'my plane.'"

"Well, it has been part of who you are longer than I have, and you call me your girlfriend, so it is your plane."

"It isn't part of the graveyard, because it went down before World War II started; look at the date."

Maggie glanced at the screen. "Not long before."

"No, I guess not. When did Hitler march into Poland?"

"September...early September 1939. My grandfather says they knew the world changed completely that day; it was their 9/11. Denmark was such a divided country at the time, and loyalties ran deep and divided. Once the Germans marched into Poland, everyone knew that was just the beginning, and that Denmark would soon follow."

"This is not going to be a good story, and some things are better left alone."

"Well, do you want to deal with it? Learn the story and get it out of your system? Or do you want it to haunt you for the rest of your life?"Maggie scrolled down the page to see what entries under G-AESY matched their plane."The data for this came out of the British Airways archives near Heathrow. There are several interesting entries here. Look at this one--someone in Florida is looking to share and exchange information. Trust me, Bill; let's move forward."

The next day, they went out to walk, breathe, and think. While visiting the Science Museum, one of their favorites, they realized why Bill always looked up. There, in its silvery, shining glory, hung the beautiful Lockheed Electra 10A.

It was an airplane built in the USA. It had been built to order, just as Amelia Earhart's had been. It first came out in 1934, featuring hydraulic breaks, dual controls, electrically operated flaps, and two-way controllable propellers. It could carry ten passengers and two pilots. It must have been some plane in its day. It looked so small hanging in the Science Museum.

Bill sighed and said, "It is barely big enough to fit the story of my dreams, too small to fit what I see…"

"I will help you make it big enough; don't worry."

Maggie was right; it was time to follow this through and resolve it once and for all, no matter where it led. They e-mailed Maggie's grandfather to ask if he could look up newspaper microfilms in his local library. Then they e-mailed the British Airways archives near Heathrow. Thus they embarked on their journey of tangibles and facts. Bill tried very hard to be open-minded. He couldn't help feeling that some of the information they had read did not match that which he had seen over and over again in his dreams.

CHAPTER FIVE – CATALINA

As Bill and Maggie were busily opening the door to the past, the middle-aged woman across the Atlantic was discouraged and disappointed and was one more time closing her door to 1939. It was also a cold winter in Florida. It was so cold that iguanas were falling off trees, frozen. Floridians were wearing coats. The world continued to mourn the deaths of so many in Haiti, and many people continued to call global warming nonexistent and political.

It had been nearly two decades, sprinkled with many interruptions from life, during which she had tried to pursue this dream. At times, one could argue that she pursued it to the point of obsession. The sorry state of the present economy had warranted that she rejoin the work force and yet again put her dream aside. Inasmuch as she understood how fortunate she was to have found a job, a good job, at a time when many could not, she had a bitter taste in her mouth that accompanied the strong feeling of disappointment. What price could be put on giving up a dream?

She felt she was so close. The last few months had suddenly opened a world through the Internet where much of the information she needed was readily available; no expensive visits to dusty old archives in Europe or having to peruse badly indexed newspaper microfilms were required. She had discovered new ways to look for information, new sites—or at least, new to her.

So again, with the same ritual of all other interruptions, she started to place the information, file by file, in storage boxes. Each file held detailed data, all of them valuable. All represented hard work and perseverance. At times, it seemed ironic that much of what she needed and had worked so hard to find years earlier was now so easily accessible through the Internet.

The world had changed so much since the early 90s, when she had met the first archivist near Heathrow. He was the one who, after suspiciously inquiring why she wanted to see a file, had finally satisfied at her answer.

"I could not believe I found it. As I told you on the phone, British Airways Ltd. – also known as BAL, for short -- was not our predecessor; our direct ancestry lies with Imperial Airways in 1939.BAL was, to a great extent, a competitor. We inherited very little archive material from BAL." And with a sigh, he added, "Can of worms you are about to open, young lady."

Through the years, she visited the archives, and other archivists strongly disputed this, crediting every airline that merged to create what eventually became British Airways as a great predecessor.

She could hear his voice so clearly, see his face. He had died a good ten years before, and she had seen the archives near Heathrow grow from an old and simple hangar storage room to a beautiful, fully functioning museum and archive. Many had since replaced the original archivist--her favorite--and others, too, had died. She had not been called a "young lady" in very many years. How much time should be spent chasing a dream?

Now the Internet and her knowledge of where to look offered the possibility that she could fill in the gaps of all that she had collected through the years. She could visualize with such clarity how to put it all together, and now that would have to wait. Unpaid bills and her dwindling bank account dictated this.

More often than not, she had to stop to reread the files, to read the ones that dealt with matters and questions that bothered her most. Some because they were incomplete, others because they had more questions than answers, and the worst ones were those that made no sense at all.

Among the latter was the file containing the pilot's statement. No one seemed to have questioned what he stated; yet there was no logic to it. While in the archives, she had read a few other accident reports from the same airline, incidents where there was no loss of life. In those, the pilots had been questioned. But in this file, the pilot's testimony had obvious holes.

The pilot clearly stated that he saw the reflection of the fire on the dashboard at the same time as the mechanic/copilot/radio operator; it seemed unclear what the second man's title was supposed to be. The investigators and the pilot referred to him using all three designations. So both men saw this reflection of the fire simultaneously, and the pilot stated that he had sent the copilot to the passenger cabin to "deal with the problem." No one questioned why the mechanic, the reference of the pilot's statement, went back to deal with the problem empty-handed. Empty-handed! Why, when he had a fire extinguisher in the cockpit?

That very airline had had a fire incident four days earlier. The incident four days earlier had been in a larger Lockheed--an Electra 14. That fire destroyed the plane and, according to *The London Times*, The famous Insurance conglomerate out of London, Lloyd's of London had been required to pay thirty thousand pounds.

Catalina could just see it in her mind's eye, could imagine the employees, pilots, and radio operators:

"Good morning, mate; did you hear what happened to that flight in France?"

"I wonder if they'll sack anyone. Good thing they are well equipped with fire extinguishers."

All of the men, with the inevitable cigarette, chatting as it is so very human to do, in their company uniforms, sharing a cup of coffee right there at Heston or Croydon or a pint at a nearby pub ...

"Pity about the aeroplane, but so glad no one died."

Catalina understood that in 1939, the world did not have the information overload of the twenty-first century, the social media cyber water cooler where everything relevant or irrelevant is dissected, discussed, and argued over. In 1939, however, people read their papers, and people conversed, especially in matters that touched the very company they worked for. With the world at the brink of war, she was quite certain that people discussed everything in great detail.

So four days later, an employee--a mechanic/copilot/radio operator--went back to take care of a fire with no fire extinguisher in hand? Someone questioned this, and some silly suggestion was made that the extinguishers should be marked better. No matter how many times she read the pilot's statement, it was not logical. If only her fantasy fueled by the...

No! That part of the search was over; she now only searched books, archives, and acceptable data.

CHAPTER SIX – WETTING THE BED

Bill felt that his nightmares and the visions in the hypnotic regressions were very real. They, however, did not match the reports that Maggie had found on the Internet. The world today, so completely informed, made it perfectly clear that often stories are inaccurate, that a source could distort and manipulate how a fact was used. As files became public years later, clearer pictures of events could be formed. Some uncovered that which many felt was best left alone.

Maggie, of course, did not agree. In Maggie's world, all war, present, past, and, God forbid, future, was wrong. Maggie was certain that there had always been very good and very bad people and that the difference was simply that today, all bad people were found out; they were caught sooner than later. People in power were not necessarily held accountable, but they were certainly caught.

"Look, Bill, of course their story is not going to match. It wouldn't have haunted you into another life if it was a cut and dry, happy tale. Think about it."

He did not need to answer. It was embarrassing enough to think about it. A few nights earlier, he had experienced one of the dreams.

He was struggling and feeling helpless. The water was cold and briny. He was afraid, and he still had difficulty breathing the fresh air after the smoke inside the plane. Nothing made sense; why were they fighting? He could see the bridge; it was not far. He needed to get back in. Surely, someone else had survived; someone else needed to corroborate his story. He tried to find a way back, but it was useless. He just swam and wondered what kind of a future awaited him ...

That was when, to his great embarrassment, he woke up Maggie by wetting the bed. She had been adamant that what he called "dreams" were absolutely horrible nightmares and no way to live. She reminded him that when they first met he looked like a sad, lost character with huge circles under his eyes.

It was then they made an appointment at the archives near Heathrow. When they arrived, the file they had requested was on a table inside a brown cardboard box with hand-printed lettering that read AW1/1869. For hours, they looked carefully at the file. It contained a wide variety of documents, letters, death certificates, more letters, and copies of telegrams. Some papers were duplicated, as were the photographs of the plane, of the five casualties, and of the bridge.

The archivist explained that there was a woman from America who was related to one of the dead. She had also worked with archives in Denmark, but as far as they knew, she had not yet found all of the gaps in the story.

The file, large though it was, remained incomplete.

As the archivist explained the airline being one of several that merged and not all the archival material had survived the years and changes in ownership of what became the British Airways of today, Bill and Maggie looked at the photographs. There was the bridge of his dreams, the bridge Maggie knew so well from her childhood. It had the three half circles, a large one in the center, crowded by two smaller ones on each side. The black-and-white photograph of the bridge had a red arrow pointing to where the plane had gone down. There were many photographs from various angles of the salvaged plane. With one of the motors missing, torn from the wing, it looked so different from the plane Neville Chamberlain had walked past in 1938. It was wounded...dead.

The hardest photographs to look at, were the images of the five corpses. They were not quite gruesome, except for one, but they made the story human and very real. There were black-and-white headshots of each of the five. Two were very badly burned, but the other three looked peaceful enough. Bill recognized some of the faces from his past-life regression. There was so much that did not match with what he had seen in his dreams and past life regressions, however.

The most annoying was the pilot's statement. It was short and to the point, and it did not match Bill's version of the story. It was so difficult to concentrate with that going through his mind.

Maggie had brought a portable scanner and was busily scanning. She noticed the concerned look in his face, and from time to time, she would smile and distract him with casual remarks and banal banter.

"I must thank my Mum for the scanner. I can't imagine what she uses it for?"

Bill nodded and made his best attempt at a smile.

There was much more to the story than the day of the accident, and the file ranged from 1939 to 1951. A man by the name of Wicks had requested special permission to work with the file in the 1950s. There was also correspondence from a German lawyer around the same time period. For the most part, Bill quietly looked and read until it was time to leave, while Maggie scanned and engaged the archivists in a bit of seemingly innocuous conversation. Focused and determined, there was a point to every question she asked as she carefully made mental notes of the answers.

The archives were only open until 1:00 p.m. Exiting into the cold, they stopped outside to smoke a cigarette. As she blew out a perfect smoke ring, Maggie said, "It is obvious that this is bothering you very much."

"Yes, it is hard to say what is bothering me the most: the pictures or the data that does not match what I saw."

"Do the faces match what you saw?"

"There are several that I recognized."

"Facts can be twisted for so many reasons. Frankly, how can you assume that the facts were not twisted? How about the telegram explaining that the pilot and his wife were to be flown to Croydon but that the press was to be steered to a different airport?"

"I missed that one."

Maggie smiled. "You missed a lot, but with a nice glass of wine, in the safety of our cozy flat..."

"Our cozy flat?"

"I already own half your closet; why not our cozy flat?"

Her smile lit up his world. If he had to go through this at all, why not in their cozy flat? In their cozy bed? All in all, he had to admit life was, if not better, certainly fuller than before Maggie shared his world.

CHAPTER SEVEN – MEANWHILE in FLORIDA

In Florida, Catalina felt far from cozy. Her new job began in two weeks. She had those two weeks to store her dream and put it away. Dealing with her research was too depressing. Every file felt so personal, and she had two weeks to hope that something, anything, would happen.

She needed office space at home; the only room where this was possible was the room she had tried to devote entirely to her project on the G-AESY. Storing away some of the books she had used for her project might feel less personal.

The list of books was a diverse collection; it clearly showed how little formal training she had in the matters related to World War II. One could even say it showed how little formal training she had in any historical subject.

She assembled the cardboard box from the office supply store. A few shelves were easy to empty; the shelves with the books on her list were harder to place.

One by one, she took each book. Some were organized in alphabetical order, by author. Those were the ones she needed to decide. Should she store? Should she keep? Should she sell?

She looked through her list. Some of the books she had read in full, but most of them she had read bits and pieces of what she needed to learn. She had added comments and the numbers of relevant pages. The shelf, just like the list, was in alphabetical order.

The A-to-Z was stuffed with a wide variety of books: memoirs from various politicians with their personal input of an era that has left such a huge imprint on humanity. Their opinions were as varied as any account seen from more than one point of view.

Like everything serious and violent, the number of casualties, not to mention those wounded and damaged by the horror, varied according to source.

Her lack of historical background was such that she chose the books with some rather unique parameters. This included, but was not limited to, books about or referencing:

- Standard Oil of New Jersey as a source of scandal or espionage
- Oil and Espionage scandals

- The Munich Pact and mentioned Anthony Crossley by name or in reference as an anti-appeaser
- The special interest group "The Focus"
- Palestinian territories in the 1930s or before
- World War II weaponry, especially Krupp
- Anthony Crossley writings
- Memoirs of British Politicians who mentioned Anthony Crossley
- Pre-WWII covert activities
- Fifth Column Movements that could be associated with the five casualties from the crash

(Full list from Original version of TBOD in Appendix A--Store, Keep, Sell)

Her five men. She felt very possessive about them; they represented the longest relationships she'd had with any man. The five corpses from 1939--her grandfather and the other four.

She carefully followed the bibliographic list she kept, and the notes she'd made for each book. Some volumes had the same repetitive notes on various historical events.

Several stated strongly that Standard Oil of New Jersey was a recruitment ground for spies. Standard Oil of New Jersey, 30 Rockefeller Plaza. Her grandfather had only been transferred to the European branch two weeks before he died. Most data she found on him had his personal address on Riverside Drive or the 30 Rockefeller Plaza address, care of a Mr. K. Blood.

Historians with different points of view wove an image in her mind of absolute human imperfection. Churchill the good guy vs. Churchill the bad guy...everything so subjective to opinions and interpretations.

Her various trips to Europe, determined to personally explore as many files as these historians quoted, often provided an anchor to what she accepted as her version, her truth, her subjective interpretation of it all.

The tremendous anger she felt at *The New York Times* for misspelling her Grandfather's name. *It is CASTILLO, not Casteillo,* was always a loud thought when she looked at the newspaper clipping.

Two Standard Oil Men Killed in Plane Crash; British MP Also Is a Victim in Denmark

Special Cable to THE NEW YORK TIMES.

August 16, 1939, Section, Page 1, Column

COPENHAGEN, Denmark, Aug. 15.--Samuel J. Simonton of Allentown, Pa., and C.A. Casteillo, a Mexican, both representatives of the Standard Oil

Company of New Jersey, and Anthony C. Crossley, a member of the British Parliament, were among five persons killed in a plane crash in Denmark today.

That anger was only surpassed by history books, or reliable, reputable--even if controversial--sources stating that Anthony Crossley had not fared well politically by losing his seat in Parliament six years after he died.

Her five men were so important to her, and the idea that they were not to others filled her with a sense of emptiness.

Then there was David Irving, the noted Holocaust denier she tried to avoid, but who had a strange paper trail that made her research collide with his work.

The strange Mr. Wicks who had requested access to the British Airways Files was a favorite subject of Mr. Irving's presentations.

As she slowly looked at each book, placing some in boxes and others on her shelf, the long journey that had led her to this point--to yet another roadblock--flashed in her mind's eye.

This one made her stop. *British Airways: An Airline and Its Aircraft. Volume* I: 1919–1939, by R.E.G.Davies.

She opened a bottle of wine and remembered the day that Ron Davies had had lunch with her, a very cold day in Washington, DC. She looked at the beautiful book and drifted away in her thoughts.

She could vividly see how Mr. Davies kindly showed her behind the scenes at the Smithsonian. He had helped her find airline schedules for the summer of 1939, including the BAL flights from London to Stockholm.

He then invited her to lunch. They left the Smithsonian, and as they were crossing the street to look for a place to eat, he looked at her and said, "Did your Grandfather speak as many languages as you do?"

"One more."

"And what exactly was his profession?"

"He was a biochemical engineer."

"You do realize, don't you, that you are researching a spy."

He had put into words what she had always suspected. Hearing it come from him gave her goose bumps, and it felt thrilling.

"I've often thought so, but how can I prove it?"

"How, indeed."

It was the one and only time they met. On several occasions, Mr. Davies had helped her and directed her by phone on where to find information and even the location of the actual Lockheed Electra 10A. She had purchased some of his books, some as gifts and some for herself. This book belonged on her coffee table. This book, signed by the author, deserved a nice place.

However, her favorite signature was the one from the book she got that cold winter day she met him at the Smithsonian--the Lufthansa book.

To Catalina,

With all good wishes to a fellow respecter of history.

Con los mejores deseos,

Ron Davies

Washington, DC

January 13, 2003

She could not imagine that the traditional curators, archivists, historians, or doctors who had helped her, would approve of the unconventional methods she had used to dig through history. This made her feel guilty when she read the line, "respecter of history."

CHAPTER EIGHT – FACING THE FACTS

Bill and Maggie had just made love like the gods. They opened a nice bottle of Sauvignon Blanc and put the laptop on the bed. This was their new ritual after lovemaking: to look at their data on the G-AESY. Every time they read a new entry, they found something else to argue about, something about which they could disagree.

"Look how this Jack Sinclair describes that they are dealing with two different jurisdictions, and each feels that the case belongs to them."

"I told you the plane fell between Nykøping and Vordingborg. It makes sense that the jurisdiction was in question. Sounds a bit like us."

"Oh come on, Maggie. These are my nightmares we are trying to get rid of."

"Yes, but I had the same past-life regression experience. I was there. The telegram about the pilot and his wife and the airports proves that. So this matter, this story, is as much mine as it is yours."

"Fine, so what bothers you the most?"

"Undoubtedly the death certificates; those bother me the most."

She had looked at them time and time again. She had the advantage of being able to read the Danish version, as well as the English translation in the file. She felt that there was a discrepancy. She studied the order in which the corpses had been brought up from the plane; this was corpse number three, so he should be the same. Rigor mortis in deaths that occurred at the same time and under the same circumstances, she felt, should be the same.

Four of the five corpses were documented as being in a fencing position, a common factor in deaths by fire or drowning. She had looked all of this up on the Internet. This corpse had his arms crossed. Even the one they pulled out the following day was registered as being in a fencing position. This corpse was described as having his arms crossed, folded over his chest. Could this mean he died a different way? Before the others?

"The death certificates?"

"Yes, it is there, plainly stated in the Danish original and the English translation that one of the corpses is different from the others."

As she showed him the picture of the corpse in question, he recognized him. "In my past-life regression, that man had blood coming out of the side of his head. I am pretty sure his arms were crossed; yes, they were crossed."

"In all of the CSI shows, the medical examiners talk about rigor mortis, and this one, he was the third corpse they took out of the plane. It is my humble opinion that the only corpse that should have different rigidity is the corpse that was retrieved the following day."

"Darling, I do not think you are capable of any humble opinions. What you say makes perfect sense. All five are registered as dying the same way."

"Well, what bothers me the most is that there seems to be no note made of this by the doctors in Denmark. There was the second autopsy, and by then, the rigor mortis would have changed, I think, but the doctor who performed the second autopsy must have seen this, too. Who signed the death certificates? The one that performed the first or second autopsy?"

Bill pulled up another document and said, "I remember reading that one of the corpses was in one of the cities, and the others were in the other. I cannot remember if it was Nykøping or Vordingborg, but let me see ... here, this document notes Mr. Maxwell's telephone call from Vordingborg at 4:30 p.m. on August

17, 1939.Look how it clearly states that the other four bodies are to be sent from Vordingborg to Copenhagen, but Mr. Crossley's body is at a local hospital in Nykøping. If you read further, it says that Mr. Crossley's body was already in a coffin that was made locally."

"Why would one body be at a different place? The bodies, I am assuming, were being sent to Copenhagen for the second autopsy. Do you know if coffins are used before a second autopsy? Did they have the green bags we now see in police shows, or did they simply use coffins? Look at this...they clearly state that the Danes are in control. Maybe with the whole fight over who had jurisdiction. Well, I am sure one could look at this in many ways, but clearly, it seems strange."

Bill considered it. "Which Shakespeare play is it about 'something is rotten in the state of Denmark?"

"Hamlet, of course!"

"Hamlet, of course, if you are English or an English major. I am sure people could easily get that one wrong in a game show. In which Shakespeare play and by whom was this stated?"

"Marcellus in Hamlet, act one, scene four."

"Oh, come on, Maggie! Is that true?"

"Let's look it up..."

Maggie went back online to prove her point about Hamlet.

Bill conceded. "Okay, you are right! Act one, scene four. I will never play Trivial Pursuit unless you are on my team. Okay, let's get back to 1939 in Denmark."

"There is absolutely nothing trivial about Shakespeare! Let's see...Denmark shortly before World War II...my grandparents discuss it at times. They describe that it was a country very divided in its philosophies. There were as many who opposed the Germans as there were who did not. I am sure it was because of their desire for survival. It is very well known that the king of Denmark wore a Star of David and was absolutely opposed to the treatment of the Jewish people. The Nazis had a huge headquarters, and I am sure locals had to work with them. I think that there was an attempt to achieve the neutrality that Sweden retained during World War II."

Unfortunately for Maggie, when they looked that up, it turned out to not be true. Inasmuch as Denmark did work hard to support its Jewish community, according to the Internet, the King of Denmark had not worn a Star of David.

"I know there was a serious resistance movement; I visited a resistance museum there. My favorite part was how they helped the Allies who under cover of night parachuted into Denmark. They had maps on silk material, along with these tiny compasses. It is amazing how much can be accomplished with such limited technology."

As Bill spoke he sounded surprised. Maggie listened and smiled knowingly.

"I have that book, Henry Channon's Diary! I found it in my office's library and read it before I met you. In the introduction by the Member of Parliament who edited the diaries, he explains that Henry Channon fully expected to be made public. It bothered me that he called our MP an ass."

Bill flipped through the pages as he said, "Our MP? Member of Parliament, you mean? You're not even British! Well, it wasn't in public."

"You know the full entry in which he refers to Anthony Crossley as an ass is from September 1938, a couple of days before the Munich Pact was signed? There is one more entry with Anthony Crossley in that book. Let me look, here it is, where Henry Channon is upset that Neville Chamberlain is helping Anthony Crossley with salmon fishing information for his book. In that one, he is just miffed, and I've read worse insults against others in his book."

"Can you imagine what politicians call each other today in private? I doubt many actually keep diaries today. They are so very rude to each other in public that in private, I am sure they say or write things far worse than ass."

"Maggie, I cannot help but wonder if we are not opening a can of worms."

"Probably. There are a few other websites that mention Anthony Crossley. I decided the best thing was to contact the woman in Florida. Her info was in the guest notebook at the British Airways archives. The archivist said she's worked with files in Denmark, and my grandfather has so far let me down; he says it's too cold to go to the library. Maybe this woman found a complete report."

"Which one was her relative?" Bill asked

"The Mexican, the first body they pulled out. He was traveling with the American, and the Mexican Castillo had a New York address. But the American ... Let me see, the American's address is in Surrey. They both worked for Standard Oil of New Jersey."

"What about the Englishman who got off the plane in Hamburg?"

"The one the file describes as a 'perfectly normal man'? Mr. Stocks? That really shows the difference between today and 1939. It sounds fishy to me! We need not question him? Imagine today getting off a plane and shortly thereafter something happens. It calls for--at the very least--a friendly cup of coffee and a conversation."

Bill sighed and nodded."I don't understand how that man wasn't questioned either. He could at least have said whether the passenger cabin smelled of petrol. Did the file also say he flew back the next day? He bought the ticket the day before, paid cash, and no one thought to question him? Just to...even to ask, 'Why the sudden journey?'"

"I told you, Bill. That one is fishy."

They drank their wine, smoked their cigarettes, and continued to discuss the files for hours on end. Their hobby, as it were, was becoming obsessive.

CHAPTER NINE – CONNECTING ACROSS THE POND

After a good night's sleep, Catalina felt ready to tackle the rest of the books. She brewed a pot of nice, strong coffee before she took up her list again. She opened the file full of the original telegrams from 1939, vividly imagining her mother's pain as she read the first one.

```
CD114 27 NEWYORK 15 1205P                        15 AGO 1939
MRS FLAVIA G DE CASTILLO
CALLE GUANAJUATO 100 MEXCTY
DEEPLY REGRET TO INFORM YOU CESAR WAS KILLED TODAY
IN AN AEROPLANE CRASH AT COPENHAGEN PLEASE ADVISE
WHAT ARRANGEMENT YOU WISH US TO MAKE MY SINCEREST
SYMPATHY
          L K BLOOD

RE 1122AM
```

Past the half-century mark, family stories change from time to time. The images in people's memories are colored by the passage of time and by their moods when telling the story.

This one always did have one tangible: her mother, a few months shy of thirteen, had been the one to open the telegram and read the tragic news. The assumption was that the telegram contained their travel arrangements to England. With most people rushing to get away from Europe, the Castillo's plans were to travel in the opposite direction.

Cesar Agustin Castillo had been transferred to the European office after many years with Standard Oil of New Jersey or its subsidiaries, mostly in New York City, but as far south as Panama's Canal Zone and Mexico City.

Reading that telegram always helped Catalina put things in the perspective she felt they deserved. She went back to organizing the rest of her books, accepting that there were far worse things than having to put a dream on hold.

It began to feel tedious, and she decided to take a break from this task and began to wonder if she should simply buy another bookshelf. So after a nice walk in the Florida winter during the longest cold streak she could remember, she turned on her computer and found Maggie's e-mail.

It was, by all accounts, odd. Catalina did not know what to make of it. She had spent too many years involved in this research to feel excited about any inquiry. This young woman had found her e-mail address at the British Airways archives. She had also noted that Catalina's name was mentioned in other entries about the G-AESY on the Internet.

Catalina was curious and wanted to get an idea who Maggie was. She looked the young woman up on Facebook and could not believe the photo; she was so familiar with that face and those smiling eyes. Like so many young people, her life was public, so it was possible to see more than one picture without formally connecting.

This was it! After all these years, it was true! He did exist—not just in her fictional book and the information from the psychics.

There he was with thicker hair. The resemblance was uncanny, both of them; Maggie's hair was longer and straight. Those unmistakable eyes...

Catalina took a thumbtack off the bulletin board: The one holding the Politik. She'd cut out the captioned picture and did not have the full name of the newspaper. "The English Pilot and His Wife" —or at least that is what she assumed *Den engelske Flyver og hans Hustru* meant.

It wasn't the best copy. It was from an old microfilm machine, but the resemblance was unmistakable. She found herself out the door, in her car, and heading back to where she'd promised herself she would never go again—to the accountant's office.

CHAPTER TEN – PARENTS & FRIENDS

Maggie was completely unaware that her e-mail had caused such a strong reaction on the other side of the pond. She even wondered if the woman in Florida would be open-minded enough to understand why they were searching.

Life was too exciting to give it much thought. Her mother had finally met Bill, and they liked each other. She was not in a habit of exposing too many people to her mother, an easy target for criticism. She also knew full well when her mother did not like someone, and although it was not necessary, her mother's approval was always welcome.

They had talked openly about having attended the past-life regression. They had no choice; many at that center knew her mother, and it would have come out anyway. As they were leaving, Mum had--with laughter and the best intentions, of course--meddled and made matters a little more complicated.

"Here are a few DVDs to enjoy and help you appreciate the pros and cons of past-life knowledge.

"Thank you very much, Mrs...."

"Oh, please call me Gitte."

"Thank you, Gitte."

Maggie's face immediately lost its smile. "Oh, mother! Not *Dead Again*."

"It's fine, Maggie. I really like Kenneth Branagh and Emma Thompson. I'm sure it's a great movie."

Maggie had to have the last word. "It's a scary movie."

Mum always won. "You were too young the first time you saw that movie. I am certain that today you will enjoy it, appreciate it, and understand it. Bill, I'm sure you are going to find it very interesting. It's a guy's type of thriller. The other two movies are cute and fun, but you'll like this one."

By the time they got back to the apartment, they had to sleep. It was a workday for both of them, and they had been burning the candle at both ends these days, sifting through all the papers Maggie had scanned at the British Airways archives. The next night, Maggie had already agreed to take Bill to a friend's party. The DVDs were left for another day.

A few of her friends had met Bill before and liked him. Maggie's friends were all very casual, and not a single one of them was married or had children. The people from Bill's world were mostly married and nice but were far more formal.

Her friends drank and partied with the freedom of the young, without much thought for the next day. That night, they were imbibing a bit more than usual; Maggie found their reminiscing annoying, especially when it came to her mother.

"Remember when Maggie's mum plotted our astrology charts? What was your rising sign? She was quite good; now that I'm older, a lot of the stuff she said is accurate."

Another friend jumped into the conversation. "Your mum told me my life was very linked to past lives through issues that needed to be resolved in this lifetime. Something about the location of the south node of the moon, or was it the north node? Anyhow, I went to a hypnotist, and you would not believe what I saw in my past life. I..."

The friend was interrupted by a longhaired musician or artist type of bloke whom Maggie had never met before—someone's friend or date who was rolling a joint and laughing out loud. "How much did you pay to have a past-life regression?"

"A hundred quid, and it was worth every penny," Maggie's friend responded.

"What a foolish waste!"

"Oh, and I suppose your cannabis is worth every cent."

"This one is. You should try it."

It was a cold winter in London; all of the windows were closed, and as the air filled with cannabis, smoke flowed in that small London apartment so that everyone there got a little bit stoned.

Maggie had not realized how much it bothered her that past lives were being mocked. Influenced by the drinks and cannabis in her system, Maggie responded more boisterously than she would have in a more sober state.

"Well, Bill and I saw the very same event, the very same life, when we underwent a regression."

All the red, bloodshot eyes stared at her; it was very quiet. Then, in unison, everyone exploded in laughter, except for Maggie and Bill.

Bill had drunk more than his share, and the smoke in the room had also made him stoned and mellow. After the laughter subsided, he figured backing up Maggie was the wisest choice. "She's right. It was very strange, but we did see the same thing."

The same girl who'd paid a hundred pounds for her regression asked, "What did you see?"

Bill smiled and winked before he answered. "That we were as wonderfully compatible in the past as we are today."

"Oh, I see."

That night, Maggie would have followed Bill anywhere and everywhere.

Bill still had more to say. "I will tell you this: women find it very difficult to resist men willing to seek the past that way. Someone told me once that such willingness makes women ready and willing to jump into bed."

With that, he planted an enormous kiss on a very willing Maggie.

The following week, there would be a very busy past-life therapy hypnotist in London—a young woman had passed his number around at a party. He worked nonstop in spite of the bad economy and had numerous new young male clients.

CHAPTER ELEVEN – PSYCHICS

Often torn between the religion and philosophies she was raised with and the ones she had espoused through her experiences in life, Catalina felt somewhat defeated as she drove to the accountant's office. The philosophies she had encountered and participated in involved the forbidden in her religion, such as psychics, astrologers, Reiki master healers, shamans, tarot card readers, and the lot.

She had, in the past year, like so many Americans, taken a turn toward the right, and it had landed her back at church on Sundays. Every Sunday, she prayed for world peace and for good health for herself and everyone she loved. She also tried to promise the God she was raised to believe in; to faithfully and respectfully honor the shape he chose for the world, so she would not try to peek into the future. The famous Isak Dinesen quote came to her mind *"God made the world round so we would never be able to see too far down the road."*She had, in fact, promised God that she would avoid psychics and, in effect, anything remotely resembling psychics.

It felt like a failure. It felt like when she started smoking after having successfully quit for months at a time. Falling off the psychic wagon was far worse than falling off the nicotine wagon. She thought she should probably stop at Walgreens and get a pack of Marlboros. If she was once again a fallen woman, she may as well fall all the way.

With the economy in such a bad state, the psychic was free and available to see her. The mystical lady was just where she had last seen her a year before: sitting in a large closet at the back of the accountant's office, surrounded by angels, with a small table in front of her. No crystal ball. No tarot cards. This lady's supernatural gifts came as easily and as readily as a friendly conversation.

She missed the setting of the flower shop, where the lady did her readings when they had first met so many years before. This room, however, was very friendly and full of angels and lace. The psychic had lost a lot of weight. It did not take a seer to read the expression on Catalina's face.

"I've been ill, dear, but I am fine now. May I hold your hands to tap into your energy?"After a short moment of silence and a few deep breaths, the clairvoyant lady began to speak.

"I see you are going back to work. It will not be for long, you are about to ... no, and you already have encountered the missing pieces. You just need to find the right voice to present the story. Spirit wants you to know it will be well accepted."

"Yes, I am about to start a new job. It feels so hard to give up on my project, again. Please tell me what Spirit says about this missing piece I've encountered."

"Spirit says that you need to trust and share with them."

"Them?"

"Oh yes, dear. Didn't I say so? There is a young man and a young woman; they need you as much as you need them. They are aware that they have to share information. Oh, wait...no, Spirit says *he* knows he has to share."

"She's the one who contacted me."

"Well, you know, dear, the soul energy that chooses the male body in an incarnation is usually not as, how can I say this? The male energy doesn't accept as readily, even when things are obvious."

The psychic hugged her as they said goodbye. She wondered if it would be a full a year till they met again.

Through the years, she had gone back and forth with her doubts and her beliefs in psychics. The truth was she had never had an unpleasant experience with any psychic or astrologer.

The fact that she had worked so meticulously at searching through archives with the help of many who were very serious about the sources of information while visiting psychics was very difficult for her to balance. The psychics she had learned the most from were all accurate in their daily and mundane information about her life; time and time again, they were correct about that which she could confirm. She just found the psychics, their information, and the entire process so very difficult to trust.

She was not ready to answer Maggie's e-mail. Fully equipped with her cigarettes and wine, she decided she needed to tackle the file marked "Psychics."

First, she had to get the books out of the way. She opened the bottle of sauvignon blanc, grabbed a few boxes, and put the rest of the books inside the boxes with the list on top.

All the books went in the box except Tim Sherwood's *Coming in to Land*. That one belonged on the coffee table right next to Ron Davies's books.

CHAPTER TWELVE – TRUST

It was snowing outside, and Bill was more than a little hung over. After they left Maggie's friends, there was a fuzzy memory that they had stopped along the way for fish and chips to appease the munchies. At some point, they had gone into a pub, and Bill, with the euphoria instilled by the cannabis and the envy on every man's face when he kissed Maggie, had decided to try all sorts of strange British beers. Something called Speckled Hen, or was it Scrumpy? Or was it Scrumptious Speckled Hen? The cab ride home was more than hazy, but he remembered they'd laughed a lot and that all was good.

"How are you feeling, my wild adventurer?" Maggie had her arms around him as she spoke.

"Pretty good."

"Don't tell me you are a Bloody Mary, hair-of-the-dog type of morning-after drinker," she teased.

"No, I am a two-egg-McMuffins-lots-of-coffee morning-after drinker."

"Uncivilized American."

"Canadian!" He challenged.

"You grew up and studied in America; Canadian in passport only, that's what you are." She looked out the window. "It really looks like it's brutal out there."

"Don't worry, Maggie, your wild adventurer will bring you back nourishment."

The cold air on his face felt great. His nostrils were beginning to freeze. Maggie was right; his parents had made sure he was born in Canada out of fear of their generation having another Vietnam. They had given birth to him in Canada just in case there was another Vietnam. He really was Canadian in passport only.

Why was he feeling so happy? Maybe it was a bit like coming out of the closet. He had come out of the past-life closet. The women looked at him with admiration, and the men? It felt good to be envied. The men, he was sure, were about to book a past-life regression session or two. Yes, he felt relieved that at the very least, in the young, happy, partying circles, he did not seem odd. He was not likely to come out of the closet at work--not in any foreseeable future.

It was so cold outside that they had to reheat the breakfast when he got back with it, even though McDonald's was nearby. After a nice shower and some very restorative lovemaking, Bill suggested they watch

Dead Again. Maggie did not hesitate, and she placed the DVD in the player.

The movie was divided into two parts that were interwoven as the story was told. One part, presented in black-and-white, took place during the 1940s. The other part, in color, took place in the late 1980s or early 1990s. The characters needed to visit people or look through old newspapers and magazines to find what they needed. It was so unlike today, when with just a few strokes of a keyboard and the right search engine, all of the information needed was found as if by magic.

In a few scenes, surrounded by bloody carcasses at a butcher's cold storage, a psychiatrist explained past lives. This was Robin Williams at his finest. Once Robin Williams's character got to his definition of karma, Bill could imagine Maggie as a child being scared of the movie. All in all, Maggie's mother was right.

"It is a good movie. I'd never heard of it before."

"I don't think many people have."

"If I hadn't been under hypnosis before, I can imagine it could be...not a turn off, but not as thrilling. The part where Kenneth Branagh hands the old man his cigarettes was brilliant! What a way to quit smoking!"

Bill lit his cigarette as he laughed at that. Maggie did not seem to be herself. In fine form, she would have had something to say or would have liked to argue that the film had much more to offer than the cigarette scene.

"You were quite chatty in your drunken stupor last night," Maggie began.

"And ..."

"And you talked about how there was safety in numbers. In the numbers of a group during a past-life regression. That it felt much safer than the one-on-one."

"Oh? I was chatty."

They stared at each other for a silent moment or two. Then Maggie, in a disappointed tone, continued. "How many times had you been regressed before we did it together?"

"Twice. Look, Maggie, I was embarrassed..."

"I know. I'm not mad; I'm just curious. A little sad but mainly curious. Had you seen me, before?"

"No. Neither in my dreams nor in the regressions. If I had seen you at all, it was in my wishes. I really want this to work, Maggie. I am in it for the long haul with you, so if I hurt you in any way, let me know and I will fix it."

They held on to each other, and he described in full detail how he disliked the therapist with the PhD who'd regressed him.

They laughed together as he explained how he had punched him, as the arrogant doctor had not given him a method of escape, such as lifting his left arm. He answered every question she asked. Every detail. This was not going to spoil what they now shared.

Maggie told Bill how she had seen him on the street and followed him into the bookstore. How she had made sure to start the conversation with something, anything, that warranted more than a yes or no answer.

She explained how she too was in it for the long haul, so as few lovers do, they became absolutely honest with each other. In their mutual honesty, they gave each other the tools to make their love story work, to make it work for the long haul.

CHAPTER THIRTEEN – MORE PSYCHICS

Catalina carefully opened the file cabinet drawer that housed the large file titled "Psychics." So many of her files had taken her on distant journeys, some over a geographic distance, such as to England and to Denmark, and other files made her travel in time to the country of her childhood, Mexico. This file was special because it had made her travel through a world of faith or fantasy—she often wondered which.

She took a deep breath and journeyed back into the past, into her youth, when she had feared little and questioned everything. She wondered at what point in life she had lost that fearlessness. She wondered if it was something one could ever recapture? It could be a useful tool for her today; one she knew she did not possess.

She looked at the written pages and cassette tapes. She had astrology charts for each one of the people she researched, plotted by sun only, as she had birthplace and date information but not the time of birth for each one. Here were the five dead that she had in different ways become so attached to. For the pilot, she only had Australia as his birthplace, and there was no use in trying to plot for an entire continent.

Then there were the psychic's scribbles-- automatic writing--full lines of words attached to each other. Together, she and the psychic would separate each word and read the messages. It was fun, but that one spoke more of Catalina's personal life, rather than guided her as to where to look for her research. Other psychics had also worked like the automatic writing old lady. They were not necessarily bad; they simply channeled subjects she either preferred to leave alone or was not interested in at all. She was not seeking the future; hers was a quest for the past.

There was a file with four psychics that had been particularly helpful. The four that had held the two watches that BAL had returned with her grandfather's belongings in 1939. There were a few other psychics who had held the watches and seen nothing at all or nothing that matched the fate of the G-AESY, but these four psychics described the event in their own words and from different perspectives. *So even Spirits saw things in different ways,* She found herself thinking.

One of them had been the lady who worked out of the accountant's office: "Tell me, dear, why do I see a bridge?"

The shaman had said, "I don't like working with the energies of the second watch...you are looking for a flag with a lot of blue in it...you don't believe me? Look it up...so it was 1939...I see what I see so clearly I cannot be wrong."

The tarot class teacher started getting dizzy and had difficulty breathing as he described the smoke. She had that on tape somewhere. He started saying he saw letters; he said "Q" but clearly drew the "G" and then said "dash" and "A." That had been a good day; she was certain she knew where her grandfather had been sitting to see that from his window.

The funny trance guy whose face moved in all directions with eyes closed. What did that one call himself? Reverend? He specialized in billet readings.

She had, of course, also encountered her share of true con artists who at first seemed to know things and then wanted much more money to "remove the spell that blocked" her. They could help her find everything for a large sum of money. (She did not consider these as bad experiences with psychics, but rather, bad experiences with charlatans.) She had learned to be polite and walk away; after all, you know what they say: *No creo en brujas, pero de que vuelan.* Better safe than sorry. Just because she didn't believe they could harm her did not guarantee they wouldn't try!

Behind the documented readings from the four ethical clairvoyants, which had described almost identical events, were three pages she had written. On top of the three pages was a little yellow sticky note that read, "If I need to go the fiction route, this could be useful."

She smiled. She had written that when she had decided to write a book about a woman searching for all of the data on the G-AESY while struggling to survive her own life. She decided to give her character numerous marriages, a sort of metaphor for all of *The London Times* she had failed at her attempts to write the story.

This was really too much. She knew it was starting, that what she had waited for so anxiously for several years was finally here. She wondered if some of their conversations would resemble what she had imagined or seen in her past-life regressions. She wondered if some of their conversations would be identical to the ones she wrote.

Was life about to start imitating art? Was she about to cross a boundary in life that would not allow her to turn back and be part of her church again? She got her car keys and drove to the beach. She walked and walked to the sound of the waves crashing against the sand. She felt tears streaming down her face; she did not want to get her hopes up and be disappointed again. Her life was and had always been far better than the characters she created to tell the story. She did, however, find the dead ends in her search hard. Though she tried not to, she often wallowed in self-pity.

She looked at the ocean and decided that the God she wanted to believe in was always there, always loving and understanding. She decided that this proved to her that books she read on re-incarnation were very important to her. Such as *The Search for Bridey Murphy*, because the source, the writer had graduated from Wharton School of Finance; a Mr. Morey Bernstein, not by an expected source on re-incarnation. The Brian Weiss books that spoke of past lives (she could not imagine accepting future ones just yet) ... and the Jess Stern books ... The God she wanted to believe in was one who allowed us to grow and live through many lives. He was not one who forced us to compact all our lessons into one limited time period. This proved to her that the world we inherited, we also gave to ourselves.

She reached her hand up to the necklace hanging from her neck on a leather cord. She caressed the stone image of Ganesh and wondered if her beliefs in that kind of God made her a Buddhist or a Hindu. She wondered if there were any other organized religions that accepted reincarnation? With a deep inhalation, she knew that this time, nothing would stop her. She would work and pay her bills, but every free moment would be spent on this, the story of the G-AESY.

CHAPTER FOURTEEN – WHAT IS IN A NUMBER?

Catalina had given up on numbers for chapters, as there was no order to how she saw the story. There was no order to tell the story. For her, it had started with a letter from her grandfather's boss at Intava. There was one sentence in the letter that did not match the self-assured picture of Warner Norton Grubb, she had seen on Wikipedia in his full US Navy uniform, not a surprise as once war broke out everyone that could joined. After offering his sincerest condolences to her grandmother and apologizing for bothering her with "cables in connection with Cesar's cremation," Commodore Grubb wrote the following on August 30, 1939:

I very much dislike bothering you with such matters; however, I think you will be very interested in knowing that up to the present time, we do not have any authentic information as to what caused the tragic accident. I am very much afraid that it is one of those mysteries that will not be solved; although, of course, investigations will be carried out.

How could such a well-educated, successful American in such a high post in the international petroleum industry write such a thing? After only two weeks, how could he assume that? When her formal research had started in the summer of 1996, she met a researcher who was working on a book about the history of flight attendants and was curious about her story. He had this to say: "It's always a problem to explain an accident like that when the pilot survives. You know, when the pilot dies, it is just documented as pilot error. So much simpler ..."

Really? Just blame it on a Pilot? What was simple? What was truth? She could tell the story with any number of voices, but there was simply no choice. With the limited traditional data and the information acquired from psychics, it had to be called fiction. She had given the character of the story one failed marriage for every time she had had to interrupt her search. She had also created another character that was searching for the same story, a character that was very bothered by the use of psychics. There was so much drama between the two characters that it had proven to be too distracting. There was, however, one chapter she always liked from that manuscript. She felt so clever that the title of this chapter was not "Psychics."

Today, life was turning the tables on her. In her manuscript, she found the pilot. She found the missing piece, the soul that was to guide her through the journey back in time. Now, in reality, Maggie had contacted her, but it could be useful. This young couple had already decided that the strange and unexplainable happens. If she had to explain to the young couple across the Atlantic how she had come about some of her information, they may be absolutely open to the possibility of psychics. She lit her cigarette and read the part in her manuscript that dealt with explaining to the pilot, the one she had created in her imagination, why and how she knew all that she knew.

The Watches

With the persuasive letter of a tear.

—Charles Churchill, 1731–1764

I'd taken notice of his e-mail address at the British Airways archives. My words and reasons had not touched him face-to-face. With tears and truth pouring out of my very soul, I sat down and began to write.

Somewhere between my third and fourth marriages, the two shortest of the five, I became lonely, empty, and sad enough to seek help anywhere I could find it. There were probably more psychics in the state of Florida per capita than in any other state. We have an incredible little town called Cassadaga.

Cassadaga, in those days, was a pleasant, small village with little streets filled with Victorian houses. One could just walk around and pick a psychic as if choosing a restaurant. The psychics' specialties were posted outside their doors, like the menus of restaurants. Some promised to help one find love; others, money and success. I chose the one who promised to help find peace of mind and balance of the soul.

Today, the psychics' from Cassadaga have websites online that are very sophisticated, offering readings by phone or other new technology. I could only imagine how they read you by computer; I had not been there in over a decade.

Peace of mind and balance of the soul had seemed the perfect ingredients to recover from a divorce. I had felt so hopeful with my wedding cake that read, "Third Time's the Charm." It had never occurred to me that the charm would be so short-lived.

The psychic's hair was longer than my shoulder-length locks. His face wore age and the abuse of the Florida sun. He dressed in loose clothing and sandals.

Apparently, this allowed the flow of energies to pass freely through his body.

"Come in, please come in. This might take a while. Were you planning to leave today?"

"Are you assuming that I plan to pay for more than your one-hour reading?"

"I don't need to assume anything; I am one of the most psychic souls on the planet. You and I, we have a long, bumpy ride ahead of us."

"Ha! One hell of a sales pitch!"

"Would you like an herbal tea?"

"What's in it?" I asked.

"Chamomile and some secret psychic herbs."

"Sure, I'll have some tea. Thank you."

"So, I see you look far younger than you are, yet another failed marriage, and of course, as you well know, more to come. Don't judge yourself too harshly; you were probably a monk in a past life or maybe two past lives. And now you need to experience more in this one."

The tea was delicious. I managed to pick my jaw up off the ground, for how did he know of my failed marriages? Observing that he certainly moved, spoke, and acted with a peace I longed for but had seldom seen, I finally found the courage to get out the words.

"How many more marriages?"

"Several."

"Divorce hurts."

"Failed relationships create tremendous growth if used correctly."

"Do I? Do I use failed relationships correctly?"

"Sometimes."

"I'd like more tea, please."

As he got up, I noticed that everything in his simple little house had a feel of happiness and light. There were so many candles, and there was a burning smell that was not really like a perfume; it was not like any incense I knew.

"What are you burning?"

"Copal. As a Mexican, you should be very familiar with it."

"Most people do not realize that I am Mexican."

"Even when you wear the Aztec calendar around your neck?"

"Oh! I thought it was a psychic flash."

"No, simply an observation. Do you wear that necklace often?"

"Yes."

"I'd like to hold it, if that's okay with you."

I pulled the gold chain over my head and handed him the necklace. He closed his eyes and took deep breaths. His shut lids showed signs of the eyes shifting underneath, and then he spoke.

"Two women are fighting over a man, one rips the necklace off the other's chain ..."

"When I found it, it did look like it had been ripped off the top ..."

He signaled that I should not speak; one cannot imagine how hard that is for someone with her birth moon in Gemini. But I kept quiet and listened.

"The one who ripped the necklace won. Not for long, but she won. The man died not long after, so he could not change his life. He was married to the one who won, but he loved the other more ..."

Now I really could not and would not keep quiet.

"That is really not nice. My grandfather died horribly at the age of forty-two. That necklace represents his work at the Huasteca Petroleum Company. I loved my grandmother very much, and she was a lovely lady. A real trophy of a woman to any man of her era; she was beautiful, clever, amazing, from a good family. She ... he would've never betrayed her, and she would've never stooped to some catfight." He sighed and took a careful look at me.

"I wonder if you are ready for your future. If you're going to lie to yourself this way, it is not likely."

"Okay, so there were some stories about how perhaps he ... misbehaved, liked the ladies."

"So be honest, and as far as your grandmother being, which I am sure she was, a trophy with all the wonderful things you attribute her with, well, take a good look in the mirror and see that you are that and perhaps more. Yet look at your record with marriages and choices of men. Good people, very good people have bad marriages sometimes. It doesn't make either one of your grandparents any less."

"You say that you sell peace of mind, and this feels more like mental abuse."

"No, it is truth, and through it, you will find what you are looking for."

"I thought psychics were supposed to go to the future, not the past."

"My sign clearly states 'Spiritual Healer.' The past is often the key to the future."

I sat down for a while and thought. He explained that if I wanted to get started, I needed a spiritual healing. A cleansing. Obediently, I lay down, and he asked for permission to touch my aura. When it was over, we spoke for a while about my energies, and then he moved on again to my grandfather.

"You have two watches. They are not yours, but you guard them and you keep them safe. Those watches have the answers that you seek. I am going to need to see the two watches to get you started with this. One is round, and the other one is almost a rectangle. I can see them put away in a box. You need to bring them the next time we meet."

He was right. Sitting in my safety deposit box at the bank, there were indeed two watches. I did not own them, but I kept them safe. I looked at them from time to time. They had arrived in 1939 with my grandfather's belongings. One was round. The other, a rectangle. One looked like it had drowned, and the other looked like it had burned. They were both recovered from the G-AESY, and one could say that the plane had both burned and drowned.

"That was not vague at all; perhaps your sign should say psychic."

"So you know what I am talking about?"

"Absolutely."

I left the next day with a few hundred dollars less in my pockets. A feeling of peace and harmony swept over me, and I looked forward to our next encounter.

I was able to return a week later. Through psychometrics, not through all of the archives, books and newspapers, my research began. He knew about the bridge and gave me the background of the people on board the plane that matched the data I later found in those very archives, newspapers, and books. He even told me where to look for some of it.

He knew there was one survivor and described the owner of the small rectangle watch my family had been sent by mistake, and that strangely, my grandmother had saved.

She could not continue to read! It was too ridiculous. In her fictional fantasy, she met the reincarnated pilot. Now this young woman who claimed that she was looking for information for "similar" reasons contacted her. Maggie was a fearless young woman just as Catalina had once been. Without hesitation, Maggie had mentioned Brian Weiss's books and asked if Catalina had read them.

Maybe this girl was some evil hacker. Maybe she had stolen her story and wanted more details.

That was not possible, as Catalina wrote on an old-fashioned typewriter.

So life had imitated art. Certain psychics had been correct in telling her she needed to be open-minded, as she would meet some of the people from her story in the bodies they inhabited today.

There was nothing left to question; in her book, she contacts the reincarnated pilot. In life, the faces on Maggie's Facebook page made it undeniable that the pilot's girlfriend contacted her. It was time to answer Maggie.

Catalina was as direct as Maggie had been and requested that they meet via Skype as soon as Maggie found the time. She attached three files, as Maggie had requested any photos that Catalina could share. The files were copies from Danish newspapers. One attachment had two pictures on the same page: the G-AESY being pulled out of the water and the pilot smiling from a hospital bed. The second one was the pilot and his wife enjoying a meal at a restaurant. The third picture was an odd one: it was of the pilot in bed at the hospital, striking matches with his bandaged and wounded hand to light the cigarette between his lips.

CHAPTER FIFTEEN – REACHING OUT

Maggie and Bill were in bed when she noticed the e-mail from Florida. Bill began to laugh. Maggie had apparently approached this woman head-on with the directness only Maggie could have. The woman was familiar with the Brian Weiss book and was a believer in reincarnation. She had looked at Maggie's Facebook page and had sent three attachments that she was sure they would find of interest. The woman also requested that they "meet" through Skype as soon as possible.

The three attachments downloaded, and Bill and Maggie could only stare, stunned. One by one, they looked at the three images. Finally one of them decided to hit "print." Holding the pictures and looking at them was beyond anything they expected. Maggie finally found her voice.

"Look, that has to be a hospital bed, and he is smoking."

"Thank you for not saying 'you are smoking.'"

"No, Bill, you are you. I am very clear about this. You are Bill, and I am Maggie; these people who look like us, this link to the past, is interesting, but we are who we are today. This is just the past--a past--which needs to be cleaned up and cleared out. Didn't the file say he broke the window with his elbow? Why would the hand be bandaged?"

"We need to talk to this woman in Florida before we look for a grassy knoll."

"What?"

"Kennedy assassination. It implies conspiracy theory. I believe that makes us even for my lack of Shakespearean knowledge?"

Maggie snubbed her nose and made her "oh, you foolish Canadian/American" sort of face.

"She wants to meet us via Skype. What's the time difference? "

"Five hours."

"What do we answer?"

FROM: Maggiestrylleri@hotmail.net.uk

TO: SecretsoftheG-AESY@hotmail.net.fla.us

RE: re: re

Thank you for your prompt reply and photos. We will be happy to meet via Skype over the weekend. You may as well know that the photos took us by surprise. Do you have any other data on the pilot and his wife?

Maggie, impulsive as ever, hit send without a second thought. The reply was almost immediate.

FROM: SecretsoftheG-AESY@hotmail.net.fla.us

TO: Maggiestrylleri@hotmail.net.uk

RE: re: re: re

I am very happy to share any and all information I have found. I prefer to speak with you. When are you available?

Maggie and Bill looked at each other. There was no reason to wait. Maggie and Bill had to get dressed. Catalina looked in the mirror and put on make-up.

Both sides of the Atlantic were nervous with anticipation and excitement. Bill and Maggie were hoping that this woman had all the answers, almost as much as Catalina was hoping they did.

As their Skype call connected, all three of them reached for a cigarette and a glass of Sauvignon Blanc. As soon as they could see each other's faces on their computer screens, greetings were exchanged.

"Hello."

"Hello to you both. I need to ask. Had you seen any pictures of them?"

"No, never before."

"Oh, you are American."

"Canadian--"

"He's Canadian."Maggie and Bill said it at the same time and began to laugh. Their laughter was contagious. They started to talk about cigarettes and how Bill began to smoke after the regression. This did not surprise Catalina, who explained to them that she had personally had past-life regressions that had caused certain physical changes in her.

Bill talked in great detail. He told his story; Maggie listened as if she had never heard the story before. He described his nightmares and the lettering on the plane. And how all of this had led them to the Munich Pact videos online, the archives near Heathrow, the information on the Internet, and her entries in the archive.

He described how there were different dreams in which he saw many things that did not make sense; that all of the dreams ended in the cold, salty water and the same uneasy feeling. He left out any incident that had ended in bedwetting, but he conveyed very clearly that this had created problems in his life.

As Bill spoke, he felt a tremendous release. He also felt that all was well and would be fine. This had to be the woman the guides had clearly been talking about when they told him, "Tell her your story." This also meant that any fear he had that Maggie might not be the one was completely dispelled.

"What is your goal, Bill? Do you feel better since the past-life regressions?" Catalina asked. "What do you want to know?"

"I still have the dreams, and that is a problem. My goal is to be rid of the dreams, to put all of this behind me. However, now that we have started to look at the story, I am curious, and it has its flip side. It is great fun to play detective with Maggie."

Maggie smiled and plunged into her questions.

"What about the bodies and the fencing position?"

"You noticed that."

Maggie's impulsiveness reminded Catalina of the day fifteen years before when she had read death certificate after death certificate and had seen the image of the man with his arms folded across his chest.

She liked all of the TV shows and novels that described autopsies and corpses. She knew that rigor mortis should be the same if all of them died at the same time and in the same way.

"I think it leads to questions. I did, however, some years ago consult with a pathologist, and he explained that there could be reasons for that; it wasn't as cut and dry as in a detective novel.

"I was allowed to work with the autopsy reports in Vordingborg. I have a good friend in Denmark who helped me read and translate, but we were not allowed to photocopy anything. We believed that we found discrepancies in that particular body. There was no blood in the nasal cavity as there was in the other four...or was it foam? I cannot remember. I'd have to look at the notes we made to know for certain. I remember that we were as excited as you sound today. It's getting late, and I assume you both work tomorrow. Look over what you have and send me questions. I will also think about what Bill said and ask him questions."

As they were saying good-bye, she added one more thing."Maggie, have you looked up the pilot on Ancestry.com?" When Maggie shook her head, Catalina continued. "Well, if I found the right one, and it is an 'if' because I tried to contact the pilot's family through the RAF, and they sent me to the wrong family. So the name is not that unusual, but I believe I found the correct Wright on Ancestry.com, listed under marriages in Surrey, 1939. At any rate, if I found the right one, the wife's name was Margaret."

That night Bill slept soundly; Maggie did not.

CHAPTER SIXTEEN – APART

Maggie was surprised by how difficult it had been to say good-bye to Bill. It was just for a few days, but she had been involved in enough relationships that had changed because of a sudden change of routine. Her life experience had taught her that absence did not make the heart grow fonder, but rather, that out of sight meant out of mind. This was doubly troublesome, as in the past, she had always been the one to walk away from a love story; this was something she could not envision with Bill.

"It would have been fun to invite you, but with the changes in the economy, all companies have to be careful not to look like they are celebrating. This convention should be all business and quite boring."

"Thanks, that's very sweet."This feeling of vulnerability was very new to Maggie, and it was not at all pleasant. That combined with trying to grapple with the news that she not only resembled the woman from her past-life regression but also that they shared a name...it left her feeling exposed.

She joined Ancestry.com and searched for data on the pilot and his wife. As the woman in Florida had said, it was impossible to know if it really was the right Wright. She had the pilot's birth date from the British Airways files as March 20, 1910, and she knew that he was from Australia.

Maggie discovered in the England and Wales Marriage Index from 1916–2005, a marriage registered in April, May, or June of 1939 for a Wright, Clifford F. C., to someone with the last name Price. The marriage was registered in Surrey NE. It said it was in volume 2a on page 365. She reverse searched for spouse, and there it was: Price, Margaret B., married someone named Wright, registered in Surrey, NE in volume 2a on page 365.

She was very happy that their last names and middle initials did not match. Also her legal name was Margrethe, after her Danish grandmother. No one pronounced it correctly except for her mother and her grandparents. That's why she preferred Maggie.

She continued to look for anything else that could be of use on Ancestry.com and found the registered death for Clifford Frederick C. Wright in October,

November, or December 1979; this had to be right, as it matched the March 20, 1910, birth date. It said Bromley. She Googled Bromley, and there it was: Bromley, Australia.

This had to be him. She wondered if in this life, things could be like in the other movie her mother had given them to watch, *Chances Are*. If anything is left undone in a past life, does a soul really come back that quickly to sort things out?

She contacted the woman across the Atlantic via Skype.

"I got on Ancestry.com, and I found the marriage entry you mentioned."

"Odd, isn't it?"

"Yes, I am not sure I like how it makes me feel."

"I can imagine that it's hard to wrap your head around it, especially if you are not fully satisfied that reincarnation is...real."

"I was brought up believing in it, so it is not that hard for me to accept, but after seeing how Bill reacts to his nightmares, I guess I am afraid of what it could open up in me."Maggie blew a smoke ring before she continued."I also found his death registry, and that one has to be accurate. The marriage we can only assume, but the death has date and place of birth. It matched, and he was born in a place called Bromley. I looked that up, too, and found that there is a Bromley in Australia."

"Wow! That's clever. It didn't occur to me. I did look up the ship manifests from Australia to England and found three possibilities...let me check my file."

Maggie watched Catalina take a binder full of papers with large lettering on the side: WRIGHT.

"How many files do you have?"

"Pretty much one file for any person or thing that is relevant, including all the engineers and specialists I could find that were involved in reporting the incident. Here we go. I remember one of the Wrights was a minister or priest, so I nixed that one. There are two more: one arrived in 1933 and the other in 1936. I also found an entry in Flight Magazine online from July 28, 1938, page 92, under 'Transfer of Officers Reserve.' Let me send this to you."

Maggie looked at the list, and there was the pilot's name. In The London Gazette from June 7, 1940, the name clearly showed the pilot to be Royal Air Force Reserve, and the number 34012, followed his name in parentheses.

"Why did you look all that up?"

"Well, I was confused because the British Airways archive has an entry that states he joined the RAF in

1947, which, with the war and the shortage of good pilots, did not make sense. Also, if he joined so late, I could not understand how he could have ended up as a wing commander."

Maggie nodded in agreement."You are right. I did see a letter when that man Wicks was looking for him in 1951."

"Oh, Wicks! Don't get me started on that one. He is in every file, and everything is confusing and questionable! Let's go back to the pilot. We did not discuss certain parts of the statement."

"Yes, I am very annoyed by the part where he says that...here, let me see my copy...Ah! Here it is, there is absolutely no doubt that he claims that both of them saw the fire at the same time. It all sounds very professional; the pilot looks for a place to land, and the Radio Officer leaves the cockpit to 'extinguish the fire.'"

"That's right! But he did not take the fire extinguisher, and that very airline had just had a fire four days earlier!"

Maggie's eyes were round and astounded."What? How? Are you certain?"

"Yes, it is very well documented because the airplane in question was a famous one, the G-AFGN. I think it was one of the airplanes that transported Neville

Chamberlain during the Munich Pact. Don't you think it is something the employees at BAL would have all been talking about?"

"Absolutely! That's a big deal. How could this guy go back without a fire extinguisher? How about the telegram where they say that they are flying the pilot and his wife to a different airport, and that the plane is to taxi straight to hangars to avoid newspaper photographers? They even switch airports."

Catalina shrugged. "I do not know how much to read into that. There is a document stating that the press had contacted crewmembers in other incidents. So for insurance reasons, loss of life...that particular entry does not bother me. I also found in the Danish archives a lot of back and forth dated until several months later. There is the matter of the pilot's license and second-class navigator's certificate. I have correspondence for that dated October 1939."

"October?"

"Yes, it's on Air Ministry paper and mentions Major Fill, who at that point was back in service."

"How could you know that?"

"I have another letter here..."

As Catalina moved around in the background, Maggie noticed bookshelves and binders, some of which were huge.

"Here we go. Danish file...Copenhagen, December 17, 1939, from Major Fill to the head of the Danish Air Ministry's accidents branch, Mr. Eskildsen. Here, I'll scan it, and you can read it. It covers a lot."

"It's coming through; I should read it, and we can talk tomorrow. I need to get some sleep."Maggie ended the Skype video call.

In Florida, Catalina looked at the letter. She had not read it for quite a while, and as she did so, she wondered why she had not underlined that which bothered her as she had with the pilot's statement. There were certainly several parts of the letter that left room for question.

The letter was from Major Fill to Mr. Eskildsen; they had each represented the Air Ministry of their respective countries in August of 1939 in the matter of the G-AESY. This was a full four months after the airplane had gone down, and these two men were still discussing the test for possible accelerants that could be found in the linoleum where the fire had been at its worst. This letter showed Major Fill in such a different light from the opinion Catalina had formed when reading others describe Major Fill. The problem with this letter was where Major Fill wrote that he 'agreed in general.' There was no real information as to what he disagreed with. Could that imply that the British Air Ministry never officially accepted the report? Was it simply that with the world in such disarray, this was just too small a matter?

Mr. Eskildsen of the Danish Air Ministry was not at all pleased with the fire expert Madsen that he had apparently not chosen. The British Airways inspectors agreed with Mr. Eskildsen and did not agree with Dr. Madsen. How odd that it seemed Major Fill had agreed that summer, but with this letter from December, it stood to wonder what had really gone on behind closed doors. Major Fill had chosen to take pieces of the airplane to be tested. That must have been unusual and a big deal.

Amid the information that Catalina had found about Mr. Eskildsen, the piece that was firmly engraved in her mind was in his obituary. It said something to the effect that Mr. Eskildsen was always proven right in the end. *Even after death?* She wondered.

No file she found was complete. The engineers did not agree upon the final report. One of the many wonderful people who had helped her, a man who had written and published several books, kindly spent the day at the archives outside of London, The National Archives in Kew. He was so sure he could show her where to look for the files at the end of the day; instead, they had simply double-checked where she had looked before.

There was a set of files that was new to her, the Foreign Office files. The historian suggested that they search for the arrival of the bodies to England. She knew that the bodies of Anthony Crossley and A. S. M. Leigh had arrived on August 22, 1939, via Felixtow, on a Danish vessel (the SS Margrethe).

They found no record of this and, according to the writer, that was apparently unusual as bodies of members of Parliament being brought into the country needed to be registered. Searching through the Foreign Office files, she eventually found some that proved useful in other ways. The writer who helped her, however, was frustrated and certain that there had to be several copies of a final report, which was the regular protocol in such matters. He named various acronyms that meant nothing to her, along with many associations or official offices. He felt the relatives of those on board might have it. She contacted or tried to contact the places he suggested, but the answer was always that files that old were not to be found. She and the writer looked at some index files that mentioned the plane but did not have the report.

Pensive and with an unhappy expression on his wise face, he finally said to her, "Catalina, your files, by their absence, are screaming."

This sent a chill through her body. Could it possibly be that there had been something wrong? Not just in her desire to justify that her grandfather had died in as suspicious a manner as she had always been raised to understand? But it did not last long; feeling and suspecting are not synonyms of proving.

He wasn't the only one. Employees at the National Archives in Kew who had helped her search on several occasions were also frustrated and would say it was "a bit of a mystery."

While searching for other files, such as the legal cases of Mr. Wicks, she had heard from the National Archives' employees that due to some decisions by some government personality or other, only sample files had been saved in such matters, and that this was a disgrace, another example of the bad decisions of...anyhow, it was a complicated but logical explanation as to why certain files were not to be found.

The official report of the G-AESY was a most unusual thing to be missing. That word again--mystery.

CHAPTER SEVENTEEN – CONTAGIOUS OBSSESION

Maggie was exhausted and finally slept soundly. It was the first time she had slept alone in several weeks, and it was hard to find a comfortable position without feeling Bill next to her. Also, she could not stop thinking about all of the information she had shared with the lady in Florida. There was one particular thought keeping her awake. *Had another plane really made use of the fire extinguisher only four days earlier?*

In Florida, it was not as late, and even if it had been, the thrill for Catalina to have someone as interested in the case of the G-AESY and happy to discuss it in detail was a gift from fate. Someone like Maggie, who was keen to question the information, made Catalina meticulously review her information. As she flipped through the pages, she took notes on what to discuss with Maggie the next day.

All files in various archives she had found were very large. They fit like pieces of a puzzle, helping fill in parts of the story. She had visited the British Airways archives four or five times, and on the second occasion, she had spent several weeks just going through the BAL file, page by page. She had been young and impulsive like Maggie and had found a hidden problem in almost everything she read.

This was also helped by the fact that the archivist, a very serious and formal English man, did at some point influence her when he saw how carefully she studied each document. H had said to her, "Remember, Catalina, in 1939, the word 'sabotage' was not used lightly; not as it is today."

The archivist had never given any specific reason to pinpoint why he said this, but it was obvious that he had taken the time to read this file carefully, and he was a man who understood these reports. He had seen something. So she went through her notes carefully; she knew that she did not know much about these reports, so she copied by hand every single document that summer.

There was a series of reports with the dates and times of anything from phone calls to cables. There was one report for the radio operator A. S. M. Leigh with nothing unusual; but his death certificate was missing. The translation was there, and in her notes from the Nykøping or Vordingborg file, she had seen it. She had also seen the dates and times of all of the sad events that his mother had been told about his death. There were details on various things: the transportation of the bodies on the SS Margrethe that arrived in London on August 22, 1939, a list of those present at the RO52's funeral, insurance information... These were sad, to say the least, as each document about the dead is sad, but nothing in them Catalina thought of as unusual.

Another report was on Anthony Crossley. This document had similar details to the other. But there were two death certificates: one typed (like the one her family had received with her grandfather's ashes) and one handwritten like the other three in the BAL file. Here the unusual thing was the body's position when found, and she felt that this was strange; she had, however, consulted with a pathologist who said there could be a number of explanations for the body position. The carbon monoxide by volume in the blood that could have been too low to render the men unconscious-- something else she questioned. But through the Internet, she found that in severe fires, this too could be explained.

The report for Intava on Mr. Castillo and Mr. Simonton was shorter than the previous two. The interesting entry was about the call from Mrs. Simonton. This was detailed in a separate page, dated

August 17th, and had a nice signature (impossible to tell whose). Mrs. Simonton had taken her husband to the airport that morning and had clearly seen Mr. Castillo giving instructions to "someone" at Heston on what should be done in the event of an accident. The person who wrote this decided to go to Heston and question anyone working there that morning from police and customs to the employees of various airlines, including BAL, Jersey Airways, and Airworks. There was no one with any recollection of even speaking to Mr. Castillo.

There were reports on BAL in Copenhagen and in the press. They were full of details of phone calls and cables. She'd tried to find out who had told the press to report it was sabotage and discovered that for some strange reason, the report of sabotage had come out of France. The flight had left London, gone to Hamburg, and had gone down on its way to Copenhagen.

There were the notes on Mr. Maxwell that Maggie had jumped at, and it did make sense that it said that Mr. Crossley's body was in Nykøbing Falster and not Vordingborg. This had even been changed; the word Vordingborg had been scratched out, and Nykøbing Falster added by hand. That was not the only correction on the page. There was something about where the bodies were taken; she finally found it in an August 19, 1939, partial report, the one that described how all the bodies were brought up. It stated that the police insisted that the bodies be taken to Nykøbing Falster, so Maggie could rest assured that all bodies had been together.

She had another report from that very day that had a long, detailed account of how discrete inquires had been made about Mr. Beuss; a handwritten letter showed how the British Airways office in Hamburg had very politely asked questions about Mr. Beuss. The report stated that he was a very nice family man who lived in a respectable residential area. It went on with details about income and his friends. What was odd was the inability to find out where he worked. It stated that they did not know what his business was, and yet the death certificate clearly stated "*Syndikus*," which is a corporate lawyer. Of course, in 1939, Germany was such a place that what was unusual and what was usual to find out could be anybody's guess. At an accident committee meeting, she noticed a mention of 'discreet enquiries' that were made about the German.

She found that the British Airways men concluded that there was simply no need to try to find out anything about the passenger who flew from London to Hamburg. That they knew where he had purchased his ticket and would get his information from the place that had booked the ticket. This was just in case they decided to question the passenger, a Mr. Stocks. The discussions of the meeting determined that there was no reason to think that either Mr. Stocks or the German passenger were to be considered as people who would be 'concerned in sabotaging the aircraft.'

That same report discussed the fire and the fact that the BAL chief engineer disagreed adamantly with the Danish fire expert's theory. This was all documented in J. H. Willans' reports, and that was something she really wanted to discuss with Maggie—the blue dye file, as she called it.

One of the reports, and the file contained several, went into detail in an hour-by-hour format. The one titled 19.8.39, in the 11:00 a.m. entry, was where she found the information that made her head spin with disbelief.

This was in reference to Mr. Stocks. The passenger who boarded in London and got off in Hamburg. The place where Mr. Stocks had bought his ticket – someone referred to simply as "P.M.," probably an employee of BAL, telephoned and found out that Mr. Stocks bought his ticket with cash, but that because of a transaction for another previous journey; in which Mr. Stocks needed a refund, the employee at Dean and Dawson of Fenchurch Street was able to give his initials and address.

Post-9/11 and with the world as tense as it is today, it was so difficult to understand why the gentleman had never been questioned. In 1939, at the brink of WWII, the feeling must have been as tense and suspect as it was in this era of terrorism and hatred. The report went on to describe Mr. Stocks as a man of thirty to thirty-five years of age and short. In full detail, it describes a conversation with an airport employee in which Mr. Stocks is told that there is no smoking on board the airplane. He said to a traffic officer, "You are behind *The London Times*," or words to that effect. The file does show that Mr. Stocks flew back on August 17th and that his luggage weighed nine kilos on the way to Hamburg and ten on the way back. It made no sense to document that and not simply talk to the gentleman. Mr. Stocks was described as 'a perfectly normal person.'

Catalina wondered if discreet inquiries of Mr. Castillo would have been made had anyone had realized that the Mexican had indeed been raised in Germany, or that his family had been affiliated with the Krupp family...discreet inquiries, indeed.

CHAPTER EIGHTEEN – CAREFUL COMPARISSONS

"Are you sure all the bodies were in Nykøbing Falster?" Maggie sounded disappointed.

"That's what it says."

"What do you think about the death certificates?"

"I am of the opinion that the only body that should be different is indeed the last one that was pulled out the following day--not a body pulled out on the fifteenth."

"I think that's the one Bill saw bleeding in his dreams, as well."

"Besides, he was a man who, by all accounts, had some very strong and different opinions. I have huge binders from *The London Times* and Hansard that clearly show that. He was, in my opinion, a sort of genius, and I have a file from the National Archives at Kew in which he actually predicts in 1932 that the Germans will start war through the Polish Corridor; that was seven years before it happened."

"Who do you think wanted to cause him harm?" Maggie asked.

"We can come to the who, later; I am very interested in what you think of the various engineers' opinions...the meticulous manner in which J. H. Willans describes how the entire system of the plane is taken apart to prove there were no leaks and no evidence of blue dye."

"These are the men who disagree with Dr. Madsen, the fire expert?"

"Yes. As I read it, the people who know and understand airplanes strongly disagreed with him. Don't forget that Mr. Eskildsen was not with BAL; he was with the Danish Air Ministry. Neither was Charles F. Thomas; he was with Lockheed."

"Okay, which documents am I to look at?"

"All of the reports signed 'J. H. Willans.' The description by J. K. Sinclair, the area representative for BAL, says that Willans seemed to be the only one who knew what he was doing. Dr. Madsen was in a constant dispute between all those with the title engineer next to their names: I. Lusty, Christopher Dykes, and Mr. Capel."

"Okay, I see here..."Maggie read the report carefully; the notes were very professional and thorough. The engineer Mr. Capel described how the BAL engineers carried out their own test and was adamant that the results disagreed with those presented by the Danish. He used the word "reverse" in regard to what BAL's findings were. Mr. Maxwell, who was given much importance, suggested even further tests to see if under certain conditions the blue dye would leave a stain.

It was very obvious to Maggie that they were a group of men with very valid points of view. There was only one thing she could say."Wow, I see what you mean."

"Well, there's the fact that J. H. Willans wrote that he also performed massive experiments on the actual equipment to look for leaks and found none. And the fact that he witnessed the way the Danish fire expert team performed theirs and had, at some point, to object. There are several entries that make the point of the blue dye. It was a very strong dye that should have left evidence. Then you see how they try to compare this to the fire in the Luxeuil incident, but that was a Lockheed 14, and it is my understanding that those fires were documented on Lockheed 14 and not the Electra 10A, as this one was. Also, the incident they mention was the one I told you about on August 11th, remember?"

"Where did this Dr. Madsen come from?"

"He was appointed by the special or secret police. I think an Inspector Strobech brought him in. I could not follow up on him, which is not surprising with the war and all.

"There was more than a jurisdiction problem with this. There was also the Danish secret police. As I read it, this was something they were not used to. The Danish secret police must have been a new entity just like the OSS, formed by need as WWII was just around the corner. I have not been able to find anything to confirm this, but it stands to reason. One thing is for certain: the Danish Air Ministry was not used to dealing with them."

"Yes, I read that, too, in the Jack Sinclair letters where he interviews and describes everyone he was dealing with."

"I can just see them arguing and trying to sort of pull rank on each other." Maggie laughed.

"You know, I found other perspectives on those details in the Danish file. Did you read them?"

"Yes, I did read the letter from Major Fill to Eskildsen that you sent me. Why did he retest the linoleum in England?"

"There was lot of doubt as to the actual seat of the fire, as they call it, but what is really telling is that the Danish Air Ministry official asked the British Air

Ministry official to take part of the evidence outside the country and retest it, don't you think?"

"Telling? That's screaming! Did you notice the entry by the Marconi engineer, a Mr. D. C. Brown?"

They each looked at the same thing:

One point which requires mention, although not strictly a radio matter, is that while examining the main aircraft battery, a burned mail flag was found in the battery compartment, although there was no other sign of burning either in or around the compartment and the battery itself.

"I did, and frankly, I do not know what to make of the fact that he found a burned mail flag where there had been no fire. He was there to make sure the fire had not gotten started by a short in the radio equipment and felt obliged to mention the mail flag? Where was the mail located?"

Again they each found the same entry on the files, each with her own data on either side of the Atlantic:

As soon as the aircraft was taken ashore at about 12.00–13.00 o'clock, the mail sacks were removed from the mail compartments in the wings and in the nose of the fuselage—in the presence of post office representatives to whom they were delivered. In the same way the passenger's luggage, the greater part of which were located in the radio compartment while a few suitcases were in the front compartment, were delivered to customs and the police.

"Well, there is definitely something wrong with all this. The mail was not near the radio compartment. I can see why this Mr. Brown thought it was important to mention this," Maggie pointed out.

"Oh, wait; I forgot to tell you about Chuck Thomas. Several years ago, I actually found the man who wrote the Lockheed letter, Charles F. Thomas. He lived in Carmel, California, and he was very sound of mind at ninety-four years of age. He could not remember the incident itself, as he had not been on-site—you can see that by the letter in the files. At any rate, he said to me that he could assure me that he did remember the men, and that anything he put his signature on, he stood by. That being said, he did tell me that after he wrote that letter, he went to Luxeuil and described the August 11th incident as if it had happened after. I was disappointed when I realized he got the order wrong. He liked telling that story because the plane in that incident was the Lockheed 14 that took Neville Chamberlain a year earlier to the signing of the Munich Pact."

"So what about this man Wicks?"

"Oh, Wicks! He is everywhere!"Catalina reached over to her bookshelf, pulled out a book, opened it, and put the page in front of the camera."Here is Mr. Wicks."

The book she was holding up was *The Prisoner Speaks* by Henry William Wicks. On one of the front pages was his photo; he looked like a nice, elegant man. The trail of letters in both the British and Danish files, his book of his experiences in jail, and an odd affiliation with Holocaust-denier David Irving told a very different story.

"Let me look at my Wicks file. It is large and complicated. The information on this man is strange and confusing, all over the place, and very...to me, he seems dark."

Maggie responded almost sarcastically'

"Dark? That is precisely what we are looking for. The letters from 1951 in the BAL file have me very intrigued."

Catalina had been down the path of sarcasm and certainty only to be proven wrong enough not to assume, as she carefully added.

"I know. That is why I started looking into him, but believe me, there is quite a lot of information on this man, and some of it is clearly wrong. I'll put it together for you and send you an e-mail. Also, don't forget that by 1951, it was no longer BAL, and I think it is very clear that in 1951, there was no issue with showing the file to Henry William Wicks."

Maggie sighed.

"That's true; there were a few memos, but no one inferred that he was NOT to be shown the report on the plane crash. Thanks."

That was the end of the video call. It was late in London, and Maggie went to sleep. In Florida, Catalina put the H. W. Wicks file away. It was a strange file, with regular copies from sources like newspapers or the Internet, but also many pages from the National Archives at Kew, large papers that were about eleven and a half by sixteen and a half inches that had the terms and conditions of the copyright rules on the back of each sheet.

Henry William Wicks had left a document or two everywhere he went. To be sure, as the archives open documents every month, there should be more to come.

CHAPTER NINETEEN – LIGHTING WICKS or THE WILD GOOSE CHASE

FROM: SecretsoftheG-AESY@hotmail.net.fla.us

TO: Maggiestrylleri@hotmail.net.uk

RE: Henry William Wicks

Dear Maggie:

I hope I can make this information make sense to you; the information I have on this Mr. Wicks is long and strange. I often wonder if he is relevant, but he keeps popping up more often than not, and I cannot help but wonder if this is one of those rare cases in life where there is smoke and no fire.

So, I will begin with one of the files I found on him: file C12533/101/18 from the UK National Archives, Kew. This is from the Foreign Office in August of 1939. It begins with this powerful and to the point statement:"Mr. Wicks is a thoroughly unreliable individual." This explains in great detail how Wicks ended up in jail for libel. It also states that his case was thoroughly dealt with by the "highest legal authorities" and that there was no reason to believe that the justice system had been ineffectual. The letter goes on very strongly to explain that Mr. H. W. Wicks is not of sound mind, with delusions of persecution.

The Foreign Office also mentions how he has "lent himself to German propaganda." It states in no uncertain terms that Mr. H. W. Wicks is not to be believed, the funny thing is as adamant as the Foreign Office is with its statement, they make it quite clear that the information is for the Danish police authorities only. I guess they did not want Wicks to end up in any other newspaper as he had the German paper *Der Angriff* that July, and the story was later picked up by *The Daily Mirror*, which was on July 19, 1939, under the very large caption "He's Glad to Escape Our Terror."

I found that in file number C10177/10177/18, it did not show the page number from the English paper or from the German one. That file has a letter from another British subject; a Mr. John Jackson who writes to his MP and threatens to also go to Germany. I guess in a 1939-sort-of-way, there was some concern that it could go viral? From today's perspective it is hard to imagine that a letter such as the one Mr. Jackson wrote would be given a second thought. I agree with H. W. Wicks and might just join him!

I saw this particular paper for the first time in Denmark, not in the National Archives file but in the local one, the Nykøbing Falster file. This information in Denmark was with a paper by H. W. Wicks –"A Case for Explanation, Should Political Expediency be Permitted to Intervene?"It looks very official, and I can only guess that is how H.W. Wicks introduced himself. The correspondence in the Foreign Office about Wicks is very entertaining, and at such a pivotal time in history, it seems a shame that this man was able to take up the valuable time of intelligent men who could have surely dealt with far more important matters. This is just fifteen days before the Germans invaded Poland, and England declared war on Germany. Well, maybe they were not that busy, as Neville Chamberlain was on a fishing vacation in Scotland. I read somewhere that the British Ambassador had already telegrammed by the 18th to show how grave the situation was; pity time and energy was being spent on H. W. Wicks.

As you and Bill did, I first encountered his name in the letters from 1951 in the BAL G-AESY file (AW1/1849). I looked him up on *The London Times* indexes available to me at a university library nearby. *The London Times* Index showed certain articles I could not find a microfilm for. (Apparently there were several editions a day of *The London Times* and not all of them made it to microfilm.) Those entries seemed to make Mr.

Wicks into an even more intriguing character. He was disputing something or other in the courts, and it came up that he had been in jail after World War II for treason.

I next found his book *The Prisoner Speaks*; this describes a year he spent in jail for libel, but he was adamant that it involved insurance fraud—on the part of others, of course. I found an entry in *The London Times* on May 1, 1935 (page 4e): "Mr. H. W. Wicks' Affairs/Application to Act as Director Refused."

It was about that time that I first saw one of the Danish files that had an entry showing that Mr. Wicks had contacted the Danish authorities and claimed that because of a big insurance fraud case, Anthony Crossley had been killed. He also claimed that three other men had died under suspicious circumstances, and this was all because of the very case he spoke of. So there I was, back again in the library with *The London Times* index and microfilm, and I found the three men he spoke of: an Italian prince Mario Colonna, and two English MPs, Sir James Blindell and Mr. Frank Clarke.

It is true that all three men were dead by August 30th or 31st of 1939--when Wicks approached the Danish authorities. I was, however, unable to find anything I considered to be suspicious.

The only obituary in *The London Times* for a Prince Colonna was dated August 25, 1939, and was for a Piero Colonna. He had been very ill according to the obituary on page 14e; Mussolini had appointed this particular Colonna to the governorship of Rome. I have no idea what Mario Colonna did, but years later, through one of the "royal bloodline" sites online, I read that he died in 1938. I guess we can put a question mark next to this one's name, as I have no idea how he died or if it was suspicious.

The next two are easily found in *The London Times*. Sir James Blindell died on May 10, 1937. It was an unfortunate car accident, with an inquest the next day. The inquest, also reported on May 12th, cleared the driver, who explained that he braked to avoid hitting two dogs because he was a dog lover (it really does say he is a dog lover). I cannot imagine that this was some murder for hire by quadrupeds! Then Mr. Frank Edward Clarke, the second mentioned by Wicks, died in July of 1938 with several articles in *The London Times* that month stating that Mr. Clarke was ill and hospitalized. I found an entry in the index for his obituary, but again, the microfilm available to me did not have this particular entry. At any rate, I believe this, too, discounts Mr. Wick's allegations.

I also looked for similarities between Anthony Crossley and the MPs mentioned above, and although their paths cross occasionally, there did not seem to be any real link between the three men. The next thing that I investigated because of the letters in 1951 and Mr. Wicks, was the mention of a lawsuit over an odd conflict--if that's the right word--with an MP named R. W. Sorensen. There are a couple of articles in *The London Times*, but it is easier to use primary sources.

I found in Hansard (the Houses of Parliament records) several accounts involving R. W. Sorensen and H. W. Wicks. This one from July 20, 1939, Vol. 350, page 46 on German Propaganda (Mr. Wicks). Has a very interesting conversation between the MP R. W. Sorensen and R. A. Butler in regard to H. W. Wicks, where Sorensen asks about "German Propaganda containing certain allegations," all this in regard to H. W. Wicks. To which R. A. Butler responds in a manner that clearly shows that he is annoyed and does not feel it is worth discussing.

Then there is this one, August 3, 1939, Vol. 350, pages 2630 to 2631, which is also found in *The London Times*. Mr. H. W. Wicks discussed how he sent a letter to the prime minister, asking to be given assurance of protection because he lived in Germany. The MP,

Sorensen, presented it. Here the odd thing is that I also found a file at the National Archives in which there is a letter from August 2, 1939. It is from 10 Downing Street and refers to "Sorensen's unstarred question no. 71..." and goes on to say, "As I mentioned to you, this is an arranged question, and I will circulate the answer."

I don't know what any of this means, because it seems to me that H. W. Wicks was not particularly important, but perhaps because he was so public with his German propaganda that it was decided to make an issue out of it.

Then we come to the one that through the BAL Archive—more letters from H.W. Wicks that you are of course familiar with. The court case from 1951 and that entry in Hansard is from April 13, 1951, Vol. 486, page 1335 Personal Statement. Before I had access to (or even knowledge about) Hansard, I was able to find this one through the newspaper microfilms of *The London Times* at FAU. Member of Parliament Sorensen explained how he 'put two questions'--all of this in regard to H. W. Wicks and his "pro-Nazi activities." He goes on in great detail to explain that H.W. Wicks landed in jail for four years and was now "pestering" and "suing him for slander." It goes on to explain that Mr. Sorensen got a subpoena from Mr. Wicks for a case that he knew nothing about. The MP was basically asking to be excused from dealing with this. Some sort of "shield" or protection! The thing that caught my attention is that the questions were pre-submitted, in the records I found they were referred to as starred questions; to me it seemed that someone in Parliament, not just Sorensen wanted the questions heard in 1939.

In response to all this, there is another entry on April 19, 1951, Vol. 486, page 1973--this one is called "Member Subpoena." This one is really fun to read: the judge is mentioned as allowing Mr. Sorensen not to appear in court only if it interferes with his work as a member of parliament. To me, this means that whatever Mr. Wicks came up with (and I do believe somehow this guy had a law degree) had the possibility to maybe stick! The thing is: then it gets juicier as another MP--this time a Mr. Eric Fletcher--comes forward to also ask for "protection" from Mr. Wicks' lawsuit, saying he has been "threatened by H. W. Wicks," so this member of parliament may have never even been named if the case ever really got anywhere. The Speaker in the House of Commons (the way I read it) does not sound too happy and seems to brush off Mr. Fletcher, something to the effect that the judge in the case needs to decide and not the Speaker.

I really think the whole thing is H. W. Wicks being difficult. I do not know much about how all of this works, and I only found it interesting because of the entry in the National Archives showing that MP Sorensen was requested to ask the questions.

The other resource is from the Internet. The Cambridge Journals has an entry with Mr. Wicks as follows:

J. R. Spencer (1979). "Criminal Libel in Action–The snuffing of Mr. Wicks."

*The Cambridge Law Journal,*38, pp. 60–78 doi: 10.1017/S0008197300093818

There is also an odd entry posted Sunday, February 22, 2004, about H. W. Wicks and a historian called David Irving. It refers to letters that Mr. Irving found written to Hitler, Mussolini, Himmler, and Roosevelt and "scores of other personalities of history."This story was told in a downtown hotel in Copenhagen, and Mr. Irving uses it as an example on how destructive obsessions can be. He describes a meeting he had with H.W. Wicks and the disturbing account of what had happened to him.

This one is tricky, and the way Wicks is described simply does not agree with what I've found. You can then go on to David Irving on freedom of speech. This speech is from October 28, 1992, in Vancouver, Canada. This entry shows you that Mr. Irving, who at some point several years ago, was put in jail as a Holocaust denier in Austria, is a very venomous man, for lack of better words. Here he goes on in great detail about Mr. Wicks, and from what I found on H. W. Wicks, the information here from David Irving is wrong. He basically states that the insurance company would not pay a claim, and that since Mr. Wicks stood in front of said company with a "placard around his neck" and became trouble, they got him for libel. I have never found anything to support that, but maybe David Irving has other sources.

I do not like the information I have found on Mr. Irving, and I did contact him many years ago, before I realized whom I was dealing with, and I asked who or what his sources were in regard to Anthony Crossley. (He mentions Anthony Crossley in a book called *Churchill's War*.) I believe there are several speeches from the parliamentary records in Hansard that show David Irving's information to be wrong. Anyhow, I contacted him again when I read the H. W. Wicks website. I asked Mr. Irving if he knew Mr. Wicks had also been in jail for treason, and that his problems with the insurance company were documented differently. He in turn asked me for my sources, and I told him to do the research himself. He said I was slightly rude. (I probably was.) If you look up David Irving's bio (there are quite a few very complete ones) you can see why even though I am not comfortable with him as a source, he has some very interesting accomplishments. The closer I look into recent books that are respected, he is here and there in the bibliographies.

Anyhow, by looking at the files at the National Archives, I can tell you that H. W. Wicks seems to have extreme anti-Semitic views in common with David Irving. The Wicks files are very confusing. In a file that was opened in 2008, reference number W0296/102 C333012, there is a letter from Wicks, one of several letters in that file. It is dated April 3, 1977, and addressed to a Brigadier Sheehan; H. W. Wicks claims to have Jewish friends and Jewish lawyers. That particular file also has a mention or two about how the 1936 libel was retracted in 1951; I have never found any evidence of that. (I'm telling you, Mr. Wicks is all over the place.)

What is absolutely amazing is that after the libel issues in 1936, which eventually landed him in jail, and then after his treason punishment, for which he also got jail time, the above file also mentions that the Germans eventually imprisoned him as well. Imagine that? What I find difficult to understand is that he seemed to have been taken quite seriously in 1977. I really do not know what to make of Mr. Wicks.

I attached a newspaper clipping from one of the files. The translation of the one from Germany is even worse. I really came to dislike this man Wicks.

I hope I did not bore you too much; it has been so nice to discuss this with someone who is interested in detail. Thanks. C.

***

She sent the e-mail. It had been a while since she had looked at the papers she had on H. W. Wicks. She wondered if Mr. H. W. Wicks had ever even met Anthony Crossley. She had found no reference to that anywhere, and it stood to reason or, at the very least, speculate that Mr. Wicks seemed to believe he knew everyone. The files were full of Lord this and Lady that, as well as mentions of relatives of the very famous.

The one very odd thing was how she had first come across David Irving's book *Churchill's War* in the cooking section, placed there by mistake. Then she bought it because Mr. Irving mentioned Anthony Crossley several times. The accounts about Anthony

Crossley in that book appeared to contradict newspaper articles and entries in Hansard. Then one day she noticed in the news that Mr. Irving had been sent to jail in Austria, as a Holocaust denier.

It was such an odd surprise when years later, that very David Irving was going on about H. W. Wicks. The facts Mr. Irving stated about Mr. Wicks did not agree with what she had found in the newspapers and the National Archives at Kew.

CHAPTER TWENTY – SKYPE & WINE

"Have you been this thorough about the entire file?"

Maggie's smiling eyes were always a welcome treat to Catalina in the evenings, and with Bill out of town, their Skype interaction was more than a daily ritual. Both women had so much to say.

"Of course I have. I guess one could say that I dissected everything and looked for links to anything else; that is what happens when you work on something for too many years!"

It was the weekend, and they--each on their respective sides of the Atlantic--opened a bottle of wine, noticing they both liked Sauvignon Blanc. They spent a few minutes laughing and talking a little about themselves. They inevitably got back to discussing the G-AESY.

"So you have taken each person in the BAL file and made a file on him?" Maggie asked.

"As much as I have been able to, yes, I have. Not everyone is as visible and as noisy as Mr. Wicks."

"Is he your biggest file?"

"No, the biggest file is, of course, Anthony Crossley. As an MP, he has numerous entries in *The London Times* and Hansard."

"It is *The London Times*."

"I guess it would be, pardon my ignorance."

"Sorry, force of habit--I have too much fun correcting Bill. Anthony Crossley--that is body number three with the arms crossed instead of in the fencing position?"

"Yes that one, and then, of course, anything I have been able to find on body number one, my grandfather, Cesar Agustin Castillo."

"In the file, they refer to them as the Mexican and the American from Intava?"

"Yes, they were traveling together, working for the same company in the oil industry. Intava is the name given to the International Association for Petroleum Industry, Ltd. If you Google them, you'll find that they were investigated for violations of antitrust laws," Catalina said.

"Your grandfather had a New York address, but the American had a local address—Surrey, I believe."

"Yes, my grandfather had just been transferred to the London office. He had just started to work in

England, about two weeks, so he was still living in a hotel, trying to decide whether to bring his family to England or not. I have the copy of a letter he wrote the day before he died, and he explains how you can pretty much smell the gunpowder, and all talk is of war. The American, Mr. Simonton, might have been ending his stay in Europe. I found a ship's manifest from September of 1939 in which he and his family are registered on the passenger list. His name has, however, a line across it, and a note that says he 'did not show up,' so he might have been planning to return to America...I do not know whether it meant permanently. I am guessing the company sent them for three to five years abroad. My step-grandfather worked for the same company and lived in London and worked with them at the time."

"Step-grandfather?"

"My grandmother remarried a few years later, to an employee of the same company."

"Oh, so what did he say?"

"He always told us it was sabotage, and sometimes the story was embellished to suggest that the 'bomb' was right between Mr. Simonton and my grandfather because a German childhood friend had given it to him in Hamburg."

"What? Why would a Mexican have a German childhood friend?"

"My grandfather lived and studied in Germany from 1908 to...1914? I think it was 1914. It was the year World War I started."

"With his whole family?"

"No, he was there by himself. His father had business contacts in Germany and people in Mexico—even today, but especially in that era—thought a European education to be superior, that such an educational background could open a lot of doors. He returned to Mexico because World War I broke out. Mexico had terrible political turmoil, and for a while, his father ended up on the wrong side of those in power. Once all that was resolved, my grandfather studied at Texas A&M University. He then did a post-grad program at Columbia University in New York City. He was a chemical engineer, although I have seen somewhere a license for biochemistry. Afterward, I think he went straight into the world of petroleum, which was huge in Mexico in those days."

"How did he end up in with Intava?"

"Well, the company he worked for in Mexico--Huasteca Petroleum Company--was affiliated with Standard Oil of New Jersey. I think the Mexican oil industry was nationalized in 1939. I do not know if the transition from foreign interests happened slowly, but my grandfather was transferred to the States around 1935 or 1936. He was also in Panama with them."

"So he spoke English, Spanish, and German."

"Apparently French and Italian as well."

"If he had lived in the States and Germany, where did his loyalties lie?" Maggie asked.

"I've often wondered about that. If he had lived beyond 1939, whom would he have seen as the good guys? I can only assume that if he had been very pro-German, he might have applied to German companies for work and not American ones. He might have been very torn, and I understand that there was a very large fifth column movement in Mexico at the time, that sympathized deeply with the Germans."

"What about Simonton?"

"That is a file that makes me wonder. He had a military background ... American military, and then he really went up fast in the oil industry."

"Why does it make you wonder?"

"Well, when I've looked up all of the other men, there is usually quite an academic background. I don't know...Mr. Simonton did go to West Point, and somewhere in the British Airways file, it says he was a pilot. Somehow his background is not similar to the others at Intava or the engineers I have looked up," Catalina pointed out.

"What do you think his military background could mean?"

"The American OSS did not exist yet, but they did have special agents. Organizations such as those are not born overnight, and I think he could fit that profile."

"Funny you should say that, because I was thinking your grandfather sounds like someone perfect to recruit for espionage."Maggie was surprised that her statement was welcome with a nod and a smile.

"Absolutely! Especially in that era, when they had to depend on the human factor--it was not as easy to spy then as it is with today's technology. The automation of espionage, as it were, thanks to all of the electronic devices...I thought at one point it would be really cool to turn the story into a spy novel. The German, for example, had a glass eye, and in that era, they used those to transport microfilms of secret information."

"Microfilm in glass eyes?"

"Yes, I saw it in the spy museum in Washington, DC. It was very common. Who would think to search an eye? People have always been very creative when it comes to the clandestine."

"So how would you make the bomb in your novel?" Maggie asked.

"Oh, it could not be a bomb. The plane did not blow up; it caught on fire. It was some sort of incendiary device like in the World War II movies. There is one as simple as a cigarette and a book of matches used to set something of."

"I think I have seen that one, where the cigarette is placed lit sideways, and as it burns down slowly, it gives the perpetrator a chance to get away."

"Right, or in the Hindenburg movie, there is one made with a simple wrist watch, although I think that one is a bomb. But the same basic principle could apply."

"So who would place the device?"

"Well, my favorite suspect would be Mr. Stocks."

"Yes! The man who gets out in Hamburg?"

"The very one. See, like if all you had were the Wicks letters...he returned on the next flight...the same day, or something to that effect. It would be really easy to make a suspicious tale out of the perfectly normal man."

"He did buy the ticket last minute and with cash."

"I know--like I said, he is one of my favorite suspects."

"One of your favorites?"

"Well, Mr. Simonton and the radio officer, Leigh--both have their hands severely burned, so a scenario where they are both touching the incendiary device could be used, and one of them could be blamed."

"What about the pilot?"

"Well, as the only survivor, again a scenario where he dumps everyone in the back with the incendiary device is possible."

"What about your grandfather?"

"No. And not because he is family, but because he was the only corpse with a concussion. Well, I guess a scenario in which he is guilty, and someone bops him hard on the head to try to prevent...fiction is so powerful that new characters could be introduced to make the story work."

Maggie was happily playing along with the potential fictional scenarios. "I know! I was watching the Amelia Earhart movie, and that was in 1938. They discussed fueling the plane in the air; they said it was uncommon and difficult, but the fact is that it was done.

In a Quentin Tarentino type of movie, you could have another plane, and the bad guys could enter and exit without a trace."

"Yes, but we begin with the five bodies of very real people who had lives and the families they left behind: a pilot who survived and went on to have a very nice life, a group of unsatisfied engineers who adamantly disagreed with the Danish fire expert report…"

"If only they had pieces of the plane to test with today's technology."

"Well, I don't know who you mean by 'they;' but the Danish National Archives in Copenhagen do have bits of carpeting and some metal pieces, I believe. I'm not sure; they may have some of the linoleum. I don't think Mr. Eskildsen ever really gave up."

Maggie was so excited by that that she placed her hands on her cheeks as she asked, "Are you joking?"

"No. Really, it's a great fantasy of mine where I find something, some evidence that would make the Danish government test the pieces. I also have two watches from the G-AESY—my grandfather's and one that was sent to us by mistake."

Young inquisitive Maggie immediately asked,

"Could you test that?"

Catalina sounded a bit defeated as she answered

"Where? And How? I have been told there is a Danish military file. That one might also have pieces, and those would be great to test, as there would be no question of tampering. Anyone can request the file in Copenhagen and go through the material; it is by far the most complete source I have used. But who knows how many people have opened that file through the years?"

Maggie requested "Could you send me the information on that one via e-mail?"

Catalina sighed and answered "Not tonight! The Danes use a funny size paper that cannot be scanned, at least not on my American equipment! But sure, I can put something together. Who knows? It might help me see if I missed anything."

The evening continued with ashtrays full of the cigarettes they had smoked, accompanied by lots of wine and laughter. The women came up with many other scenarios of what-ifs on August 15, 1939, on board the G-AESY. They eventually said goodnight and ended their Skype call.

CHAPTER TWENTY-ONE – THE PLANE

FROM: SecretsoftheG-AESY@hotmail.net.fla.us

TO: Maggiestrylleri@hotmail.net.uk

RE: Danish National Archives

The G-AESY file at the Danish National Archives in Copenhagen is larger than the one at the British Airways archives. It contains many of the same documents that are found in the BAL file. It has more photographs, and if memory serves me right, many of them are larger and clearer than those in the file you saw. It also includes various drawings of the plane (I'm pretty sure those are in the BAL file as well). There are reports and correspondence. I'll separate the information in those categories to avoid confusion.

Photographs

There are photographs of the bridge from two angles--one with a red arrow pointing to the bridge itself. You said you are familiar with Storstrømsbroen, so the arrow points to the column right of the three semi-circles. The other photograph of the bridge shows farmland; it is taken from far away, and the red arrow is pointing to the water. I wonder if the arrow that points to the bridge points to where the pilot was rescued? It says that he swam and was thrown a life preserver...something about a painter on the bridge.

There are several photographs of the plane being pulled out of the water with a large crane. There are photographs of the plane on land with the motor missing on the left side. There is also damage on the bottom of the plane, but there is some question as to how much of the damage was incurred as the plane was being pulled out. Other than that and the broken windows, the plane looks whole and clean, from the outside.

There are photographs from the inside of the plane, from the front to the back and vice versa; these show great damage. There are several of these, and some seem to focus on the cockpit and others the toilet. It is hard to tell, as they are in black-and-white, but you can see that the description of how seriously burned it was matches the photographs; it looks horribly burned.

There are a number of photographs of certain parts of the plane; these have been disassembled and are displayed. I believe that some of the pieces displayed in those photos are the pieces in the very archive box. I understand that they are the filler caps and spill box mentioned in so many of the reports. There are others that could be the heating system pipes; the ones in the box, I think, are part of the filler caps, but that is only a guess.

There are photographs of the seats of the plane on the ground, along with some other parts. At any rate, there is photo evidence that the plane was thoroughly taken apart and studied. There are also five photographs, one of each corpse from two angles, the right and the left sides. The bodies are nude and show all of the burns. Two are on large metal trays with the head lifted a little by a small sort of block. The other three bodies are on a large flat sink. I have seen similar modern versions of those on TV shows like CSI.

An odd thing about these is that the bodies' weights are recorded, and the description in the files states that there are two heavy men, Castillo and Beuss. However, in these photos, Simonton looks large. His was the last body brought up on the day of the crash, so maybe it could have been bloated by the sea; however, Leigh, whose body was not pulled out until the next day, looks very slender. You can see his muscles clearly defined. I just looked up the data, and oddly enough, I do not have Mr. Simonton's weight. Maybe he, too, was a heavyset man.

Drawings

There are two very large drawings that look like a professional illustrator made them. These are of the bridge. Showing exactly where the plane went down, they show the sixth column to the right of the semicircles, explaining the approximate distance from the bridge.

There is one very rough drawing of the inside of the plane; it shows where each body was found. It shows lines to separate the cockpit from the passenger cabin as well as the back to separate the toilet. It has eight circular lines to represent the seats. Then there is a second very professional looking version of the same, and that is signed "Th. Moller" from the criminal police in Nykøbing Falster. I am pretty sure you've seen that one in the BAL file. This one has a list of the order and how each body was found.

There is another large drawing that shows where the fire started. This drawing looks very professional. I have never understood this drawing because the motor is missing on the "G-A" side. The wing with that lettering and the part where I read "Fuselage" leads me to understand the drawing focuses on the "ESY" wing, which has its motor. But I am sure that's just me.

Papers

- A memo from August 4 about precautions for the distillation of isopropyl ether. (I think this was for the tests they needed on the G-AESY.)

- Weather report from the Copenhagen Airport.

- The pilot's statement.

- Letter from the salvage company called Zone Redingskorpset. The salvage company pulled the plane out of the water. I do not know if it was also in charge of the bodies. The salvage company had its own divers, as I understand it, but it is interesting to note that the rescue divers were not used to pull out bodies; instead, a self-taught local diver/carpenter was contacted (I met his family in 2002).

- A letter from a Mr. Knud Lauritzen to the Danish Air Ministry inspector, Mr. Eskildsen, about a similar fire on KLM. (This fire was on a different type of aircraft, a Fokker F-XII, but the point of the letter is to ask if any passenger had the type of lighter that could ignite inadvertently.) This man was in the shipping industry and may have simply been someone Mr. Eskildsen knew.

- A letter thanking Knud Lauritzen but explaining that the fires cannot be compared, as the fire in the G-

AESY was of a very violent nature (meget voldsom natur).

- A list of eighteen documents retrieved from the G-AESY. (None were found in any file I have ever had access to.) I would be interested in seeing some of them:

- Journey logbook for the G-AESY.

- Schedule of weights for the G-AESY.

- Passenger and baggage list.

- Manifest or general declaration of the cargo from Heston.

- Manifest or general declaration of the cargo from Hamburg.

- Passenger list from Hamburg.

- Letter from Air Ministry of June 16, 1939.

- Reports from the police in Nykøbing Falster, Precinct 19, describing in great detail how each body was found as per the diver Christian Andersen of Kalvehave. These are both in perfect English and in Danish. There is also an actual account by the diver himself. He was not the only diver down there.

- Report on radio equipment by DC Brown Marconi Engineers.

- Handwritten letter from a medical university about Mr. Crossley's body (liget af).

- Detailed reports from the fire expert, Dr. Madsen—one in Danish and a "rough draft translation."

- Letters from a Danish tobacco store, WO Larsen, addressed to Danish Air Ministry Inspector Eskildsen, asking for help and information on behalf of a friend of Herr Beuss, a Dr. Berkemeyer. It also includes the letters from Berkemeyer, dated August 26, 1939, and September 8, 1939. (These are all related to the German passenger Herr Beuss; they are all requests from his friends seeking information.)

- Letters between Danish Inspector Eskildsen and English Air Ministry Inspector Fill.

- Letters from Jack Sinclair and I. Lusty (Ivor Lusty) from BAL in response to Mr. Eskildsen's requests for data about the motors.

(This is because the serial number on the motor on the plane did not match the serial number on the logbook.)

- Detailed fire report that was disputed in findings by the British Airways engineers. (I have never understood if perhaps this is the final report, because it is a Danish report, and there are no others recorded in the files at Kew.)

I have many notes on the autopsies; those are, however, from the report I was not allowed to copy. They are rough translations of what we found in Danish.

Another thing missing is that there is no mention of interviewing or even attempting to interview those in charge of fueling the plane at the Hamburg airport, in spite of the fact that for the Madsen theory to work, the tanks had to be overfilled. In the report, there is in a fuel record of the total amounts used both at Heston airfield and the Hamburg airport. There is no specific notation that either amount could be too large. These are Heston, 160 gallons, and Hamburg, 727 (160 x 4.54) liters. The report for the fuel receipt, however, has either a 550 or 650-liter amount, and the type of fuel was Shell ethyl aircraft petrol.

In the Danish report, which goes far more in depth about the pilot's statement under the heading "Hearing of the Pilot," there are two entries that I think are worth mentioning. The first one describes how the pilot "looked over his shoulder;" when he did this, he noticed maps in the radio compartment on fire and how the radio operator runs back to deal with it. There is specific mention that the door between the radio compartment and the cabin was closed. I believe this can only mean passenger cabin. This does not make sense to me. I believe the windows were movable, so breaking them has never made sense, but if the pilot could break a window with his elbow, why didn't the survival instincts of the passengers set in to do the same?

There is also this on the last paragraph of the pilot's hearing: an explanation about leaking "a little fuel" in something called a primping pump. This does not seem to attract any attention, in spite of the fact that the whole investigation revolves around looking for fuel leaks. The thing is that the pilot explains how the "mechanic"--you saw how they go back and forth with A. S. M. Leigh's job description--but the point is that he says, "the mechanic had fixed this leak right away."

I fail to understand why this was not relevant to the BAL engineers. Maybe they never read this report? But I think it is the one they disagreed with. I do not recall reading anything with regard to that from them. I still cannot grasp how a "mechanic" who can fix something like a little leak in an instrument panel a few hours earlier does not take the fire extinguisher with him when he goes back to put out a fire. There is no logic to this.

I know that is also one of your big questions. Anyhow, there is a section in the Statens Luftfartstilsyn report from September 1939, under the heading

"Hearing of the Diver Chr. Andersen." In it, the evidence of the diver's testimony has to be corrected as to the location of one of the bodies; Mr. Eskildsen of the Danish Air Ministry notes the correction as to where the last body was located. That correction can also be seen in the official police diagram. I also find this odd. I find it very odd because there is a personal account taken by the police where the diver goes into great detail as to how it was difficult to find the body and to retrieve it.

There are reports in the Danish files that three diver boats were searching. They mention a company called Zone Redingskorpset and Christiani &Nielsen. As I believe I told you before, I met with the diver's family (his two daughters), and they told me that he was called in because the salvage divers were afraid. The two daughters described the phone call, and here one has to acknowledge that these are memories of two little girls. I heard a psychologist say on the radio once, "The human mind sometimes adapts the order of events to create narrative." Who knows how accurate any family's stories are, but the diver's family had a nice and detailed story to tell.

The diver's daughters said that K. Andersen was a John Wayne type of gutsy adventurer. They were part of a group an archivist and a policeman gathered for me in

March of 2000;our little group, including a witness who remembered the plane going down and the smoke; again, this man would have had to have been a very small child at the time, but his memories were full of details, and I believe he was married to the diver's daughter. Memories are often mistaken, and we tape-recorded our meeting; I have it transcribed and translated by my friend. In my notes, the diver's daughter remembers her father being picked up and all the commotion. This is the report I was referring to earlier--from the Vordingborg police file--we read that the diver was sent a telegram at 4:30 p.m. He was summoned, and he made a few phone calls to make sure he was being offered payment for the dive. Once at the site where the plane sunk, someone informed him he was probably not needed as there were already two divers down there. In that long statement, it says that the other divers came up and said they had found the machine. K. Andersen put on his diver's suit, and with the line the other divers had attached to the plane, reached the machine. He then described opening the plane door and a body falling into his arms--that was my grandfather, body number one. The statement also says that there was another diver nearby, but as soon as he saw the body, he went upwards--the last he saw of him were his clog shocs! (I am not making this stuff up; my notes say "clogs.")

He goes into great detail about how he finds and retrieves each body and how he closes the door to the plane's passenger cabin as he leaves with each body. This is the only account in very specific detail from the diver. He describes how difficult it was to get the last body out the next day and how he was also involved in the search for the missing motor. One of the diver's daughters was allowed to read the report out loud to us--did I tell you we recorded it in Danish, and then Birgitte translated it? We visited the bridge and shared pictures; someone said that because the water was cold, he was given a shot of Gamel Dansk between each dive. I am sure that since you have Danish grandparents, you are aware that it is pretty strong stuff. At any rate, the body with the corrected location was from the next day. So it would not have warranted a warm-up drink.

A local archivist placed an ad in a local paper. That is how we (my Danish friend and I) found the diver's daughters and the witness. Here, too, it is odd that there were no relatives or children of the "rescuers," the people who pulled the pilot out of the water.

I also met with other locals, and one had published a short article called "Som Jeg Husker Det."

My Danish is beyond limited, but I do believe that means something to the effect of "as I recall" or "as I remember it." Anyhow, the story explained how to him, a Mr. Viggo Sigvardt, then seventeen years old, that plane crash was the beginning of World War II. Again, as interesting as all that I have found through the years is, there is no real smoking gun.

Let me know what you think about all of this or if you have any questions. Sorry for any typos, especially in Danish. I must say I do envy your fluency in the language. I put it together as best I could. C.

CHAPTER TWENTY-TWO –THE FIRE

FROM: SecretsoftheG-AESY@hotmail.net.fla.us

TO:Maggiestrylleri@hotmail.net.uk

RE: Answer to your question.

Hi Maggie,

No, of course I understand that there are holes in the story, and that there is great room for doubt. That being said, I think it would be really nice to find real concrete proof. I'm just questioning what we find.

At any rate, yes, the Dr. Madsen report that I make reference to is the one by the Danish fire expert, the one that all the engineers from BAL and Lockheed disagree with. Notice that on page 2 of his report he states, "No small quantity of some highly inflammable material, giving a strong flame, had been present."

That is why it is so disputed by the engineers; all the petrol they used had a blue dye, and this dye does not come off with water. Dr. Madsen goes on several times to speak of the intense flame. That is not what is described in the pilot's report. He sees "some maps burning." The fire specialist, Doctor Madsen, describes in detail a very large flame. Then he goes on in his report to explain that the spill box he is blaming is tight, and that it is the other side, where there was no question of fire, and that one is loose.

He does go on to say that after further testing, he does indeed find a leak, but there is no evidence again of blue dye, and Mr. J. H. Willans, who witnesses the tests, disputes this.

Mr. Willans explains in the most meticulous detail how all pipes and caps are tested. One by one, and that there is even issue with more pressure than would have realistically have occurred in the circumstances the tests were trying to replicate. He is adamant that no leaks were found.

I know you've seen that report. It goes on to say that the fire had to have started in the cabin in the front left-hand corner. I have been very candid with you that due to my extreme lack of knowledge about this, I have used any and all help available to me. So I must tell you that a psychic told me years ago to look for Willans—I had never mentioned his name! When I asked what he was talking about, the psychic said to hurry up and find him, that he wants to tell the story and is old and ill.

I did not know what to do or where or how to look. But I contacted every Willans I could find. (As you saw in the BAL files, his name is often changed to Williams.)

I contacted every engineer's association I could find in England, and since I was looking for Willans, I figured, what the heck? So I added the names of the other engineers who agreed with him. I ended up meeting—both online and through regular mail—numerous, very nice Willans families, but not the one I needed.

As you know, I eventually did speak to Charles Thomas, the representative and engineer for Lockheed. He, as you may recall, did not remember the actual event, but he did remember Mr. Willans and said that he would have never put his name on anything he did not agree with. Anyhow, because of the influence of the psychic, you can imagine that I am most affected by any of the Willans reports.

There are also the letters from Jack Sinclair about all the Danes in the BAL file. In those, Dr. Madsen is described as a brilliant chemist who knows a lot about fires but is limited in his knowledge of aircraft. In the letter about the Danish Air Ministry inspector Mr. Eskildsen, the very man described that he felt hampered by the "new department of the police" and how Dr. Madsen was part of that department and had been imposed on him. In the letter about Inspector Strobech, the head of the secret police department, there seems to be a lot of damage control and apologizing that revolves around the autopsies.

In the other letter is an interaction between I. Lusty, the engineer from BAL who took over from J. H. Willans, and in that one, I. Lusty disagrees completely by explaining how because of the design of the wing, the theory does not work. I did find a trail through the aviation journals—Flight Global, or something like that—on the engineer, I. Lusty, and he ended up with Boeing in the US. It's nice when I can put a face to the reports.

It might also be worth mentioning that I looked up the Lockheed airplanes track record; it seems to show that it was the Lockheed 14 that was prone to the fire, not the 10A. I meticulously researched each incident, plane by plane in a book about Lockheed, and the G-AESY, which was known to Lockheed as Plane Number 1102, had a fire somewhat similar to those that that occurred on the Lockheed 14, but other than the first-built prototype, which is registered as dbf (destroyed by fire), that's the only 10A I found. Also, keep in mind, that I say somewhat similar because the fire of the G-AESY was in the passenger cabin and not in the cockpit. So it was a unique and strange fire.

Anyhow, I find the Jack Sinclair memos the most interesting and informative part of the entire BAL file. I wish he had written a file on everyone and not just the Danes and Major Fill of the British Air Ministry. He had a very interesting face, Mr. Jack Sinclair; I have several photos of him from the Danish newspapers. He was a smoker and does not look very tall (compared to the Scandinavians). He had strong, powerful features. If only he had written at least one more report, one on J. H. Willans. Although I do believe that in more than one entry, I have read the comment that Mr. J. H. Willans seemed to be the only one who knew what he was doing! C.

CHAPTER TWENTY- THREE – JACK SINCLAIR'S OBSERVATIONS & THE AUTOPSY DISSECTED

After several messages and missed calls, the two women were back on Skype, Maggie smiling excitedly with youthful exuberance and Catalina smiling with the cautious optimism that comes with age and experience.

"I sent through all of the papers related to Sinclair I could find, and I believe there is something there." Maggie was holding up the document to the camera as she spoke, pointing to each sentence she commented on. "This paper from August 15th, titled 'From Mr. Sinclair,' says that the pilot noticed smoke, not a flame. It also says that he had time to move the R/O, which must mean 'radio operator,' and then smash the left cockpit window with his elbow. It also says that he climbed through the emergency exit."

"I know, Maggie, but there are several things about that. The signature on the paper does not look like the ones in his reports from the 22nd of August. The paper has no BAL heading. So, I believe this is all based on phone calls from Jack Sinclair, and the corrections, such as switching the window for the emergency exit, were probably made by a second or third person, not by someone who spoke with him. I do find that the statement...let me see here..."

Catalina picked up a document and read from it. "'Check is being made at once as far as possible to see what luggage was loaded into the cabin in London, and I am arranging for the same to be made as far as possible when passing through Hamburg tomorrow morning.' I do not like the 'as far as possible.'"

Catalina continued. "It is odd, isn't it? As I understand it, there was supposed to be a complete manifest. When they are looking into Mr. Stocks, there is record of how much his luggage weighed on the way to Hamburg and the way from Hamburg a few days later."

Maggie sighed with frustration, her feeling of "Eureka! I found it yet again," deflated by the facts. "I see; you are right. The initials signed at the bottom do not match Jack Sinclair's from his other papers. Well, I think that the letters from Jack Sinclair, the reports from J. H. Willans, and the seven-page report from Ivor Lusty tell a very interesting story. First, how there are problems in the question of who was in charge; not only between Vordingborg and Nykøbing Falster, but everyone seems to back off when Inspector Strobech into the picture. That report on Inspector Strobech, Head of the Secret Police Department, and the entire paragraph on the post-mortem...that does not sound like a jurisdiction problem; I mean look at this: 'We had always held a view that a postmortem was most desirable, particularly when two of the victims were to be cremated, and since the cause of the accident was still unknown, I was personally most surprised that he, as Head of the Secret Police Department, had not insisted from the beginning on such an examination taking place.'

"This is very strange, and I am still very bothered by the discrepancy regarding the body rigor mortis; the only different one should be the last one."

With arms up in the air, a sigh came from the other side of the Atlantic as Catalina agreed. "I have always felt the same way, but I consulted with a pathologist who explained that this could possibly have a number of explanations. The autopsies that I got to look at also note some differences between where blood and foam was found in each body. I was not allowed to copy those, but I remember my Danish friend and I felt that this supported our suspicions. They were very thorough, that much I can tell you, because I remember how we assumed that if my grandfather had not died that day, he would have probably died young. In his autopsy, there was the description of a big tumor wrapped around his spleen.

"The original decision as to what killed them was made so fast that there is the following entry on the commercial manager's report: 'M. Lybye discussed the position generally and the point that there seemed reason to believe that the local medical examination had been fairly quick. (The last body—Leigh—was recovered on Wednesday at 05.30 hours, and by approximately 16.00 hours, the death certificate had been made out.)' I mean, don't forget they needed to get him to the hospital and take the photo of the corpse, which shows absolutely no postmortem cuts."

"That is ridiculous! I cannot imagine that that's enough time. I see where you found that, and in that same document, they dispute that if Madsen's theory is correct, then the doctor's statements have to be incorrect. Oh! Here is another entry that really says something in the interview with Dr. Madsen, the fire expert. Here, look at the last paragraph..."

Maggie held up another report to the camera, she turned the paper around and began to read out lout, at times turning the paper to point at something, Catalina did not have the heart to tell her she could not see a thing:

"'Mr. Lusty, on the other hand, whilst admitting certain facts in Dr. Madsen's theory, was not satisfied on all points and felt that although no doubt a very brilliant chemist and scientist, Dr. Madsen's knowledge of aircraft construction and engineering was not perhaps, of so high a standard. Mr. Lusty also felt that Dr. Madsen was regarded in the light of a man who never makes a mistake and whose pronouncements the police authorities would accept as final without question.'"

"The fire expert was appointed by the secret police," Catalina said, "and in the end, they were the ones running the show in Denmark for this investigation; you can see that from the report on Mr. Eskildsen."

"I know, I agree, and I have found several entries on Ivor Lusty. He apparently went on to have a brilliant career and knew his aircraft. The other men who dispute the findings I have also tried to track. For example, Christopher Dykes, also another great engineer who understood the design of aircraft, had aeronautical training from Cambridge, which leaves no doubt as to his credentials. The engineer J. H. Willans also went on to be respected in the field. The engineers refused to sign off on the Danish report findings to the point that it had to be stated in the BAL conclusions 'that sufficient evidence does not exist for a cause to be attributed thereto, nor as to the exact location where the fire started. 'I still have to find an actual report that looks like the one or two from other incidents I looked at, with, of course, far smaller files!"

Maggie started sifting through her papers.

"I also found in the Ivor Lusty seven-page progress report, the entry you talked about, the one stating that 'Mr. Willans appeared to be the only man who was attacking the problem in a logical way.' In that one, I get the impression that Major Fill with the British Air Ministry was already set on what to say before he even saw the plane."

Catalina was again surprised by how Maggie carefully questioned all she found. It was such a treat to discuss any aspect of the G-AESY with anyone but especially with Maggie.

"My favorite line in that report is 'I stated that the lives and history of the passengers might well have been the subject of an investigation, but this again, I was told, would be adequately cared for by the police.' There is no real bio on any of the passengers from the police file I saw. But it is true that when you read that Major Fill arrived telling everyone that 'petrol had been spewing out' on the flight he took, it does sound like he had already spoken to the Danish authorities and had made the same conclusions. I changed my mind, however, about him when I found the correspondence between him and the Danish Air Ministry man, Mr. Eskildsen."

"I think I am beginning to confuse who was who."

"Okay...I'll make a list and send it to you."

"That would be great. I think you forget that you have been working with these files for so long that they are very familiar to you, like old friends. Whereas I can get easily lost in all of the 'who is who' in 1939."

"I probably do. They are very real to me, all of them! For years now, they have occupied my thoughts. I'll make an easy list with bios so we can be sure you understand who is who from it."

"Well, I do believe you are about to become my very personal Jack Sinclair!"

Laughter flowed on both sides of the Atlantic as that video call ended.

CHAPTER TWENTY-FOUR – UNTAGLING WHO IS WHO

FROM: SecretsoftheG-AESY@hotmail.net.fla.us

TO: Maggiestrylleri@hotmail.net.uk

RE: List from G-AESY (People)

J.H. Willans

First engineer from BAL on the scene. There are three reports on the aircraft by him. He disputes the findings of the Danish fire expert and is called a senior assistant to the chief engineer. I. Lusty replaces him with no particular explanation.

Mr. Eskildsen

Danish Air Ministry inspector. States that he is dealing with the secret police for the first time. Doubts Dr. Madsen's theory to the point that he requests a test on the linoleum to be done in England, even though it has already been done in Denmark. As you say, the war was about to start, and I do not think that anyone would want to be on the secret police's bad side. Anyhow, Mr. Eskildsen noticed that the motor on the plane did not match the serial number of the Pratt Whitney motor on the plane. It was explained as some neglect to update the logs after maintenance. I just feel it is very important to note that Mr. Eskildsen of the Danish Air Ministry seemed to notice everything and include everything; he also held on to the pilot's license for a long time, and many requests had to be made.

Major S. J. V. Fill, OBE

British Air Ministry, accidents department, which went into operations in December 1937. Major Fill arrived at the scene on August 15, 1939, by telling everyone in "lurid" detail how much his plane smelled like petrol and how it was overflowing—"spewing" was the word used, I believe. As far as I was able to find out from the archives at Kew, he was one of a few assistant inspectors (inspector grade II) for several years. There are entries in which he complains about their pay as not being sufficient when they travel, and in July of 1939, he seemed to be competing for a promotion and got one, but the other assistant, a Captain Wilkins, got a higher one. Then he got a promotion. There were only a handful of inspectors in that era; this, of course, changed with the war and how important air travel became.

I like the letters from the Danish file when he corresponds with Mr. Eskildsen. I do know from the file at Kew that the man who seems to have been chosen for the promotion that Major Fill was vying for was quoted as having "criticized the machine." So it seems that the man who got the promotion did so in part because he went out on a limb and pointed out all the flaws in a particular airplane; neither the plane nor the airline is mentioned, but it is stated that the manufacturer threaten to sue. The "makers" of the plane; actually it says machine? Your guess is as good as mine, could it be a Zeppelin maybe? Did they have helicopters in 1939? A lawsuit was never filed so I can only guess that whatever this man found whether in how the "machine" was maintained or in the actual manufacture, must have been accurate.

Who knows how people think and if that's how the other guy got promoted? Maybe Major Fill wanted to make the same type of footprint. This is just my assumption of course.

Jack K. Sinclair

BAL area representative for Scandinavia. He did not seem to be an engineer and did not voice opinions on the aircraft. He reported on everything that happened and offered to help with certain translations, so one can assume that he was fluent in Danish. This was important so as to rule out faulty information being passed on to BAL because of a lack of knowledge in the local language. He was a handsome man; there is a photo of him in one of the newspaper clippings I got from the salvage company's museum. It's from *Berlingske Tidende*from August 16, 1939. Jack Sinclair had the inevitable cigarette between his lips and a nice Clark Gable type mustache. He had a beautiful profile and was looking down, wearing a hat as men did in that era, his pinstripe suit and the white handkerchief slightly visible in the breast pocket. I tried to draw him once and noticed the ears were somewhat large, but not to be noticed at first glance. I cannot quite decide where the photo was taken, the background is a doorway, and the caption simply states who is in the photo with Sinclair, misspelled as Zinclair. In the photo, there is a Mr. Bache behind him--this man is in uniform—and the caption calls him *Trafileder fra Lufthavnen*, His uniform is not very official looking, and more like an airline pilot's. I know he is with the Danish Airlines from some of the folders; I'll get to him later.

Ivor Lusty

BAL assistant to the chief engineer who replaced J. H. Willans (no explanation for that is given). I. Lusty was an (or the) assistant to Mr. C. T. S. Capel, MBE; they were known in 1939 for developments in advanced techniques of airline maintenance (check out Flight Global again). He arrived on the scene on the 17th in the afternoon. He explained how Major Fill had described to Mr. Eskildsen about his journey on a Lockheed 10A and how the petrol was "belching" (sorry, it was belching, not spewing) out from the filler well on the left side. (It is funny that it is the same side as the G-AESY incident because other reports stated that the caps on the left were tighter than the ones on the right in the G-AESY.) Anyhow, as you know, Mr. Lusty did not agree with Major Fill and found he influenced the other people. He also disagreed with Dr. Madsen. He was given access to certain tests that he felt proved Dr. Madsen to be wrong. He explained, piece by piece, how there was no damage to the parts of the plane under the floor 'petrol pipes,' no sign of being burnt as there was above the floor. He went on to explain that when he had pointed this out to the Danish Air Ministry man Mr. Eskildsen, this man had said to him that 'he was completely at a loss.' Mr. lusty went on to explain that he was asked for suggestions on how to look for answers. Here Mr. Lusty described Major Fill as going back and forth.

Dr. Madsen

Danish incendiary expert. He had two assistants working with him who were not mentioned by name. He was given the job by the Danish secret police and arrived at conclusions that all aircraft engineers disagree with. Brilliant chemist but little knowledge of aircraft engineering. Also, if you read his original report, he stated that what he had described was accumulation from previous flights, which is something that would make the lack of blue dye even more questionable.

Inspector Strobech

Head of Danish secret police. Ivor Lusty called it "The Political Police," and another report by the commercial manager in Denmark (I think this might be Mr. Maxwell, not sure) called it the "special branch" of the Danish police. I believe this shows that it was a relatively new department. He seemed to be the man everyone has to listen to and work well with.

Jack Sinclair's report shows that they felt he went from antagonistic towards them to willing to work with them. I tried to look him up while I was in Denmark. I found nothing, and as you know, he could have been friendly or unfriendly with the Germans in April of 1940 and "sent away," as so many Danes were when the Germans occupied.

Herr Knud Lybye

He was with DDL, Det Danske Luftfartselskab, the Danish airlines, and was mentioned sporadically. I believe BAL and DDL were affiliated in some way because BAL asked for his help and consulted in the matters of getting the postmortem; he also consulted the authorities on their behalf. I also think I saw both logos together somewhere.

Mr. Pritz (or Prutz)

This man was with Intava, the petroleum association my grandfather and Mr. Simonton worked for. He might have been there locally—I found entries for Standard Oil of New Jersey in the Danish phone books of the era, but Intava seems to have been far more than just Standard Oil. Or he could have been flown in as a representative from Intava for the accident. There is also the possibility that he was there for the investigation itself with regard to the petrol and the blue dye; I found an ad on eBay from Aeroplane Magazine dated September 1939, a one-page advertisement stating BAL used exclusively Intava oils and greases. By then, I don't know if BAL had fully merged with Imperial Airways. The logo on this ad is that of the griffin on the side of the G-AESY, so probably not. Also, when it came to identifying the bodies and their personal effects, there were Mr. Haley and Mr. Ashby of Intava, so I believe we can assume that Pritz or Prutz was Intava's man or one of their men in Denmark.

Captain White

This man was also with Intava but in London. He contacted BAL about Mrs. Simonton's statement. There was also a Mr. Bedford in the London office that contacted them.

Station Leader Bache

(In Danish, it is *stationsleder*, which I think means, "station leader.") This one was also DDL, and it says he was from the traffic department. I know Sinclair's papers say somewhere that he was of invaluable help.

D. C. Brown

Marconi Radio Engineer who took apart all of the wireless equipment to prove there was no fire there. He was brought in from England. This was the one who made a special note that a burned mail flag was found where there was no fire.

Charles F. Thomas

Lockheed Aircraft Corporation. His title when he signed the letter was "Assistant Factory Representative." He too was an aircraft engineer, and he also disagreed with Dr. Madsen's theory of the fire. (As I told you, a few years ago I found Mr. Thomas living in Carmel, California. We spoke on the phone a couple times and exchanged e-mails.)

I called Lockheed to see if they could help me in any way, and they put me in touch with a writer whom they said would know if there were still anyone around from that era. That was in 2003. So imagine her surprise and mine when I found the very man, Chuck Thomas. He assured me that although he did not remember the incident itself, as he had not been to Denmark, he stood by what he wrote. His actual words were something to the effect that he never put his name to anything he did not believe. He also remembered the other engineers. In his letter, which he was happy to re-read after so many years, Mr. Chuck Thomas explained that he had studied the photographs and discussed or read all reports made by the various engineers. He explained that due to "the lack of evidence of dye from fuel being found in the fuselage," he was of the opinion that it was not possible for the fire to have started the way that the Danish fire expert had explained it. Mr. Thomas described how whether this was from "gaseous or liquid form," it could not have happened that way. He mentioned that, in his opinion, whatever had happened was not due to the airplane (remember, he did represent Lockheed) or the maintenance. This exonerated BAL.

I cannot stress enough how adamant he was that he never put his name on anything that he did not truly believe. The letter goes on to describe the tests performed by the BAL engineers and piece by piece of the airplane, describing how, due to the lack of any physical evidence, that the fire was started by a "would-be-smoker" had to be "discredited." I read a report somewhere which interpreted Mr. Thomas' letter in a far different voice, as more of an official reply from Lockheed explaining that the "fuel leaking observed" in apparently many such airplanes was "not a thing which is dangerous."The point of that report was to question whether manufacturers are sometimes slow or even reluctant to make changes to improve safety. In the case of the G-AESY, I, of course, see the story from a very different point of view.

The letter ends saying that he was returning to Amsterdam, but he thought he remembered going to Luxeuil to investigate the Lockheed 14 G-AFGN incident. On this point, he was mistaken as that incident occurred on August 11, 1939, and not after the G-AESY crash. Then the war broke out, so he must have returned to the States. His recollection was going to Luxeuil and then to the States.

I looked up the fuel on Wikipedia and found that most aircraft fuel in America today is dyed blue and is 100 octane compared to the 87 octane that was used in 1939.

There are names of some others, but I did not read in any of the information available to me anything that led me to count them as of any importance. Unless, of course, someday I were to be allowed full copies of the autopsies; then I would trace the doctors' careers as I have traced as best I could the engineers'. C.

CHAPTER TWENTY-FIVE – TEQUILA

She took a long drag from her cigarette and gave up on the Sauvignon Blanc. Maggie was stirring things inside Catalina's soul that called for something far stronger, like tequila. It was inevitable that she would ask for one more list. That list would be the hardest list to compile.

The journey of the past sixteen years, compressed in a week or so, combined with Maggie's contagious excitement of youth, had Catalina looking through all of the papers and data in a manner she never had before; she studied every detail meticulously in order to explain it to Maggie. The information at times seemed new to her, and then she found a notebook, papers full of notes or stories, and realized she had indeed worked with those facts in the past.

The Danish pictures in the papers showed photographs of Jack Sinclair, the pilot, his wife, Mr. Eskildsen, and Major Fill. The pictures brought them all back to life as they paraded through her thoughts.

She took another long drag of her cigarette and sipped her Tequila. She walked to the file cabinet and pulled out a notebook; it had a plaid cover and had "Denmark 2000" in bold letters. As she flipped through the pages, she said out loud to no one in particular, perhaps simply to the walls in the room, "This is about real people."

She flipped through the pages and came to an entry...

The meeting had gone far better than expected; really, it became more of a reunion, and now we were driving to the bridge. My friend said how it was her favorite bridge in Denmark, the last leg of the drive from Copenhagen to her grandfather's house; this bridge was the smell of Christmas food, the fun of birthdays, and the great joy of Easter and the beginning of spring at her grandfather's Parish.

The policeman and the elderly archivist were sitting in the front of the car. He glanced back through the rearview mirror and said, "Bridge of joy, hope, and childhood? I should think not. We have at least ten suicides a year here every year; why, just last year a fellow tried to pull me in as he was jumping. I managed to save myself, and fortunately, he did not drown."

Swedish helps me understand Danish when I have a general idea of what is being discussed. This time, however, my friend had to translate. I thought it had been information for me, for my "quest," as I'd come to call my research.

The others were there already. I could see there were so many differences between the Danes and Swedes, with whom I had once been so familiar. We got out of the car; it was cold. The archivist, to whom I was so grateful for all of the people and information he had found for me, needed to be helped out of the vehicle, as he had severe arthritis.

There we were, the eleven who had met and talked about the G-AESY, its passengers, and the rescue diver, all afternoon at the Vordingborg police station, sharing what we knew about August 15, 1939.

"If you look out, straight ahead to that pier, and move your head to about one hundred meters from there, that is exactly where your grandfather's plane went down." The policeman was always ready with the facts.

I looked where he told me, and on an impulse I blessed myself. It felt like the only appropriate thing to do. In a way, I must have prayed for the five men who had occupied my thoughts for years.

She had to laugh, reading this, and thought how little she had known then, how many more years they would continue to occupy her thoughts.

Erick, Anthony, Samuel, Alfred, and my grandfather, Cesar.

Yes, the next list would be very hard to compile for Maggie.

Finally I spoke. "Pity they never found the motor."

Someone answered; it's hard to remember whom. "No, and they never will. You see, those waters are now full of American and English planes. It's like a huge graveyard. This bridge, Storstrømsbroen, was the landmark for Allied pilots during World War II; when they reached the bridge, they made a turn and were off to bomb Berlin. The Germans had anti-aircraft guns on the bridge and shot as many as they could down. An undetermined number went down. If you were to take a boat down there and look at the pillars on the bridge, you could still see the bullet holes."

In Danish, they all began to presumably describe what they knew of the guns and the planes. I felt empty and sad inside, looking at that huge graveyard and imagining how all of the pilots and crew had died, including the ones on the bridge they had killed, as well. Real people, either way--real people who probably had families who loved them, just like my five. And now these waters attracted people who liked to end their own lives by entering those very waters after jumping from this "Bridge of Deaths."

She did not finish reading; she felt tears streaming down her face, but not because what she had written was particularly touching or well written. In the ten years since she had put pen to paper and had written that, so much war had taken place, so many more violent deaths.

She could not understand how in an era in which so much information is at our fingertips, at the click of a button, a tap on a keyboard, an era when no one can run away from the sad truths of war, how so many chose to applaud war. America had not yet invaded Iraq when she stood on that bridge. Was that trip in 2000 or 2002? The naiveté of the origins of war that she had possessed when she wrote that was forever gone. It was replaced by the bitter feeling that, as a world, we could be foolish and reckless enough to make the same mistakes and to ignore the behind-the-scenes manipulations and decisions that lead to war.

She found it hard to remember what she was looking for when she stood on that bridge looking out, searching for an almost romantic war story like

Casablanca's "Here's looking at you, kid." There was no romance or beauty in war; all war stories of any war had very dark origins and conclusions.

Then she remembered a book and pulled it out of the storage box: Bruce Catton's *The War Lords of Washington: The Inside Story of Big Business Versus the People in World War II.* She looked at the strong, red cover and the smoke coming out of the dollar sign. She had not read the book; she would get lost in the names of the people of power unless they were common knowledge to her generation, such as Truman. It was the book's flap that made her think and dig. It said, "The fight was between those who believed that a democracy at war should be a cooperative effort of all people, of big and little business and labor alike, and those who wanted a limited war to be fought in such a way as not to threaten any vested interest of big business or any privilege of the War or State Departments."

Warlords were indeed found in every war.

CHAPTER TWENTY-SIX – HOMECOMING

Bill's return from America was full of surprises for both of them. He had managed to spend a few hours outside in the sun and looked younger and so different from the man she had met at the bookstore. Bill felt that the mood in the convention showed that companies were more secure about the future.

"There were some really nice parties; it was very different from last year's fear of being reported for how the 'bail–out' money was being spent."

Maggie could not stop hugging and kissing him. "I guess you are safe. I saw nothing in the news about your company's executives basking in the sun at an expensive resort, but you do have a nice, rested, I-just-came-back-from-vacation type of tan."

"It was nice to feel the warm weather. I did not have a single nightmare while I was there, but I did miss you. I missed you very much, Maggie."

"Well, if things are better, why don't the reports of the economy sound better?"

"Businesses need to feel secure before it trickles down?"

"Oh, come on! It's for the benefit of the few."

"Yes, and there is a solution to that. Be one of the few! It's easy to talk, but the truth is that you like nice things and good restaurants, and I do, too. It is nice to be so established and secure as to be like Bill Gates and do wonderful things, but the truth is that most of us are making sure we build a future."

"You're right. I would like to believe that somehow I'll always live well, travel, and enjoy certain luxuries."

"Why didn't you study business?" Bill asked.

"It went against my core principles...I wanted counsel people...and marry some coldblooded businessman with no principles!"

"One who could provide financial security and a life of luxury?"

"Exactly."

"What if that financial security came with strings attached?"

"Strings? Strings that could choke me?"

"Perhaps."

"How?"

"Well, I have had time to think, and there is the problem with my nightmares; I really do not think that

London is the place for me. It is where I get these dreams, and my company offers great opportunity for growth in other countries, far away countries."

"Oh, I see. Well, what if you gave hypnosis another chance, and if you still decide that

London haunts you, we move?" Maggie asked hopefully.

"How much of a chance?"

"What do you mean?"

"How many sessions is a chance?"

"Have you already agreed to move elsewhere? Without talking to me?"

"Oh no, Maggie! I know better than that. I considered it on the plane, and you are, of course, the first person I have discussed it with."

"Okay, that's an acceptable scenario, as it is absolutely hypothetical."

"No, Maggie, it is not hypothetical. I am willing to work on this thing, but only for a short time. I do not plan to allow this to invade the kind of life I want to lead."

"But you need to be realistic. Like the John Lennon song that says 'life is what happens to you when you are busy planning other things.' So many things can happen in life that we cannot control. Like meeting me, for instance."

He could not resist her smile and her eyes. "Fair enough, but I know that only a fool would not, at the very least, try to control what he could control. It is just common sense."

"I'm not sure I understood before now how practical you are."

"I am. Very."

"So you were not exaggerating when you explained how you explored all practical solutions to tackle your problems."

"All, and if I saw one today, I would take it before accepting reincarnation and all of the baggage that comes with it."

"It is true. It comes with a lot of baggage."

The conversation went on for a long time; it was, however, interrupted by lovemaking and wine. Bill had returned from his few days in America with yet another surprise: he no longer smoked.

"What if, when I have another regression, I need to start smoking again? It was not good for you; my smoking had you smoking so much more."

"That's a valid point. I am ready to quit smoking. We can have the hypnotist give you a hypnotic suggestion to stop smoking and another to detach from your old self so that you will not crave cigarettes."

"Would that really work?"

"My mother found it much easier to lose weight with a hypnotic suggestion. I think she experienced a past life where she had to release her old starving self—apparently that was what made her so hungry—and that helped her to lose the weight."

Bill chuckled. "Yeah, right. I was beginning to take you seriously."

"I was serious! She had a past life in which she did not eat enough to satisfy her needs, and she was exaggerating her food intake to compensate in this life. It worked."

"So, we request a private session. We request a session to help me sever whatever links me to that past. Not one in which I need to relive all of the cold, salty water going into my nose, when I am not sure if I am going to be able to breathe."

"Well, Rome was not built in a day. It is not like in the movies. This is not Robin Williams in *Dead Again* as the psychologist who cured claustrophobia with one regression, one session; you have to promise me that you will be open to more than one session."

Bill shrugged his shoulders and looked at the pile of papers Maggie had accumulated in his absence.

"You are the one who is hooked on this story; look at your file of documents. What is all this?"

"It is the names and backgrounds of the people in the investigation. How they disagreed and how their conclusions were made."

"So, what do you think?"

Maggie thought for a moment. "I think that it makes a lot of sense that a fire expert who is not an engineering expert cannot make the final conclusion as to what happened on an airplane. I think that the personalities and egos also intertwined in how it was all approached."

"How can you know about their egos?"

"Because one of the men from BAL was really thorough in explaining to the offices in London what was going on. There were others who wrote reports explaining what they observed around them, as well. It was a very odd time, and I think it is like that Hitchcock movie, *39 Steps*, where everyone could be someone else, everyone a spy."

"What? Now it is like a movie?"

"In 1939, with all that was about to explode, people were beginning to decide what they believed.

Were their convictions more important than their survival? Were they willing to oppose or not? Denmark capitulated in just a few hours in the spring of 1940; there were only sixteen dead on the Danish side, and the king and important leaders decided to accept it as long as Denmark was respected. It was a decision to survive; Germany and Denmark were very linked before the war."

Bill began to look a little worried. "Of course, there are always at least two sides in conflicts, but from the old letters or reports we have seen, you cannot tell what the people thought or followed."

"True, but it makes it easy to suspect all of them! And there are discrepancies, and you can see how they did not even trust each other."

"Well, that was because the plane sank in between two police jurisdictions."

"But the ones that took over were the secret police."

"The secret police?"

"Yes, one of the engineers who complains about them explains that it is a new organization, and that he had never had to deal with before. I couldn't find any information online, but I guess it is logical to assume that to prepare for war, countries had to create certain departments. There is another reference to them as the 'political police.'"

"It is an intriguing story."

"Absolutely it is. Here, let me show all I have."

The discussion now turned solely to the incident in 1939. Paper by paper, they went over the meticulous accounts of how each part of the Lockheed Electra 10A had been taken apart and studied. There was no doubt about how thorough the investigation had been, especially by those who questioned the final conclusion and were determined to refuse it. Maggie identified with them.

CHAPTER TWENTY-SEVEN – PRIVATE HYPNOTHERAPY

Bill and Maggie continued for a few days with their negotiations over how many hypnosis sessions were enough to prove whether it could solve his problem or not. The number agreed upon was five. Maggie agreed that if after that, there was no change, and he felt he needed to leave London, she would follow him regardless of what country he chose or got sent to.

They decided that the hypnotist needed to be very well recommended, which meant another meal at Maggie's parents' home. Bill and her father talked about sports, business and world politics. Maggie helped her mum with the meal. It was agreed that Maggie would get the information they needed and that Bill would not be subjected to discussing it with Maggie's parents.

The hypnotist that Maggie's mother recommended was a woman. This woman, according to Maggie's mum, was capable of making anyone feel safe and secure. By the time they said good-bye to her parents, Maggie had already made the appointment.

It was agreed that Maggie would be present. Maggie made sure she drank large amounts of caffeine so that she, too, would not end up hypnotized.

The melodious sound of the female hypnotist's voice guided Bill to a space of peace within himself; Maggie wished she could be a fly on the wall of Bill's brain.

The hypnotist guided Bill through a forest; the forest was so alive, the firs, the wildlife, the leaves creaking under his every step. With each step Bill took, he went deeper and deeper until he came to a spot where he could relax.

The hypnotist had a small office, and the sounds from adjacent offices could be heard. She guided Bill to incorporate the sounds in anything he saw or heard in the past life. Bill's breathing became very even, and he looked as if he were so light that he might float away.

"Open the door, and tell me what you see." The hypnotist's voice was so light and sweet. There was laughter coming from somewhere, but Maggie noticed that Bill was elsewhere, in a time far away and long ago.

"I am on the street." His voice had a different tone and a slight accent that was not his.

"Tell me the name of the street." This time the gentle voice also had a power to it.

"I don't see names."

"You can identify it because you know the street."

"Looks like a familiar street." Bill spoke slowly and carefully, the movement under his closed eyelids showing that he was looking around.

"Look around."

"A few people walking in the street, sidewalks, lights, windows, commonplace things on a street, buildings."

"Describe the buildings."

"They are gray buildings."

"What else can you tell me?"

"Few, a few birds on the edge of the roof. The buildings look like they were built with big blocks—not huge—but larger than..."

"Walk about and see if you can locate a paper or something that will indicate where you are."

"I am walking. I turn to the right, and I see stores and stairs."

"What type of stores? Anything that indicates where you are."

"I can see words...I cannot make them out. I see people, mostly ladies, shopping. I can clearly see myself as I move. I am getting close to a window, and I can see myself. I'm looking through the window, but I can also see my reflection on the window."

"Describe yourself."

"I am a man wearing a dark coat, and look like...kind of young...early twenties."

"Can you tell me your height? How tall are you?"

"No."

"Your build?"

"No, I don't see it."

"Move closer to where your residence is."

"I have to walk back, turn, and make a left. Yes, I have to go upstairs."

"What is your address?"

"I, I only see a number...530. It is not a fancy building; it is an old building."

"Permit yourself to go inside. Go inside your home. Once inside..."

"Small apartment with old furniture."

"There must be something in your apartment that will help you see what the date is. Take a look around and see what is in there."

Bill's eye movement under his lids showed he was observing, but he was silent for several minutes.

"I'm looking through...I am looking at my place."

"Is there a particular piece of furniture?"

"A sofa, circular table, papers, and newspapers."

"Walk over to the table and look at the newspaper. Look for the date."

Bill takes a very deep breath.

"I think the date is sometime in August of 1939."

"Do you know your name?"

"I think my name is Clifford."

"Wonderful. May I call you Clifford?"

Bill's breath is more even now, and he nods slowly.

"Clifford, will you tell me what work you do?"

"I am pilot. I work for a big company."

"Do you know if you are going to work this morning?"

"Yes, I will probably go to work, because I am wearing a suit. It is a dark suit, white shirt; my tie is a dark blue or black."

"Move forward to the time that you go to work. See yourself at work. Tell me about the people who you work with, the people who are there."

"I see people working in an office. It feels like a regular day."

"Are you going to be flying today?"

"I think maybe not today. I am not really sure."

"Is there anything significant you wish to tell me?"

"I am a little confused and nervous. I start feeling that way when I go in the office."

"Can you look at a desk and see the date?"

"Not really. I don't really see papers that show today's date. I see a woman behind a desk; I think her name is Margaret."

Bill took a deep breath before he spoke again.

"No, I don't really remember her name."

"Say hello to Margaret. Ask her the date."

"I think she said the date is August 18th."

Bill got restless, and Maggie was quietly taking notes. She thought that the BAL papers showed that the pilot, C. F. C. Wright, and his wife had not returned to London from Copenhagen until the August 19th. Bill's breathing got heavy and fast. His face did not look relaxed.

"Why do you feel so nervous?"

"I think it is because I am about to have an important meeting."

"Do you know what the meeting is about?"

"I think it is about the flights; they are telling me what to do. Well, I haven't got most of the information about this flight, and somehow I know it is important, and there is a meeting."

"Don't question what you see or feel; follow your feeling."

"I think there will be important people, but I don't know who they are."

"Can you tell me the city? The country?"

"I don't really know. I know I am somewhere in Europe, but I don't really know where I am. I know I am home, or my city, but I cannot tell you exactly where I am."

"If you could, Clifford, try--"

"I say hello to Margaret and one of the guys at work. I go to the second floor, and I see lockers, a table, and a place to sit and wait. I can see the street through the window. The room is empty. I don't know if it is empty because it's early or because they are already gone. I sit in this place, biding my time. I take out a cigarette and start smoking the cigarette. My foot is on the floor, and my knee is bouncing. I am nervous. I can see my black shoes. I spend a little longer in that room and look at the time. It is 9:12. It is a.m. I go down the stairs and find this long hallway. I see a room to my left, and there are people in it. I walk in...will I get the...I am losing the fear. I am ready to hear what I want to hear. I see three or four men."

"Do you know these men?"

"Yeah, they work for the same company."

"Would you tell me their names?"

"I know them, I feel close to them, but I cannot tell you their names. I am shy. I just take a seat. I hear someone coming in the room; we stand up to receive this man. He is our...superior. I think I know who he is."

Bill was quiet for a moment, and his breathing became very steady.

"He is wearing a nice suit. He looks well put together, tall but not too tall, older than the rest of the men in the room. He is maybe one of the owners. His position is very high, and we see him as a person of power. I don't really know his name. He called the meeting.

"He has a secretary or someone who whispers a lot. That man has a suitcase, and it is placed on the table. He starts speaking to us. He is pretending to be friendly. He looks at us as if we are beneath him. He is going to explain. He opens the suitcase, gets out papers. He explains the importance of a flight that we are making in the future, maybe tomorrow."

After a short pause, he continued."He starts explaining that there important people and that their treatment during the flight should be special. We listen; now the two other men are asking questions about the people we are transporting."

Bill's speech, at times, was not clear; the hypnotist started to pull him out of that lifetime and into a comfortable place where she proceeded to explain to him that he did not need cigarettes. He did not want cigarettes, and he would no longer smoke.

She went on to explain to him that in the next session, he would be able to pick up where he left off and that he would remember Clifford clearly, but he would know how to detach and not be so nervous.

Bill and Maggie set up a second appointment for the following week. The office was located near many nice restaurants; they strolled quietly down the street until they found a nice Italian restaurant with a menu to their liking.

Maggie was twirling the napkin as she asked.

"Well, do you feel like smoking?"

"No, not really, but I had not been smoking."

"So what do you think?"

"I think she's a nice lady. She has the kind of voice that makes me feel comfortable. I liked that she ended the session when she did. It was okay."

The napkin was tightly wound at this point as she asked,

"Did you see me?"

"No."

With a sigh she added

"You said you were young, in your twenties, so maybe you were somewhere else."

I don't think so. I did recognize...someone from the other regressions."

"Someone?"

"I'd like to wait till the next session to see what happens. I would rather not talk about it.

"At all? Or just about someone?"

"Maggie, you are so stubborn."

"Well, the date you gave did not match at all. You said August 18th, which would have been after the plane crashed and before he returned from Denmark."

Bill was pensive, and for a while, they ate in silence. There was no sense of animosity from either one; they knew at the end of the day they had the same goal. After ordering coffee, Bill was certain that he was no longer craving a cigarette.

"Do you really think the hypnotist has a method that can help me detach from Clifford? Detach for good?"

Maggie's gentle answer had a touch of determination.

"I do believe that is possible, but I am surprised that you are not questioning everything. You seemed to have several discrepancies from what we know to be true."

Bill did not seem to be interested in the discrepancies.

"Well, it felt very real. The nerves and fear had absolutely nothing on the fear of facing the cold salty waters and the fire. It was an anxious or nervous fear combined with desire, the kind you feel before you interview for something hard to get that you really want."

Maggie was still trying to make her point.

"But that doesn't sound like you. You know what you want, you prepare well, and you get it."

Bill was trying to avoid the conversation.

"I know, but it was very real, the kind of desire that you want it so completely you can almost taste it before it is yours...a goal, a job, entrance to an incredible school."

Maggie pushed on.

"The way you describe it, it sounds like a special flight that may have been compensated. Do you think they were getting paid a lot more?"

She asked the right question and finally got Bill to open up more.

"Well, this is the same airline that flew Neville Chamberlain to sign the Munich Pact. It was Neville Chamberlain's first flight. So this airline, it stands to reason, flew important people. To qualify as the pilot for such flights, it is simply logical that the type of meeting I saw could have taken place. It would have been a big deal."

Maggie was animated as she said, "In that era, in England, yes. The owners would have absolutely been of an upper class that would have been snobbish, felt superior."

Bill nodded in agreement and added, "I am guessing that being Australian and not of the upper class would have also made someone feel that he was being seen as inferior. I mean the upper class pilots did it for fun; not to pay the rent."

"I absolutely agree. I still cringe when I read how they referred to people from other lands in that era? The Jewry and the Mufti, the N word was politically correct. I cannot imagine being part of such mentality. But please do tell; who did you recognize?"

"One of the corpses. He was smiling...this is where I need to draw the line for the time being."

"What about the secretary, was it me? Could you have been a year earlier?"

"It was not your face, but I know I did not force the names out."

"You had a different accent...I would not say Australian, but it was not your Canadian/American accent. It was also not your personality at all. When you did this before with the therapist that made you 'feel inferior,' did you see any of this?"Maggie asked.

"Now that you mention it, yes, I did. That man did make me feel as if he felt he was superior, so maybe that is where those feelings came from. If any of this is real, who is to say where the line between the past and the present ends?"

"Well, it needs to be closely tied together, at least in certain souls that carry over issues or karma from past lives."

"And do you still insist that the fact that Clifford did not join the RAF until 1947 is what proves the karma?"

"No, I do not feel that way anymore. There is reason to believe he was RAF even before 1939. I have been thinking very much about the behind-the-scenes action and spies. I believe that a good pilot who had already survived the G-AESY incident could be invaluable. So he was maybe one of the reconnaissance planes that took photos from the air. That is why in the list of inflammable materials the inspectors were looking for, cellulose was mentioned several times, and in many of the reports the commercial planes carried cameras to photograph targets; I think that that type of operation could be undercover work. I know not everyone is a spy, but in 1939, it seems very fair to believe that almost everyone who could be useful was recruited as a spy. I have a *Fly Past* article from 1983 that describes a mission that took place in July of 1939 in which pilots got 'considerable footage' of Germany. That would be at least two weeks before August 15. The war was coming, and both sides were already spying on each other."

Bill frowned as he spoke, "Maggie, how did you come up with that?"

Quick with her answer and oblivious to his frown, Maggie continued."The woman in Florida said she contacted the RAF. They allowed her to send a letter to the Wright family in 1996 but would not put her in direct contact. She got an answer to her letter and visited with a married couple in Peterborough, the Wrights, who turned out to be the wrong Wrights."

"The wrong Wrights, with a W?" Bill had to smile.

"That's right: with a W. She was sent to the family of, I believe she said, a Clifford Frederick Wilbur Wright, and not Clifford Frederick Cecil Wright. That family was surprised that the Captain Wright we are interested in ended up as Wing Commander, as did their relative who had flown during the war, had been shot down in France, and had earned some medals. But looking through *Flightglobal* magazine and some other sources online, I found some entries with Clifford Frederick Cecil Wright. These were from 1938 and 1940. In those, I saw a record of military involvement, at the very least. Either his involvement was under the radar, or whoever wrote the letter that said he joined the RAF in 1947 when Mr. Wicks was looking for him in 1950–51, was wrong. Or..."

"Or?"

"Or what are the chances of yet another Clifford Wright in the RAF with the same three names?"

"Three? Very unlikely, but I suppose that it could happen."

"Why didn't she contact the RAF again?"

"Of course she did. She was told to send another letter; she said that her time in England was limited and that she handwrote such a quick letter. She said that in retrospect that handwritten note was not the type anyone was likely to answer, and they didn't."

They both started to laugh. Maggie went on to tell him how when the woman in Florida told her the story, while making a very bad imitation of the British accent, she'd repeated her conversation by phone to the RAF that she had had:"Excuse me, but you sent me to the wrong Wright." Maggie laughed while rolling her eyes and saying, "Americans!"

CHAPTER TWENTY-EIGHT –CONTAGIOUS ENERGY

Catalina was more obsessed than ever to find the glue that made the story of the G-AESY come together. Meeting Maggie had given her a different perspective and a youthful energy to infuse into the story, the type of youthful energy she had possessed when she'd begun to search.

As she looked through the many files that she had accumulated in her years of research, she could only think of how events define, individually and globally, eras and peoples. How people are changed by events in life. Some events are so large and arrive with such force that they define entire generations almost instantly. Especially today when, as a world, all of us witness everything in a firsthand way—a kind of almost-being-there feeling—through the media. Others of these events are subtle, and it can be hard to pinpoint long-term when the changes these events produce actually occur and how they are noticed in hindsight.

This was a thought that was stirred by the many historians whose books she had mostly stumbled upon.

A few of these she read from cover to cover; some she studied, underlined, and marked. She did this to try to understand the world that surrounded her grandfather in 1939. Some of the quotes that impressed her were carefully tacked to her bulletin board next to the newspaper clippings of August 15, 1939.

Among those, the words of Donald Cameron Watt's How War Came were printed the largest.

"Wars are made between governments, but they are fought between peoples."

She found herself reading Chapter 21--The Amateurs Attempt to Prevent War. The way the famous historian went on to explain how powerful public opinion in England had been in the ultimate success for the war to begin truly made her wonder. The historian explained that had the British people in 1939 been as "irresolute" then as they had been in 1938, the war would not have begun, and each country would have had to rely on itself. Mr. Cameron Watt called it a sauvequi-peut, the way Hitler and Von Ribbentrop are described in assuming that England would not get involved, if Poland were invaded--the details of the behind-closed-doors dealings by so many.

Her attraction to those particular words was because of the wars of her generation. The idea that public opinion could dissuade powers from violence in any generation was important. It made everyone's opinion have serious responsibility. If people realized that, how willing would they be to encourage war? It was that first sentence that made her wonder if the people of today had really as much of a voice as the people of the 1930s.

She had found numerous accounts that stated that FDR wanted to join World War II, but that public opinion had stopped him until America was attacked. But her generation had been so loud in disapproval of war; America was as "divided" and as "irresolute" and very loud about how divided it was in late 2002 and early 2003. Like a rabbit out of a hat, those who wanted war used the dirty word and record of appeasement and Neville Chamberlain as an example over and over again.

As one of the five men who died in the G-AESY was a visible anti-appeaser, this was one of the few parts of history about which she tried to achieve an understanding. Most books she found seemed to make Neville Chamberlain the weak appeaser in a far more polite manner than the voices of today, when anyone accused of being an "appeaser" is spoken to (or about) in a very rude fashion.

Among the books she found there was, however, one--Chamberlain and the Lost Peace--describing a very different Neville Chamberlain. Another different description of Neville Chamberlain was also found in a book written by Anthony Crossley, the third body brought out of the G-AESY. Anthony Crossley wrote in the last chapter how he saw the world situation in March of 1938. He clearly felt that there was the threat of war was on the horizon. In it, he was complementary of Prime Minister Chamberlain, stating that the world would be a safer and happier place if the dictators took up fishing like Neville chamberlain.

On page 3 of the same book, Anthony Crossley described how he tried to avoid a fishing outing out of respect for the then-Chancellor of the Exchequer, Neville Chamberlain, feeling that Mr. Chamberlain would not want to see anyone from the House of Commons. However, he received a phone call letting him know he was welcome to join the then-Chancellor of the Exchequer who was quoted as welcoming, even though it was "just before the budget!"

She continued to wonder if the voices of people were really as strong today, so strong that they had the power to prevent war.

"Hi Maggie. So Bill quit smoking? You are going to have to open all the windows if we have another one of our drinking, smoking, and brainstorming sessions."

On each side of the Atlantic, they opened their bottles of wine and lit their cigarettes. Bill was away for only one night, and it was the first time since he'd stopped smoking that Maggie smoked in the apartment. It felt like breaking her parents' rules in their home when she had been at an age when that would have mattered.

"You can't imagine how much I miss the 'smoking Bill.' It was such fun to have a ciggy after lovemaking. This new version is very nice, and I know it is so much healthier not to be a smoker, but it was fun. I have decided to smoke as much as possible before I quit."

Maggie was serious, but Catalina had to laugh.

"I cannot begin to...if I try to count how many times I have quit. Bill was not the only one who started smoking with you, as you might remember."

"Of course! Blame it on the Brits. I see on the news there is a movement called the Tea Party in America that is named after the rebellion in Boston when America was part of us."

"Yes, there is indeed. Are you very familiar with American history?"

"Not according to Bill; he had to explain the grassy knoll to me. The American Revolution is different, as America was a part of England then. Our National Archives at Kew have many of the documents related to that era."

"Oh, wow! That makes sense. I have always been so focused on the 1930s that I never stopped to think of what other treasures that building holds. Can you imagine the correspondence describing the 'wrong' side misbehaving? Well there is no question of all those documents being open to researchers, at least no question of the fifty-year restriction."

"Is it a fifty year rule? I thought it was seventy five to prevent anyone being alive."

"I wonder if there are files that warrant more than fifty year restrictions; you might be right. I have heard historians and researchers being interviewed saying seventy-five. The relative of Anthony Crossley who explained to me that her grandmother had eventually seen a file that showed it was sabotage spoke of the fifty year rule."

"Where was it?"

"She said it had to be recorded in parliament as he was of the House of Commons. I could not find it. I got an appointment to use the reading room and searched, but maybe I did not look in the right place. The staff was very helpful and seemed to know what was available. Perhaps it is like so many family stories that become different as the years pass. It could also be that she saw the same file we saw at the British Airways archives, and that since the word sabotage appears here and there, it was not read carefully."

Maggie had to frown."Okay, so I got excited at first."

"I did too! As have some of the archivists who have helped me through the years. It is a very human reaction to that file, until you read it carefully. Especially when you are already predisposed to understand that it was sabotage. I grew up with that story that my grandfather was killed because the Germans wanted to kill the MP--that my grandfather was collateral damage. All the psychics I took my photos and the two watches to used psychometry, and everyone always insisted that it was sabotage and espionage and insisted I look for that. So I was predisposed to assume it was sabotage. You were, too, with Bill's nightmares."

"So you took the two watches you showed me to psychics before you searched any archives?"

"No. Not before, but certainly before I became serious and meticulous in my search. I had already seen the BAL archive once in 1993. I took the watches to the first psychic about three and a half years later. That was before I spent three weeks studying the files in the summer of 1996."

"Was every psychic's information correct? Well, not that you can prove that, but, I mean, was it the same?"

"Every one that had precise and detailed information matched. I only took them to five, and four of them had already been accurate in other ways. The fifth one had, at least locally, a very good reputation, but her reading was very vague, and she apologized for not picking up enough. The bits and pieces she did pick up, were in agreement with the others. She was expensive, so I never went back."

"I know you said that some psychics mentioned the bridge, and another gave the lettering on the wing. But what matched in a way that amazed you?"

"All four described by age, physique, and attire the same man as the owner of the second watch. Their descriptions and the story they told were almost the exact words...it was in essence the same story. One of them told the story in Spanish, and it was like a translation of what the others had said. They each spoke in their own words. The description fit one of the bodies to a T."

"Did you tell me which one it was?"

"I'm not sure if I did. It was the youngest, the last body out; the radio operator."

Maggie let out a pensive sigh before she added."I think that is the one Bill saw in his past-life regression. It's the only one that makes sense. I was thinking that the German had medals, so we can be pretty sure he fought in World War I...the medals and the glass eye. The American also had a military background; that's a common factor in several of the five."

Catalina nodded in agreement as she said: "In a way, my grandfather did too. Texas A&M University was a very military oriented school when he was a student there. I also need to look it up, but I am guessing that Anthony Crossley might have had to be military reserve? I know there is an entry in Hansard where he states something to the effect that if war were to start, he was one of the few who was of the age that he would have to fight."

"Do you think you will ever really know what happened that day?"

"Who knows? In my mind's eye, I do see a picture. It starts with this."She held up the British Airways

Summer Timetable from 1939. "I got this from Ron Davies at The Smithsonian Air and Space Museum Collection. *"April 16th until further notice. Flying to Belgium, Denmark, England, France, Germany, Hungary, Poland, and Sweden"* In the fourth page it shows our flight. 'The Viking Royal Mail Express."

Maggie tapped on the screen and said.

"Put it up to the camera. Look! Operated by Lockheed Electra Airliners with a cruising speed of 165 miles per hour! How fun. Look at the top...passenger lists closed five minutes before departure. Now that was an era when one could fly on a whim."

"Really! On a regular day, it boasted Stockholm in seven hours, Copenhagen in four hours and forty minutes, and Hamburg in three hours."

"The G-AESY was pretty close to Copenhagen."

"It had been airborne about an hour when it went down."

The both said simultaneously "The fuel should have been low."

Laughing Catalina added,

"Maybe. I don't know if they refueled normally in Copenhagen; I know they did in Hamburg. But again before the leg to Stockholm...I don't know. The schedule calls for a twenty-five minute stop in Hamburg and a twenty-minute stop in Copenhagen. From Copenhagen to Stockholm, it states two hours between departure and arrival."

Maggie had taken a screen shot and was scrutinizing the details. "Look at the regulations and general information: they were allowed thirty-three pounds of luggage free of charge. It has to be suitcases, not trunks. Cameras had to be handed to an official of the company because most countries had restrictions."

Nodding, Catalina said, "That had to be because everyone knew war was coming and that aerial views, like those today with satellites, could be most helpful. "You really think everyone knew?"

Maggie's eyes widened as she nodded with her youthful enthusiasm. "OF COURSE! Everyone knew, especially those in government. That is why I question a British MP going fishing."

Catalina shook her head and reached for a small book; *1939* in bold red numbers took up most of the cover with black and white photos of familiar WWII personalities framing the bold read numbers. As Catalina flipped through the pages of *1939* by Richard Overy, Maggie started to laugh.

"*1939?*And what are all those tabs? You marked the entire bloody book!"

Catalina joined in the laughter; it really did look absurd. Maggie's laughter was light fun and genuine; Catalina's was self-deprecating but not self-critical, somewhat modest. The transatlantic bond between the two was becoming more than a common interest.

"I did; I think I underlined at least eighty percent. I know I wrote this for you before. Here it is on page 23. 'On 19, August Halifax sent information to Chamberlain, who was on a fishing holiday at Lairg in Scotland.' From this book, I get the impression that many were in denial of the impending war."

Maggie's sighed, and her shoulders bounced up and down in frustration."Is it a reliable source?"

"I believe so, he is a college professor on your side of the pond."

The two women went back to the airline timetable, because that made more sense.

"So the London Departure was at 8:15 a.m., and in my mind's eye, I can imagine the group that boarded in London. I can see my grandfather getting into a taxi in London from the Cumberland House Hotel near Marble Arch. I can see Mr. Simonton driving from Surrey with his wife and probably a little girl in the car as well. Anthony Crossley with all his fishing equipment. I see all of them arriving, but Mr. Stocks is already there smoking his cigarette."

"It would have been nice to read a detailed account of how Mr. Stocks was questioned. I was thinking: did you try to find out whether he was interviewed by any newspaper?"

"I had very little access to the German papers, but I could not find him in any English one. I looked for it at the newspaper library in Colindale...nothing, but Stocks is not exactly a key word that would pop easy answers in any search."

"It is pretty odd that when the pilot and his wife flew back to London BAL deliberately misinformed the press, at they had to document how to avoid the press, and yet the press did not find the strange passenger that got off in Hamburg, Mr. Stocks, or apparently look for him."

"Yeah, but I think that in 1939, people were more private. It would have been far more difficult for a reporter to get a hold of the passenger lists. I don't know," Catalina sighed.

"So do the passengers go in through the same door and meet the crew?"

"I don't think so. I think the crew boards like Amelia Earhart in the Hillary Swank movie, through the top, but they refer to it as the emergency exit, and as you may recall, J. H. Willans pointed out that it worked perfectly, but the pilot's statement says it was not used."

"In your mind's eye, to whom is your grandfather talking at the airport that morning?"

"Do you mean from the papers at British Airways in which they state that Mrs. Simonton saw Mr. Castillo leaving instructions? Or just my wandering mind?"

"Yes. Both. Either. Whom is he talking to?"

"Well, it simply says someone; it does not say a man. In my mind's eye, he could very well be speaking to a woman."

"To a woman? No it was 1939, and it was in a man's world. In a place full of men, I think the 'someone' had to be male. It would have surely been specified if it were otherwise."

"That makes sense; you must be right."

"Did your grandfather smoke?"

"Oh, absolutely. Chesterfields. I understand quite a lot."

"Do you think any of the others smoked?"

"Well, in Herr Beuss's personal belongings, there is the description of a silver match box; I think there was a cigar cutter as well. So he must have at the very least smoked cigars and a pipe, maybe? I guess it would have been on the list. Mr. Simonton is anybody's guess, maybe. I seriously doubt that Anthony Crossley smoked; he was an athlete. He actually played tennis at Wimbledon, many years earlier to be sure, but I cannot imagine Mr. Crossley smoking."

"I was wondering what your files of the passengers look like?"

"Large and small."

"Of course."

"Death certificates, photos, and any type of bio I have been able to compile, which, in the case of Anthony Crossley, is enormous, and in the cases of Mr. Simonton, Herr Beuss, and the radio operator, are very limited."

"You know, I would really appreciate if you put together the bios for me."

"I had a feeling you would ask; I just don't..."

"I'll trade you for all my notes on Bill's regressions."

"Well! That is certainly an interesting offer."

"It is an interesting offer, and if you are fair about it and include even your observations, I promise to take very good notes and make my own observations."

And so there it was; one of those life changing events that smacks an individual like a blow to the face, as if by physical force. There was the glue she so desperately needed and had not known how to ask for.

"Every word he utters and every expression?"

Maggie was ready to become a spy.

"I'll record it and take notes if you give me your word that you'll never tell him."

"Agreed!"

CHAPTER TWENTY-NINE – BODY NUMBER ONE

The weather in Florida was still unusually cold. Catalina only had a few days until her job started, and the time she could spend on her research was about to become very limited. She went to her two file cabinets and pulled out all of the information labeled Castillo. That's where she would begin, not because he was her grandfather, but because his was the first body brought out of the plane.

Her grandfather's watch had stopped at 1:17 (or 13:17); that was the time the water damage had made it stop. That was what the rusty watermark showed. The British Airways files stated, "the bodies of the four passengers were recovered at approximately 20.00 hours on the evening of the accident, Tuesday, the 15th of August. The fifth body that of Radio Officer was recovered the following morning at 05.30 hours."

It made perfect sense to write the details of each man as she knew them in the order in which each man was removed from the wreckage.

FROM: SecretsoftheG-AESY@hotmail.net.fla.us

TO: Maggiestrylleri@hotmail.net.uk

RE: Bios on the 5

Hi Maggie,

As promised, here is the beginning of the bios on the five men. I decided to write the reports about the men in the order they were retrieved from the sunken plane, the way they were detailed in the drawing of the plane.

Body Number 1

Cesar Agustin Castillo. Mexican Passport number 988. Issued on July 11, 1939. Born June 27, 1898, in Mexico City, Mexico. Height 1.82 meters. Weight 90 Kg.

Body number one was found with his back leaning against the passenger cabin door. As the door was opened underwater, the body fell out. The diver's family story was that the cabin door had already been open by the salvage divers, but that they got spooked, and that was when their father was called. The records show that a diver with knowledge of the local waters was brought in after the aircraft had already been located, which makes no sense. (I believe this is why the reference to John Wayne was made.)

The death certificate states that he was a chemical engineer and lived in New York City. (The death certificate was translated into both English and Spanish.)

Remarks on death certificate are as follows. Mortal accident was the cause of death. There are wounds on the face from third and second-degree burns and signs of pressure on the forehead, body, and extremities. Dried foam around the mouth, drowning and fluid in the lung, light red livid spots. Cause of death is noted as drowning. Burning and poisoning by carbon-oxygen. It has--in Latin--*rigor livores* and is translated as death stiffness and livid spots. There is an entry, number 11, where it needs to be stated whether need for further tests is necessary, and the answer is simple nej (Danish for no). The death certificate is dated August 16th at 8 ½ F.M. I am assuming that is 8:30 a.m. (the Spanish translation shows it as such as well.) In the section of additional remarks, it is stated that the body was brought up together with three others eight hours after the accident. There is the remark "Extremities in 'Fencing' position."

No list of belongings or luggage. I am guessing it was made and given to the Intava representative in charge of collecting both Mr. Castillo and Mr.

Simonton's belongings. I have record that there was a list in the Vordingborg archive; I remember being surprised he had German coins in his pockets, as prior to that day he had not set foot in Germany since before World War I. It was an odd, casual mix of German coins. His fountain pen was a Waterman; Crossley, the poet, had a Mont Blanc.

There are various telegrams trying to make arrangements for the cremation. The Catholic Church did not allow cremation in 1939, and this complicated matters. Mexico only allowed ashes to be transported; so transporting the body was not an option.

The Danish autopsy papers from the file in Vordingborg (those we were allowed to work with for a few days but not copy)...I cannot tell you if they are from the first autopsy or the second one. The death certificates are by the date and document number 11 (mentioned above) from the first examination, but I have never understood why the information from the second autopsy is not acknowledged as some sort of addendum to the death certificates.

The notes I have from the autopsy are as follows:

At the autopsy, widespread second-degree burns have been established, especially in the face and on the back. Soot particles have been found in the airways. No signs of violence have been found. Enlargement of the lungs have been established; the lungs are filled with foaming liquid, and foam has been found in the upper airways. These findings are of such a nature that are found in drowning. No signs of violence have been found. (I don't know why they have this twice; it should have been no signs of illness, I would assume; maybe I read it wrong.) Theses are notes a Danish friend helped me take by recording the information and then translating it.

There are closing remarks for all five, which read: in connection with the autopsies, examination of blood samples, etc., from the abovementioned five persons, will be performed, especially with regard to the presence of carbon monoxide and prussic acid.

There is a second report from Copenhagen, which makes reference to the dissection on the August 18th. In that report, they do perform blood samples and liver tissue. However, to make the conclusions work, the doctors make reference to Dr. Madsen's report. Their finding is that there is no carbon monoxide or cyan in the samples. Then it states that reference needs to be made to statements, and they describe what they were told happened according to Dr. Madsen's theory and the pilot's statement.

In that report, the levels are stated at 10 to 11 percent by volume. I found a PubMed website that has an entry from the California Criminalistics Institute in Sacramento, California: "Victims of fires are sometimes discovered to have less-than lethal levels of carbon monoxide (CO) in the blood and no significant ante mortem fire damage. Such occurrences are often linked to flash fires involving volatile hydrocarbon furls."

The study uses temperatures in the rage of 500 to 975 degrees Celsius. So, between Madsen's theory and the pilot describing how he tried to go back in after he landed the plane on the water and climbed out of the window, thus reigniting the fire, according to Dr. Madsen's report and modern science, this could be possible.

They thus declare that none of the persons had been poisoned by carbon monoxide. They also say that the soot particles found in all breathing ducts show they were all alive during the fire. (Maggie, please keep this in mind when you get to body number three.) At any rate, it is declared by that institute that Cesar Agustin Castillo died of drowning in connection with a shock condition caused by the burns.

There is a picture from two sides of Mr. Castillo's body from Denmark. There is also a picture of his face only from the BAL File. I have, through my family, copies of telegrams and letters as well as other communications from Intava.

Cesar Agustin Castillo

Castillo was born into a family of means in Mexico City, Mexico. His father, Victor Manuel Castillo, appears in Who's Who in Latin America. He was a lawyer and had a very interesting international history. Cesar Agustin Castillo had three younger sisters. One did not live long, and the other two survived him by many years.

In 1908, when he was ten years old, he crossed the Atlantic en route to Germany, where he remained for six years. On board the ship, he was known to be a very mischievous child. His paternal aunt, Dolores, who was in charge of him and who as even a very old lady showed an incredible strength, both in character and physical strength. She loved to tell me stories about the mischievous child in 1908. Of her many stories of his mischief, my favorite is when, because of his bad behavior, Aunt Dolores picked him up and carried him out over her shoulder. The ten-year-old boy was so undaunted by this that, as his arms were behind her, he grabbed her skirts and lifted them for all to see her undergarments.

His father decided that the best education was in Europe, and he chose Germany, Heidelberg. The family story is that great grandfather had strong business affiliations with Baron von Krupp. I attempted to find data from the Krupp Archives in Germany but failed to find any (just via phone and e-mail; I never visited, which always makes a huge difference). There is, however, a writer in Chiapas, Mexico, who has seen letters showing that the family even stayed with the Krupp's at a Castle in Germany.

According to the family stories, Baron Von Krupp was so fond of my great grandfather, Victor Manuel Castillo, that he had the state shield from Chiapas (the area in Mexico that the Castillo's came from) especially made for him in Bavarian crystal. As I've said to you before, I contacted the Krupp Archives directly and found no data on their relationship, which is said to have been both personal and professional. There is no doubt that if you use Yahoo with the word "Mexico" (I always find that Yahoo and the country gets great results when looking for footnotes of history) and search for Victor Manuel Castillo, you will find that he belonged to the kind of international circles that could have easily included Krupp. If I can find papers about this, it could be important, as Baron von Krupp left an interesting trail in World War II.

Castillo remained in Germany until 1914, until the outbreak of the First World War The fact that he never returned home to Mexico during the six years and that he lived in Germany made those of his generation I knew as a child describe him as someone who kept his Germanic ways (there were odd little details, such as he ate like a European, with both hands always on top of the table). His holidays were spent in summer camps in various other European countries, which is how he is said to have spoken five languages.

There are many stories about his few years in Mexico. His father was involved in politics, and Mexico was in very politically complicated times. One of the stories is that his father had his assets frozen and spent some time in jail.

This story was always a favorite when my old aunties (his father's sisters, who all seemed to live to close to a hundred years of age) told it. They told the story in which my grandfather, then in his teens, was the hero, because he helped feed the family by selling stamps from his stamp collection. I believe all of these stories to be true, if perhaps a little shaded in brighter hues of enhanced family pride or by the family's imagination through the years and generations, but true.

When he was ready for university, he attended Texas A&M. On Ancestry.com, I have found various entries in which he crosses the border to go back and forth during school breaks. During that time, he was able to visit his family regularly. He was of the graduating class of 1920, and in the Texas A&M yearbook, next to a photo that has him sporting a military uniform, it says, "C. A. Castillo; Mexico City, Mexico; Agriculture." (That entry confuses me, as I always thought of him as a Chemical Engineer. There is another very elegant photo that shows him at age twenty-one and says he studied agricultural chemistry. It shows that he had the rank of private and lists the company he was in each year since 1916. He is also credited with being veteran of Lost Cause; vice president of the Latin American Club; Wanderer's Club member; and member of the Chemical Society. It says that his nickname is 'Casti', (my family never used that nickname). His little bio reads as follows.

Here is a hard worker, conscientious, steady and dependable. He has made many friends at this college who will regret to see him leave this country in May, when he returns to Mexico City, his home. Casti is probable the most widely traveled student in this college and can speak most any language, even "dog Latin." This big natured boy is going to make success in life because he has unusual ability coupled with lots of energy and determination to make good. No doubt he will show Carranza [president of Mexico at the time] and his gang how to rule the country.

There are various other pages with the different clubs he belonged to. In those, some of the students are wearing military uniforms, but he is not. One of those says he is an associate editor for the school paper, *The Battalion.*

The following year, he continued his studies at Columbia University in New York City. It was a one-year program, and I am unclear as to what he actually studied there. I have a nice little gold charm with the Columbia University emblem on it that has '21 engraved on the back. He was already engaged to my grandmother, so it might have been a gift for her.

He married my grandmother right after he finished his studies. She was from a nice family, and her father was a successful man, in the oil business as well. They had two daughters, the youngest of whom is my mother. I do not really have a complete and clear picture of his various positions before the Huasteca Petroleum

Company and Standard Oil of New Jersey. I do know that as newlyweds they lived in Port Arthur, Texas, and he worked with a laboratory developing serum against rattlesnake bites. My mother's memories are very vague; she was two months shy of thirteen when he was killed, and that is not an age when kids pay too much attention to what their parents are doing.

The job with Standard Oil of New Jersey required a move to New York City and another to Panama. The final move before his death was to London, but as you know, he was barely there two weeks before he met his fate in Denmark, on his way to Stockholm.

I also have a license from Mexico, dated 1924, authorizing him to work as a microbiologist. This is also from a school of agriculture. I have some books that were his about chemistry and fuels, and a stamp collector's catalogue from 1937.

Here is the hard part to get into, and frankly, I notice that I am procrastinating, and I did promise you that I would be honest and thorough and would include my assumptions and observations. So here it goes. He had a reputation as a ladies man. Some in my family say that he "misbehaved," and that, at times, he arrived home with lipstick stains on the collars of his shirts. Of course, as a modern woman, I do not find any of this disrespect to my grandmother acceptable in any way; she is truly someone whom I love (she died many years ago, but my love for her remains), so this is hard for me to get into. At any rate, he was said to attract women with great ease. That was the reason I had to assume that Mrs. Simonton would have noticed someone talking to him when others did not.

That and the fact that he traveled so much, as the whole world has seen in the news lately with the famous golf player, is not a good combination for fidelity. I would like to believe he loved my grandmother, for she certainly deserved to be very loved. His last two letters to his father are mixed (I'll get to that later).

The thing is that when I was a teenager, my aunt (my mother's older sister), on more than one occasion, at cocktail hour, when one tends to get chatty, told me that my grandparents would have gotten divorced had he lived and that she knew there was another woman in the picture, one with whom he had a son.

There are other sources from which I heard stories that would support that something was very wrong with their marriage in 1939. Now to his letters, in his last letter to his father (dated August 14, 1939), he informed his father that he was not "bringing" (to London) his wife and daughters. There is also the fact that any psychic who has touched his watch always goes on to say how women surrounded him, and that there was one very strong relationship other than the one with his wife.

The very odd thing is that at least two psychics have also mentioned Panama as the country that this woman was from or lived in. I assure you that this was without me saying a word! Well, it is odd because at his Aunt Dolores's funeral in the 1970s, which my mother did not attend (we did not live in Mexico at the time), someone who attended told me a story about a man who looked just like my grandfather's photos. This man had asked how they were related to Aunt Dolores, and then this man who so closely resembled my grandfather said, "This family to which I am so strangely linked." That man was also described as having a Panamanian accent. (Such an accent could be confused with other Spanish speaking Caribbean nations.)

So Panama keeps on coming up in all of the stories, whether from members of my family, psychics, or the fact that he actually traveled there so often that my grandmother decided to move there. I found a ship's manifest that documents her return from Panama—just my grandmother, her two daughters, and their nanny. The story always was that she thought Panama was too hot and decided she much preferred New York City. You would think that when moving from one country to another, the husband would be with them? Perhaps not.

The other thing psychics always say, and they always apologize before doing so, is that my grandfather was involved in espionage. Some of the gentlemen who have helped through the years and are savvy about the era are also very keen on the idea that he must have been a spy. David Kahn, in his book *Hitler's Spies*, has entries of recruitment in Latin America and, specifically, Mexico. In that very book, there is also a strong link to Standard Oil of New Jersey.

I do believe that the psychics who have helped me are very good at what they do. I try not to believe them, because I was raised to believe that it is against my religion or, better said, the religion of my upbringing.

However, there is in the laws of probability no reason for different psychics, who have never met, to whom nothing is told, to come up with the same story. There is always espionage, there is always a son—not just a child, but a son—and there is always the apology before espionage.

I could go into more detail, but frankly, I think that you probably will think this is detailed enough, and of course, if you do not, I know that you will bombard me with your questions, which is fine. (Don't be offended; I enjoy your enthusiasm.)

***

She was too tired to go on. The emotional strain of putting into words some of the facts wore her down. She saved the draft; it was not to be sent until she had detailed every single man. There was the possibility to perhaps exchange one at a time for the recordings of the regressions. This was certainly something to consider.

CHAPTER THIRTY – THE DEVIL IS IN THE DETAILS

Maggie e-mailed to ask about Catalina's progress, as all of the other information she requested had been sent so fast. When she heard that the first one was several pages long and was not the shortest, she suggested that perhaps they should be divided and sent, as they were ready.

FROM: Maggiestrylleri@hotmail.net.uk

TO: SecretsoftheG-AESY@hotmail.net.fla.us

RE: Re: Bios on the 5

Hi,

I cannot wait to read the others, especially the autopsy information on body number three. I like how you started with the bodies in the order in which they were pulled out of the wreckage. Of course, as the airplane sank nose first (I know I read that somewhere in the BAL file) and then settled at the bottom under the water, the air bubble would have carried the bodies to that end. It is actually really odd that all five bodies were not in the back, carried by the air bubble the same way.

Because the last body ended up in the front, all burned as it was, for the pilot's statement to fit (in my opinion), the pilot would have had to hear a screaming, burning man right next to him. The cockpit door was closed, right? So the backfire, as described when the pilot swims around and opens the door, cannot get to that part of the plane. Nobody describes the cockpit chairs as all burned, not like they describe the ones in the back. Were they made of a different material? The others were what? Textile and horsehair?

Then Dr. Madsen's report does talk about very high temperatures that would work with the PubMed report you found online. But when I looked at it again, it said it had to burn for five to ten minutes, and there does not seem to be enough time, again, to work with the pilot's statement, because he would also have had to been burned. Dr. Madsen says it had to have been a passenger who lit a match or a lighter; that is the only way his fuel gas theory works. It would also have to strongly smell of fuel for that to work, and the four men back there were all well-educated, well-traveled men. The only two with severely burned hands are the radio operator and Mr. Simonton; they were both familiar with aeroplanes because Mr. Simonton, you said, had been a pilot.

So it simply would not make sense. There was no smoking allowed. The summer timetable from the airline shows that smoking was not allowed. Also, the pilot statement says that there was a map on fire in locker D; well, in Dr. Madsen's theory, they would have never seen a small fire in locker D...it would have been a huge flame! Also the place they keep on calling the seat of the fire is not distinguished as locker D, which does not make sense at all.

I appreciate that certain events seem like private family matters. I am personally sure that people had two and three families (men that is) in that era; it was so easy to get away with it, and today look how many are found out!

But the ability to have a sort of secret life also would help give one the ability to be a good spy. The fact is that they died in 1939, so no matter what anybody's affiliations were, it was before the really bad stuff happened in World War II. At any rate, the formative years that your grandfather spent in America, the nickname Casti...his loyalties could well have been with the Americans. He would have been the perfect recruit for them.

Have you tried to find your uncle in Panama? Do send them as you write them? I imagine the others are not very long except for Anthony Crossley's, as you promised to include the newspaper entries. I saw online in Hansard that he has many entries there, too, which I am afraid I was too lazy to read!

Also, if there are any of the personal documents you would not mind scanning and sending, it would be interesting to see them.

Always curious,

Maggie

FROM: SecretsoftheG-AESY@hotmail.net.fla.us

TO: Maggiestrylleri@hotmail.net.uk

RE: re: re: Bios on the 5

Attachment: Cesar A. Castillo; Death Certificate

Hello Maggie,

You are too much! I, too, think that the pilot's statement and how the bodies were found contradict Dr. Madsen's report, and I find it very strange that it is not brought up in any of the papers I found. In perusing other files in the same box for the same airplane, I read one of a pilot being questioned on particulars; the choices he made that could have contributed to his accident. He was what I would call being "grilled by the chairman"; this was a pilot named Captain Moss. It even includes an appendix on Captain Moss's flying ability. There is nothing like that for Captain Wright.

Mr. Simonton was a pilot, and it was assumed that he was sitting in the back (because of a postcard that was found in the pocket behind the second to last seat addressed to Mr. Simonton's brother). It was also assumed that he was trying to go to the cockpit, to run to the front and try to help fly the airplane.

I think the time of the fire—five to ten minutes— does work, from the time the fire was witnessed to the time the airplane went down. Altogether, since it sunk so fast, it says it sunk in about four minutes, and presumably the fire was going on all that time.

But the body locations and taking into account the air bubble is difficult to explain. I do know this: the seats were supposed to be wider in the back. I believe then that the larger passengers, Herr Beuss and my grandfather, were likely to be in the back. Mr. Simonton was traveling with my grandfather, so one can also assume that they sat together. Herr Beuss is described as very heavy; he was four kilos heavier than my grandfather but considerably shorter, and four kilos is almost nine pounds. So we can also assume that Mr.

Simonton was polite and gave the German passenger his seat.

That would place Mr. Crossley more to the front, and would have made him more likely to be burned (more so than he was), but his burns are similar to Mr. Castillo and Mr. Beuss. Also when the air bubble settled (remember, we talked about how there had to be an air bubble also mentioned in the files, and that would make the bodies shift position), maybe it was when the door opened and closed. If the story from the diver's family is accurate that other divers had already been there, maybe they opened the door, and the air bubble pulled the bodies in that direction like a vacuum; at least two bodies got pulled toward the door. The third one was partially in the toilet, so it could have floated there with the air bubble and gotten stuck.

There does not seem to be much importance given to why or how the bodies were found, but there were two sketches made to show where they were found, as well as a note in the Danish report that the diver's memory was incorrect and that he had to be reminded where the last (I think) body was found.

I'll send the next one as soon as I have it ready. C.

Attachments. Open Attachment Download

Genpart.

B 2

Medicolegal Ligsynsattest.

Lov af 4. Maj 1875.

(Denne Blanket maa **ikke** benyttes til Børn under 1 Aar.)

Form. Nr. 23 a.

1) **Fulde Navn.** (for gift Kvinde, Enke, separeret eller fraskilt tillige **Pigenavn).** Ugift, gift, Enkemand, Enke, separeret eller fraskilt. Er afdøde ukendt, oplyses Kønnet.	Cesar Agustin Castillo. Pas No. 988.
2) **Født.**	Fødselsdag og Aar. 27/6. 1898. / Fødested (For Landet: 1) By eller Sogn 2) Amt). Mexico.
3) **Stilling og Næringsvej** (egen, Mandens, Forældrenes eller Forsørgerens; eventuelt om under offentlig Forsorg eller Aldersrentenyder; for Børn født udenfor Ægteskab Moderens Navn og Stilling). For Børn under 14 Aar: Hos Forældrene eller i Pleje, og da hos hvem?	Ingeniør, kemisk.
4) **Bopæl** (sidste faste Opholdssted) Folkeregisterkommune.	Adresse: / Folkeregisterkommune, Amt: Mexico.
5) **Dødsdag. Findedag.**	d. 15/8. 1939 19 Kl. 1-2 E.M. / Alder (evenl. Skøn). d. 15/8. 1939 19 Kl. 9-10 F.M. / 41
6) **Dødsstedet** (eller Stedet hvor Liget først fandtes). Stedet for Ligsynet. (Er Liget transporteret, da hvor langt og hvorledes.)	Storstrømmen, udfor Nr. Vedby Strand.
7) **Dødsmaaden.** (Naturlig Død, Ulykkestilfælde, Drab, Selvmord).	casus mortiferus.
8) Findes paa Liget **Tegn paa Vold?** Findes andet af særlig Interesse? (f. Eks. vedr. Ernæringstilstand, Defekter, Tatoveringer.)	vulnera ambusta grad: III - II faciei impr. frontis, trunci extremitatumque. Størknet Skum om Munden. Lyserøde Ligpletter (livores rubelli.)
9) **Dødsaarsagen** (saavel paa Dansk som paa Latin). paa Dansk: / paa Latin:	Drukning (Forbrænding, Kulilteforgiftning. submersio (Ambustio, veneficium (C O))
10) Hvilke sikre **Dødstegn** (Dødsstivhed, Dødspletter, Forraadnelse) konstateres ved Ligsynet?	Rigor Livores.
11) Er der eller det oplyst Anledning til yderligere Undersøgelse, eventuelt legal **Obduktion?**	Nej.

Supplerede Bemærkninger til Punkt 6—10 opføres under Anmærkninger paa Blankettens Bagside.

F. M.
Undertegnede Læge har d. 16/8. 1939 Kl. 8½ i Forbindelse med Hr. Politimester Jørgensen synet Liget af Cesar Agustin Castillo og forefundet ovennævnte sikre og utvivlsomme Dødstegn.

Oluf Olsen,

Amtslæge.

(Lægens Navn og Adresse *tydeligt* skrevet.)

Indført i Jordpaakastelse	Sogns Kirkebog d.

Se Anmærkninger paa Bagsiden.

Attachment 2011034125205_00016.jpg.

Anmærkning til P. 6—10.

Idet der sondres mellem Lægens egne
Iagttagelser og andres Angivelser oplyses
her: ¹) om Redningsforanstaltninger eller
Oplivningsforsøg er foretagne; ²) om Læge
kom til Stede før Døden, i saa Fald hvor
længe forinden; ³) Ligets Leje og Forhold
til Omgivelserne paa Findestedet; ⁴) i Til-
fælde af Selvmord, den formodede Bevæg-
grund; ved Forgiftningstilfælde oplyses saa-
vidt muligt Giftens Art og det indtagne Kvan-
tum. Kortfattet Beskrivelse af de nærmere
Omstændigheder, under hvilke Dødsfaldet
har fundet Sted. Det angives, om Afdøde
vides at have lidt af Sindssygdom eller af
kroniske Sygdomme som Tuberkulose, Kræft,
Syfilis o. l.; ligeledes om Afdøde vides at
have været hengiven til umaadeholden Ny-
delse af Alkohol- eller narkotiske Midler.

1–2) Nej.

3) Liget blev tilligemed 3 andre
bragt op af Dykker fra den for-
ulykkede Flyvemaskine ca. 8 Timer
efter Ulykken. Ekstremiteterne i
"Fægterstilling."

Attachment 2011034125205_00017.jpg.

CHAPTER THIRTY-ONE – SYNDIKUS

FROM: SecretsoftheG-AESY@hotmail.net.fla.us

TO: Maggiestrylleri@hotmail.net.uk

RE: Second Bio of the 5--Erich Bruno Wilhelm Beuss

The second body to be pulled out of the airplane was that of the German passenger who boarded in Hamburg, Herr Beuss. His was the body found in the lavatory compartment, and not Mr. Crossley—sorry. I did find the entry from the report dated the August 19, 1939, on page 6, number 23. This is in relation to where the bodies were found by the diver. I saw the translation they received, and it was not the detailed one that I found in the files from Nykøping. The one on the BAL files is a very basic one, with no real details. This particular one you must have in your own copies (but as promised I describe what I find to see if either one of us missed anything). As the airplane is known to have gone down nose-first, the location of the bodies--especially the three found in the back and most specifically that of Mr. Beuss--is assumed to not be the location where the people were, but rather where they floated.

Mr. Erich Beuss was born in Wilhelmshafen, Germany, on February 8, 1892. He was a *Syndikus*, which I understand is a corporate lawyer. His place of residence in 1939 was Hamburg. He was 1.72 meters tall and weighed ninety-four kilos. His face was badly burned, and he also, according to the photo, had some bad burns on the left leg and on both upper arms. This is my observation from the body photo in the Danish archives in Copenhagen. I was able to recognize the family resemblance when I found his grandson, so it was not indistinct.

The death certificate has similar entries to those of the first body. (Did I point out before that the death certificates were never reissued with the findings in Copenhagen, because they are dated before the second autopsy?)

7) Mortal Accident.

8) Wounds of 3rd degree and 2nd degree of face and neck [You can see clearly in the BAL photo that his face is much more burned than Mr. Castillo's or Mr. Crossley's]. In left shoulder blade region and extremities. Light red livid spots.

9) Burning and poisoning by carbon oxygen.

10) Death stiffness and livid spots.

11) No [need for further autopsy].

The same time and date are given as the first body, and there is a similar additional remark as to how the body was found by a diver in the passenger cabin. As well as the same description of the "Extremities in 'Fencing' position. Body brought to surface eight hours after accident."

My notes from the Vordingborg autopsy files are as follows. (I know the language is awkward, but I wanted to keep it as my friend translated it, in case you as a Dane can read more into it.)

At the autopsy, a number of second-degree burns have been established, especially on the head and on the limbs. Soot particles have been found in the airways. A few minor extravasations [perhaps with your Danish, you can make sense of this word--I think it refers to wounds or scrapes] on the skull have been established, but besides this, no signs of violence have been found. Enlargement of the lungs have been established; the lungs are filled with foaming liquid. These findings are of such a nature as those that are found in drowning. No signs of illness have been established.

Then there is the same additional remark making note of the fact that blood and tissue tests will follow.

For Herr Beuss, we do have a list of belongings from the Nykøping files, as well as from BAL--that one is signed Jack Sinclair. The other men had lists of belongings in the Danish file from the police, but our time was limited, and we did not choose to make a thorough list of those. You have, of course, seen the list and are aware that it includes his extra glass eye in a case. (I cannot remember, nor do I have notes of any mention of his glass eye from the autopsy, and I was not allowed to make any copies, but surely the eye was his, as he is the right age to have fought in World War I, and this was a common loss.) I visited a Spy museum in Washington D.C. where I saw that. He had three small green stones, a pen, pencils (these were silver)...all common personal effects. For our purposes, what stands out are the silver matchbox, cigar cutter, and four German badges or orders. (Hence the assumption that he fought in World War I, as well as his age.)

As you recall, they did investigate him, as he was German, and they found out that he lived well, had a wife and two sons, and was liked and respected. A friend is mentioned, a Max Pusher, an insurance agent. That same man contacts British Airways after the war ends on behalf of Herr Beuss's widow. There is mention that a friend who had been awaiting him in Stockholm was the one to tell his wife he had perished, and then there are two letters of inquiry from a law firm, Berckemeyer & Katterfeldt, in the Danish file.

The letters are not official and go through friends, who are also friends of Mr. Eskildsen. It is through a famous tobacco shop in Copenhagen, Wilhelm O. Larssen (you might know it; I was familiar with it), that this correspondence takes place. The letter has the eagle of the scales of justice with the Nazi swastika in the middle. This appears in both letters, one from August 26, 1939, and the second one from September 8, 1939. I do not think that by 1939 there was anyone who could have escaped registering with the Nazis in Germany. Herr Beuss was also heading to Stockholm. I read that German people had no choice but to join Hitler, or the repercussions were unbelievable by 1939.

Germany was such by the summer of 1939 that just to be able to travel or to be able to keep your orders or medals, one had to be cautious and publicly respectful of the powers that were. Herr Beuss, one can only assume, would have had to play along. By the end of the war, when his family claimed their insurance, to which one can also imagine they were well entitled; they had to claim no affiliation whatsoever to the Nazis. This, of course, is ridiculous, but I have met Germans who explained to me that it was the basic introduction, and suddenly no one was affiliated with the Nazis when applying for anything that involved England or any Allied country. It would be most inappropriate to judge, as who can tell how anyone would react under such threatening pressures. The German people were as much victims of Hitler's madness as the people of the countries he attacked.

I looked for Beuss's family for years and unfortunately began with the A's, because after umpteen searches, I finally found a grandson about my age in the W's. His bone structure was unmistakably that of the second body pulled out. I contacted him. He is a public figure who at first was very friendly, intrigued. He wrote to me a little about his family, but when I mailed him some photos and copies of newspaper clippings, he never contacted me again; nor did he ever answer my e-mails.

I read about him here and there in Yahoo Deutschland. I did not send many e-mail messages; there is no sense in badgering people, and maybe he is just busy, but my very own family members have given me the silent treatment, changed the subject, or made blatant remarks like, "The secrets of each generation need to stay as such."

There is no doubt that 1939 is an era where in any family, if a closet is shaken hard enough, skeletons are bound to fly out (probably in large numbers). As such, families are reluctant to get involved, but again, as we have talked about with each other, it was 1939, and the real horrors of war had not been perpetrated. Our five bodies deserve the benefit of assuming that if they had lived, their choices would have been impressive and helpful to society. What can I say? I'm attached to them, and I would like to believe that.

Anyhow, as you know, there are a number of documents you have seen in the BAL file. They are all basic formalities...a little internal feuding over who should have written the letter of condolence to the widow.

I found one German paper with news on the accident; it is written in gothic German, but I believe the name is printed as Reuss and not Beuss. I have had several Germans look at it, and nothing stands out.

You know, the next one is long and complicated. I will include anything I consider relevant, because there are so many entries in both newspapers and Hansard! Simply too many to include all. Maybe someday you'll take the time, and you'll read the entries in full, online.

C.

CHAPTER THIRTY-TWO – MORE QUESTIONS THAN ANSWERS

FROM: Maggiestrylleri@hotmail.net.uk

TO: SecretsoftheG-AESY@hotmail.net.fla.us

RE: re: Second Bio of the 5

YOU CANNOT BE SERIOUS! ARE YOU JOKING? There are many things here that make me think. First of all, how did the biggest body get inside the lavatory? I keep trying to visualize it, and all I can think of is that he ran for cover. Also, the diver's report says *"Dor til Passagerrummet paa Klem,"* which is Danish for "the door was ajar." The report has them trying to figure out if the door was forced open by the salvage. Maybe they ripped it off the hinges. The newspaper pictures of the plane being pulled out by the crane show it being pulled out nose first and probably not slowly. I have seen the newsreel of the G-AESY being pulled out of the water at a museum; The Danish Museum of Science and Technology part of the Zonen Salvage Collection. It does seem that the plane was pulled out with force, and some of its damage might have been caused when it was retrieved on August 16, 1939.

Another odd thing is where was our diver when the airplane was salvaged? Don't you think that you would have heard or read mention of that? He was a builder, a carpenter, and it seems that his only job was getting the bodies. There is no record that he helped hook up the chains for the crane; it is odd, isn't it?

The three green stones...we don't know what Herr Beuss did yet, but he had four badges or orders from World War I and the glass eye. This German would be perfect for a spy novel! It is a pity that his family was not more interested. I guess you are right about the fear of skeletons from the past. That is something that is less and less likely to happen as we all get caught by cameras on phones and posted on Facebook these days!

I know you looked for the lawyers' families, and that you were unable to find anyone, but again, it was during an era many seem to feel would best be left forgotten. What ever happened to the fear of repeating mistakes once they are forgotten? History of war and suffering should be the kind of subject made so tasteless as to deter people from wanting to participate in any war.

I wonder what the three small green stones were for. I have seen his list of personal effects, and he has the personal effects of an elegant and well-to-do gentleman.

I cannot understand why when he was a *Syndikus*, an in-house counsel for a company; they failed to find out what he did. Do you know that most arms deals in World War II were made in Sweden? He had to represent a company that did business in Sweden; he was not traveling with his family.

Also, why was his face burned more than the other two bodies found in the back? Because of his size, we did say he probably had to sit in the back where the seats were larger, so he should look like Mr. Castillo and Mr. Crossley.

I am still certain that as you said, at that point you really had to be (well, I am going to use very different words) connected to the Nazi party to be allowed to travel. And his personal belongings and "papers" are for a business trip. What could the three small green stones be for?

If the third one is too long, maybe you can send it in parts. Just a thought.

Maggie

CHAPTER THIRTY-THREE– THE BRITISH MP

There were several large binders labeled "Anthony Crossley" in her office, as well as a full file cabinet drawer that was specifically for Anthony Crossley. Of course, the only place to begin was as she had begun with the other two passengers of the G-AESY.

She looked at the photo of Anthony Crossley's body at the morgue in Denmark from the Copenhagen files and realized for the first time that this had been taken from a different angle from any of the other men.

So had the photo in the British Airways archives. The one in the coffin did not make sense; it was simply from a further distance than the others, but the one from the morgue...well, as this corpse was that of a man in public life, a politician perhaps, maybe the decision was made to photograph him without showing his entire body?

The other bodies were photographed from the side from a ninety-degree angle. Mr. Crossley's body was photographed from a forty-five degree angle, which showed less of him. This made her look closer.

His hands were in the position of a fist; the only other body that displayed such a closed hand was the last body, and those hands were quite burned. Unlike Mr. Crossley's, one of Mr. Simonton's hands had its fingers completely spread apart, and the other much burned hand had the fingers curled in, but not tightly. Herr Beuss' hands had the fingers loosely curved in. The only hand similar to Mr. Crossley's was the side where Mr. Leigh was the most burned, that hand. It was shaped as if making a fist to hit someone or a determined angry person. She wondered how that hand shape matched the arms folded across his chest.

The pathologist had explained that Mr. Crossley could have folded his arms across his chest in the universal emergency landing position. That would probably be with fingers open—or would it? She tried both ways. It made sense to make fists; she just could not get out of her mind the way the doctor showed the position. The doctor's hands were open. The psychic's description of the way the arms were crossed at death, however, easily matched the closed fist.

She ran back to her cigarettes and wondered if using information acquired through psychics made her a fool. Television was full of shows showing psychics helping police solve crimes. She took a long drag and looked at the bodies.

If she believed in reincarnation, then the body was just a shell, a wrapper to be left behind when the soul moved on to perhaps a bigger and better life. There was always that little word--if. Doubt often crept into her thoughts and made her question the validity of all that she had learned through psychics. All of that was, at best, very hard to prove; most likely it was impossible.

Was it a matter of faith? The type of faith needed for religion? Were the many books with anecdotes about how people found items or families from a past life made up? How much value and weight could she in good faith give the information from the psychics and the past life regressions?

She took another long drag from the cigarette and blew the smoke out with a sigh. If that, too, had to be included when she told the story, would it be accepted? Would it be mocked or ridiculed? If only she could tap into Maggie's strength and sense of conviction. Maggie would surely start typing away, writing in her attitude of freedom and acceptance, saying or shouting to everyone, "See! There is a grassy knoll in this story!"

The files were so large...*The London Times*; Hansard; the official report edited verbatim of the proceedings of both the House of Commons and the House of Lords in the National Archives, UK; a file for "other newspapers"; Anthony Crossley's poetry books and one about fishing; notes from all of the books that she found in which Anthony Crossley was mentioned (unless it was just one of the Munich Pact anti-appeaser books). The files were large, long, and heavy. She remembered when she sent Anthony Crossley's granddaughter copies of all of *The London Times'* articles, the package looked like she was mailing a phone book, and that was before she had gone back to study and copy the full articles. She'd been researching the people with whom Anthony Crossley interacted, as reported by *The London Times.*

The Kew files binder, holding the files from the National Archives, was copied on the enormous sheets that are used at the archives. Year by year, little by little, she found new files. Anthony Crossley had certainly gotten involved in issues between 1931 and 1939 that made the "front benchers" in the British government take notice. There not as many files from Kew as from other sources, but all of the Kew files were certainly interesting.

She had visited the library at Parliament; there she paid to have certain papers copied and had always wanted to go back. That was not to be, but one day, as if by magic, she found that all of the Crossley entries were readily available online! She read every file available since 1931 in which Anthony Crossley was quoted. It was a way to form an understanding of his personality, and what she found the most amazing was that several psychics, by simply holding a book or two that Anthony Crossley had written, without even opening the books, described the personality that she could clearly see in the words written from the sources available to her; the personality matched (sometimes, unfortunately) the one that psychics had described.

On the Internet, one of the first entries she found was a quote from the Henry Channon papers in which he refers to Mr. Crossley as "that ass, Crossley..." A psychic had told her that people reacted to him that way at times.

One thing was for certain: Mr. Anthony Crossley was aware of how he could antagonize people. He wrote it himself in his own epitaph years before when he changed seats from Oldham to Stertford in the House of Commons while addressing a conservative association:

"Crossley was a curious character. He had not much tact. He was much too intolerant. He was not nearly polite enough to all those people to whom a politician should be polite-even if he would like to see them at the bottom of the sea. But he had his good points, three of them. He was a fighter. He took more interest in the cotton trade than any Oldham Member has ever taken. And he always told what he considered to be the truth."

She knew that in the many words she had read--spoken or written by Anthony Crossley--there was at least one more reference to someone ending up at the bottom of the sea, and she found that uncanny.

There were speeches in Hansard that clearly showed the "not nearly polite behavior". There were entries in books and the parliamentary speeches that displayed lack of tact, to be sure. It really felt that there was an inherent honesty in anything she had come across that bore his name.

It was not going to be fun to put this one together; it was full of entries that made her wonder if it was better to let sleeping dogs lie. She decided that it was important to try to do it in the Anthony Crossley sort of way: "And he always told what he considered to be the truth."

As she set out to convey the information to Maggie, she could not help but wonder if she would sound much more like a fan than a researcher.

FROM: Maggiestrylleri@hotmail.net.uk

TO: SecretsoftheG-AESY@hotmail.net.fla.us

RE: Body Number Three (The British MP)

Anthony Crommelin Crossley

Born August 13, 1903. (He celebrated his thirty-sixth birthday two days earlier.) British passport number: 426354.Height: 1.75 meters, weight: 72 kilograms.

He is the only one with two death certificates available in the files. One of them is typed (Thankfully! Did you notice the handwriting on them? I almost needed a class in cryptography. Fortunately, the one my family received was typed). This one, too, is from August 16th, before the second autopsy. Has the same time as all the others (8 and ½ F.M.). The translated answers are as follows:

7) Cause of Death. (Natural or accident, etc.)Mortal Accident.

8) Any signs of unnatural death. Wounds from second-degree burning of face and body. Dried foam around mouth. Light red livid spots.

9) Cause of Death. Drowning, burning and poisoning by carbon-oxygen.

10) Outward signs of death. Death stiffness and livid spots.

11) Is there any reason for postmortem examination or further investigation? No.

Additional Remarks

Body brought to surface with three others by diver, from the machine, eight hours after the accident. Both arms folded across chest.

As we have remarked, this is a difference, a big difference from the other bodies, including the body brought up the following day, but a pathologist explained to me how this could be explained. It is not like in the TV shows, when any difference means there is something wrong. You can imagine how disappointed I was that this could be scientifically explained, as it contradicts what the psychics say.

From the Vordingborg (Nykøbing Falster) archive, we took and translated the following notes (There are Vordingborg police reports and Nykøbing Falster files; the jurisdiction problem has the information very mixed up): "At the autopsy, a number of second degree burns in the face, the back, the arms, especially the left arm, have been established, whereas the legs only have a few burns. No signs of violence found. An enlargement of the lungs has been established; the lungs are filled with foaming liquid. At the coroner's inquest, foam around the mouth was established. These findings are of such a nature that are found in drowning. No signs of illness."

Please remember, Maggie, that we were not allowed to copy from this archive, and that we read and recorded, but it was not great quality. Another difference that is important to note is that in that report there are no soot particles. I also noticed a difference in the hands and angle from the morgue photo.

As you have seen the documents in the file from the British Airways archive, I'll just go over it briefly. There are papers for the schedule of the body to be delivered in England with that of A. S. M. Leigh. There are correspondence and notes of conversations from his family. I did see some sort of list of belongings in the file I could not copy, as I distinctly remember a Mont Blanc pen (I've always wanted one).

His fishing equipment was described in a container made of lead. We spent an evening with my Danish friend's family, and her father was very particular that this would have made it very heavy and was odd for it to be made of lead. We were careful and did not feel we had made a mistake. I trust my friend, and I looked up in my Danish/English dictionary: lead is *bly*, and tin is *blik* or tin. I guess the clerk typing the information in 1939 could confuse *bly* and *blik* in certain handwriting, just as easily. I remember this conversation well, as someone said that the weight of the lead would have contributed to the airplane sinking so fast. Observation: if this were a spy novel and not a long, boring list for you, I would make it a lead container keeping something very safe. Note: No sign that it was damaged or near the fire was found.

The articles from *The London Times* will be sent to you as agreed. I found a few other English newspapers—mostly different versions of his obituary and other personal and political articles. I am enclosing a list, and you can feel free to ask about any article; the ones that might catch your eye are sure to be more detailed in Hansard and maybe even the National Archives at Kew. I will start with 1932; in 1931, he is only mentioned once with the election results (for his first seat, Oldham).

I believe Oldham was also Winston Churchill's first seat at the House of Commons. I have to tell you, Maggie, that after typing all of these entries from the research and work I did so many years ago, I cannot help but feel sad that the articles will end in 1939 with Anthony Crossley's death.

I assume anyone would agree with me that had Mr. Crossley lived longer, he would have certainly tried to make his country a better place. I mean, I don't know; I'm not British, but as an American, I love to see politicians who really stand for something, and sometimes, but rarely, even those with whom I disagree. His tombstone could have said, "Here is a man who, had he lived, would have made the world a better place."

Thanks for the FedEx Account Number; I will send the articles. C.

CHAPTER THIRTY-FOUR – *THE LONDON TIMES*

FROM: Maggiestrylleri@hotmail.net.uk

TO: SecretsoftheG-AESY@hotmail.net.fla.us

RE: *The London Times* **and Anthony Crommelin Crossley**

Anthony Crossley appears in *The London Times*(notice how I did not write *London Times*) in a wide variety of ways. As I promised you, I sent you photocopies of each article with an index and summary of each to Bill's company with the FedEx number you gave me; it felt great to send it that way--not something I could afford at this point.

There are about ninety articles ranging from 1931 to 1939 in *The London Times*. When I researched Anthony Crossley in the 1990s, they had a nice index bound in large red books. When I went back to check something, all of the indexes were online and, I assure you, incomplete! It was so frustrating! So there might be more. Did I tell you he too has a military background? A lieutenant in the Shropshire Yeomany? (I cannot read my own notes.)

In the entries ranging from 1931 to 1934, there is not much; various election results as he enters politics. The rest is all about workers' rights, especially in regard to those in his contingency and matters such as unemployment insurance, depressed areas, and the cotton trade. A few stand out in one way or another, they are:

-Trying to get a tax exemption for artists that paint in other foreign countries. Did I tell you his wife Clare was an artist? It is the only entry that could be construed as 'self-serving.'

-He discussed a visit to Germany in a political capacity as some sort of "labour exchange," and he explained certain things he observed that could be implemented in England. I found a distortion of this one in a history book to make him sound like a sympathizer to the Germans. (I wish I could find that book; it had a blue cover).

- In a matter on the water supply, he plays the House and gets everyone to laugh with a cute little quip. (In later entries where he is adamant in regard to other matters, especially Palestinian territories, he seems to grab the spotlight again).

In 1935, things start to get interesting as Austin Hudson, the Parliamentary Secretary to the Ministry of

Transport, appoints Anthony Crossley as a private Parliamentary Secretary. Apparently, this is quite a big deal, and that it is doubly impressive that he received this appointment twice.

His voice in different issues seems self-assured and louder. How cool that in 1935, there is a discussion about women being appointed to committees. I found this fantastic; no wonder England elected a woman to be Prime Minister in 1979. I remember that year well in the USA, and a woman president was inconceivable. Well, that was my opinion, but for Anthony Crossley...well, for him it was a matter that made his "blood boil" when he saw that the amendments said that one woman should be in this committee or that. I think he means that any spot should be acquired because people are capable and not because a "minority" is needed to show balance.

The entries in 1935 are all interesting but you will see soon enough for our purposes the other one worth noting is a Council of Action--one where there are definite rumblings of war, and he points out that he is of fighting age, and the other opinions are coming from "old men."

In 1936, he gets very international with a visit to Spain and adamantly defending the Palestinians. Many of the other MPs use terms such as the Mufti and the Jewry, but Crossley makes it a point that he chooses to call them Palestinians and not Arabs. He goes on to explain that they have lived in "that country," (I do not understand why it isn't "that colony") for fourteen hundred years.

There is a mandate being discussed--I am guessing the mandate he claims that the British government is tied to is the Balfour Declaration, because every time I look any of this stuff up, it comes up. Anthony Crossley's point of view that if the future could be foreseen and the contradictions of trying to help two peoples were not going to work. We are so used to conflict with Israel and Palestinians that of course he was right. His words are, of course, far more elegant than mine; I learned a beautiful word from that entry. Axiom: something that self-evident, that there is no need to prove it.

Like I said, that is how sure he was that the issue of Palestine as the Balfour Declaration had created it had "no real chance of cooperation for an indefinitely long period." Imagine that in March of 1936, and here we are, as a global society, still dealing with this.

The other two I'll note of that year are one with a Catholic point of view in November (His granddaughter told me he converted and then asked his wife to marry him; she did not become Catholic, so the family is half Catholic, half Church of England.)And as someone with one foot in and one foot out of Catholicism, I also found a December one on divorce; here he wanted the word "persistent" added before the word "adultery." (I guess a quick slip is okay, but if it happens often, you are out.)

Amongst them, some of the best ones to get to know Anthony Crossley are his letters to the Editor, which I think you'll enjoy.

In 1937, there are some really huge entries from Parliament. He meets with Generalissimo Franco, addresses Central Europe, and, to me, there is an absolute feeling of impending war and doom.

He continues with an Adamant defense of the Palestinians and their rights in such a way that he does eventually earn international recognition as "The Voice of the Arabs in Parliament."

-As an American, I found this one fascinating from December:"Attitude of the USA under an insult". The United States "Isolationist" policies. How America knows that it will not be directly physically affected by the impending war and how a "blatant" deliberate attack like "the sinking of the Panay" would end the American public from an isolationist view. There is an amazing book called *The Irregulars* by Jennet Conant, which explains to what great lengths your country went through to end the "Isolationism." Anyhow, here he disputes that those who believe America is willing to lend a hand are not forming their opinions based on "the facts."

Well, I do not know if I mentioned that his mother was an American (as was Winston Churchill's). She was from the Marshall Fields family in Chicago. I remember going to a really elegant Marshall Fields store in Chicago; I think it's a Macy's now. I haven't been there in ages...okay, and I am rambling like a fool. I do not know if I will ever tell you all that the psychics have said, but if I ever do, this entry on America makes some of what was said make sense.

Again, several entries in which he voices an unpopular pro-Arab stance; sometimes, this gets him in trouble as his fellow house members have good memories. As you read the full entries, you'll notice that in spite of the decisions made in that era, the people in power sure seem more concrete than many today. That being said, decisions made in that era, such as those in regard to the Palestinian Territories in which Anthony Crossley is so outspoken, left a very wobbly foundation.(Did I say wobbly? How British!) Anyhow, as with anything else, if the foundation is not solid and stable, nothing it is supporting will ever be, and that was a strong argument in all the back and forth.

Aside from the entries on the Munich Pact that you are so familiar with, more on the Palestinian Territories especially the White Paper of 1939 in which Zionists' views were completely opposite to Crossley's (The Arab voice in Parliament). There is, of course, his death certificate and obituary.

The BAL file shows that a brass plate was requested saying,

ANTHONY CROMMELIN CROSSLEY

DIED 15 AUGUST 1939

AGED 36 YEARS AND 2 DAYS

I will give you more details about that in the entries for body number five, A. S. M. Leigh, as they were transported together back to England on a ship baring your name, the SS Margrethe.

At the National Archives at Kew, I found a file from 1932, W 1428/95 20 January 1932. There was a note on it that says that there was nothing new in the attached newspaper article, but due to the fact that an MP wrote it, it could have provoked controversy. It was initialed by an L.C. The same Lord Crichton wrote a summary of a speech along the same lines given by Mr.

Crossley. They were trying to figure out how much it was desirable for MPs to "state their private opinion." Lord Crichton went on to express the point of view that he felt Anthony Crossley was "unduly influenced by German propaganda." Because of that, the potential threats were being made far more than Lord Crichton felt they were; the making-a-mountain-out-of-a-mole hill attitude. Who knows when people began to agree with Anthony Crossley? Winston Churchill explained in one of his many books that he gave his first "formal warning" in May of 1932 at the House of Commons, and I also read somewhere that in 1933, H. G. Wells published *The Shape of Things to Come*, where he also predicted the next great conflict to begin in Poland.

Reading the article and other attachments in the same file, Crossley stated in no uncertain terms that World War II would begin there, in the Polish Corridor, and seven years later, it did. (I mean, according to Wikipedia, Hitler invaded from the North, East, and West, but it sounded good! My knowledge of history is embarrassing; I actually failed the subject more than once.) I have a number of files from the National Archives, most of which are related to the articles in the newspapers directly or indirectly.

I have four of his poetry books (I believe there are one or two more). I do not find his poems easy to understand, but that is not saying much, as poetry is not really appealing to me. There are lines in one poem, however, that I like to think about. I don't like the title of this poem, but I like the lines from it on page 88, especially the last one in the book *Prophets, Gods and Witches*:

Across the stars a veil is spread,

Like grey souls fleeting

From earth, remote and disinherited.

Ours is the meeting

Heart with Audible Heart; yet hear the whirr of

The souls new-bidden

To the stars!   Love have you fear? Shall love with life surrender?

Shall love   lie dead?

Hush, for the stars are hidden.

End of report on body number three. C.

She poured a glass of wine and looked at a picture of Anthony Crossley she had found in a book at the New York Library, a book he wrote while at Eton. It was a much better photograph than the one from all of the obituaries in the newspapers. She sipped her wine and thought that she was looking at the face of a man who would have surely made the world a better place, had he lived longer than thirty-six years and two days.

CHAPTER THIRTY-FIVE – SECOND REGRESSION

Maggie chose a small digital video and audio recorder from an electronics store on Oxford Street. The store sold a wide variety of amateur spy gear. She had so many devices to choose from; many of the recorders were hidden in easy, everyday things. She wondered which type spouses who did not trust each other used? How many video cameras hidden in pens, key chains, and other such items found their way into "closed" meetings? The world had certainly changed since 1939, and become such that spying was no longer limited to Big Brother. Technology had given Little Brother the means to spy and report.

She also wondered if this was better--if the world of 2010, with so much openness, was better than the world of 1939, with so much secrecy. Could all of this knowledge and openness prevent wars? Could it help people in danger? Could it hurt? Were information and truth tools for peace? For the time being, Maggie decided that it was better for her to be a little secretive.

She did not plan to tell Bill that she was recording his sessions.

Session number two was longer than session number one. Bill was obviously very comfortable with the therapist. Her mother was always very intuitive when it came to matching people up for practical purposes (not at all for romance).

True to his word, Bill was showing that he was determined to give this therapy a fighting chance. She felt the ease of a person who knows that either way things worked out, it would work out. The alternative to the therapy not working was simply living happily elsewhere with the man she loved.

This time, preoccupied by the video equipment, she had forgotten to drink coffee. Her curiosity was not as piqued as the last time, and Maggie felt very relaxed. Thus, the melodious voice of the therapist took Maggie deep into her own subconscious, deep into a magnificent journey of her own. This was not as the woman she had seen in the group session several weeks before. This was an enjoyable diverse journey into several different lives.

She traveled through a wide variety of time periods and even flew to the future inside small space capsules. It was one of the most wonderful adventures she had ever had. It ended with the familiar smell of Bill's fresh breath, always sweet and clean now that he did not smoke.

"Maggie, you were supposed to be my life support, and you slept? You slept through that?"

"Through what?"

The therapist laughed and said it would be interesting to see who Maggie had been in that era. Bill and Maggie looked at each other in that knowing manner that only two people very much in love can and laughed. The therapist knew better, so she did not pry. The third session was booked for a few days later.

Hand in hand, they walked to find a restaurant for that evening. There was a very nice menu in the oriental restaurant they chose.

"You know, this is a very nice area; expensive. I think she makes very good money," Bill said.

"I think she started out with money; I can ask my mum. That is probably why she is such a good hypnotherapist, because it is more of a labor of love than a career to make money. Maybe she's married to money?"

"Well, that was certainly something you slept through; it did not match the archives, and I don't think it matched the information you've been getting from your new friend in Florida."

"She said that her information from psychics contradicted a lot of the information from the archives, as well. I am not sorry at all that this happened. I did not sleep. I got hypnotized as well! We got a session in tandem; it was such an extraordinary experience..."

"As the pilot's wife?" He interrupted.

"No. Not at all. I went through so many lives. And as fast or short, I don't know how to say this. I cannot explain...each glimpse, each peek was really illuminating."

"Illuminating?"

"Yes, like a lightning bolt that cannot hurt you. I saw something like...no, it was not like it; it *was* the French revolution."

"Who were you?"

"A woman. No one you would find in a book, but I was helpful to people. I was educated but not one of the aristocracy. I was happy to see the people take power, but I walked away from the violence. I was aware that it was there, but I had a job. I taught people who needed knowledge to read but not in a traditional school."

"Maggie, that does not sound like a quick peek."

"I told you, it was illuminating. As short and quick as each bit was, I knew all that was important to know about each life at once. It was like looking at a detailed painting for a few minutes in which all of the details are observed and absorbed. It left me with such a complete sense of being one with the universe."

Bill was happy and relaxed. Perhaps Maggie's lack of curiosity in all that he had seen and said was for the best. She was glowing as she went into great detail about each and every one of her glimpses. As she spoke, he realized she was radiant; there was something even more special about her today, and she made him feel so complete.

Once back in their cozy apartment, holding her, he started to laugh. Bill laughed and laughed and finally said, "Oh, Maggie, you must have been influenced by the hypnotic suggestion. You have not smoked one cigarette since we left her office."

Maggie joined in the laughter and knew this was for the best. When Bill fell asleep, she went to her computer and scrolled through the long e-mail she had received from Florida. True to her word, she hooked up the digital recorder to the laptop's USB port; she turned to look at Bill sleeping peacefully, smiled, and attached the video file to a short e-mail with the subject, "Re: Here it is," and hit send.

Catalina made herself a cup of chamomile tea, looked at her e-mail, and smiled at "Re: Here it is." She opened the attachment and began to look and listen. The sound of the hypnotist's melodious voice began to relax her. Catalina was already very tired and so willing to let go. She felt her bare feet stepping on the ground of the forest the hypnotist described. She went deeper and deeper into her subconscious, her body asleep, and her mind awake. She was sitting by her desk with her arms folded underneath her. She could hear the hypnotist's voice saying, "You are Clifford, and today, you are going to fly." She could hear the male voice saying, "I am checking all of the equipment. I tap some of the gauges lightly with my fingers."

She could hear their voices in the background, but she floated away. It was a very strange feeling, for she could see it all very clearly, and yet somehow she knew that she was not really there. She saw the airplane. At first, she saw a cockpit, and two men sitting in it; their backs were to her. She could see their hands holding the strange steering wheels, half open circles. She could hear the sounds on the plane. She could not see their faces.

The scene suddenly and abruptly changed, and she could see the airplane. It was in the water; it was sinking. She could see inside; she was inside; she was floating in and out of the plane, seeing the inside filling with water and the outside. It was all in a sort of slow motion, the type of slow motion she had experienced when she had a serious car accident.

Inside she saw a body facedown and floating in front of her. She reached out and was able to turn the body so she could see the face; he was fully clothed, but the wounds on his face from the archive photos were there. He opened his eyes, and she heard her own voice say, "I did not know his eyes were so light." There was her grandfather's face; he opened his eyes, but she knew he was dead. He was dead, but his lips began to move very slowly, and he said, "Search."

She slept for a while and realized the recording had ended. She remembered that she had had similar dreams through the years to the one she had just experienced. She wondered if she was dreaming what she wanted to hear or if there was really some spiritual force asking her to search. Every time she had tried to let go of the story, the story found a way to find her.

The next time she watched the video, she planned to drink coffee and find a very uncomfortable chair; that hypnotist was just too good. She was in the mood to get back to the Anthony Crossley bio she had promised Maggie.

CHAPTER THIRTY-SIX – VIDEO TAPE

Maggie was glad that Bill had to stay in Zurich for two days on business. It would give her a chance to listen to the tape of the regression she had missed before Bill had the third regression. Since the second regression, Bill had been sleeping very soundly and seemed eager for the third regression, he had to reschedule, because of the Zurich trip and had tried unsuccessfully to move up the date. This had made Maggie very curious as to what was on the tape.

She checked her e-mail and carefully read both of the long e-mails on body number three. No soot particles--and the hand position was different. To that, she added the lack of fencing position and the pictures taken from a different angle, which made four differences.

She read the articles from *The London Times*; Anthony Crossley seemed to have an opinion about everything and was happy to share it. Just like the online entry of Henry Channon "Chips" calling Anthony

Crossley an ass, it seemed that he was someone who could make people angry. Angry enough to perhaps...

No, Maggie, stick to the facts! It was so annoying when her thoughts sounded like her mother scolding her.

Some of the subjects really made Maggie wonder. It almost seemed that nothing had changed; we were still struggling with the same issues today, seven decades later! She could be reading the newspapers today. On the Palestine entries, she made note of the days and looked up the information online at TheyWorkForYou.com. Year by year, she could easily see that Anthony Crossley had said far more than what had been reported in *The London Times*. It was really incredible that in 2010, so much sounded so familiar.

She got on Skype, but the familiar yellow sign that shows "not online" was next to Catalina's name. She sent her a quick message, requesting that they speak.

Then she made herself a cup of very strong tea and turned on the video recording from Bill's past-life regression. When she heard the hypnotist's harmonious voice, she yawned. She stopped the tape, made a second cup of strong tea, and then pressed fast forward. She knew it would take a while to get to the good parts. When she pressed play, she realized she had gone too far and had to rewind. After a few attempts she finally got to the part she wanted, and she listened carefully to a different nuance and accent in the voice of the man she loved.

"Clifford, today is August 15, 1939. You have to fly. How do you feel?"

Bill's breathing got very strong, and his face looked anxious.

"I must be worried, because I feel a pressure in my chest."

"Okay, Clifford, take a deep breath and relax. You are going to be an observer; you are going to see the story as an observer. Tell me the story; you are an observer. Is that alright with you?"

"Yes, it is."

"Take another deep breath. Inhale, Clifford, and relax. Now exhale slowly. You are detached, and you can stop whenever you want."

"The takeoff was fine. I am getting nervous, annoyed. The copilot is getting very pushy, and he is telling me how to fly the plane. I tell him I know how to fly the plane without his help. He boarded the plane with a small suitcase. He is looking at it; he has it up front. He is still annoying me, and I make it perfectly clear that I am the captain on the plane. The copilot needs to go to the lavatory. He takes something from his suitcase with him. He is taking too long, and the passengers are very loud and arguing. What is taking so long? And why is everyone is so loud? I have to go back to see; the copilot is in the back, talking to a man. I am ordering him to get back in the cockpit. A man shouts at me to get back to fly the plane. Everyone is arguing and loud, except one man; he is asleep. I see blood; he is not asleep, and I see blood down the backside of his head."

Bill's breathing becomes very agitated, and the hypnotist, with her lovely voice, asks him to leave that place of discomfort, to relax and breathe slowly. The hypnotist continues with suggestions that he never has to feel fear and that he does not like to smoke. She helps Bill relax for a while and then guides him to awaken refreshed and relaxed.

"That is quite a story."

"Why did you take me out before it ended?"

"I needed time to let you finish the session relaxed, and my main interest is your well-being, not your story. Also, I had taken the liberty to push you into a specific day that we knew could be very difficult. Look how cute Maggie looks sleeping."

The hypnotist and Bill laughed and discussed the regression and how the next one would be handled before Bill woke Maggie up. She had turned off the camera, so she had sent her entire dinner and her conversation about her regression to Florida as well.

Bill was right; the number of passengers and the number of bodies did not match. There should only be one passenger in Hamburg; in the regression, he said "the Germans." Also, in 1939, could you really walk away from an aircraft? Was there such a thing as an autopilot in the Lockheed Electra?

The hypnotist really worked as a labor of love; she had given Bill a very reasonable price for five prepaid sessions. How could she not let him finish the story? What if Bill decided not to do a third session? What if he said he felt fine and did not want to know, that he would just stay in London.

Where was that woman in Florida? What time was it over there? She had surely also heard the recording; maybe because the data did not match, she thought the whole thing was foolish. Maggie wanted to know the whole story; a deal was a deal. No, Catalina had also said her psychics had told her a story that did not match the archives. What if it matched Bill's story?

She got back on Skype; it was yellow, not green. Her only choice was to send another message and an e-mail; maybe she had a Blackberry. She made it as urgent as she possibly could:

FROM: Maggiestrylleri@hotmail.net.uk

TO: SecretsoftheG-AESY@hotmail.net.fla.us

RE: WE NEED TO TALK.

CHAPTER THIRTY-SEVEN – CAN OF WORMS?

The sound of an incoming video call from Skype was exactly what Maggie wanted to hear. She had a list of questions about the information on the e-mails and the search she completed online.

"Hello. Finally! It has never taken this long to find you."

"I have to get ready for my new job. Had a lot of loose ends to tie up in my real life."

Maggie smiled. "Well, don't forget that I still need your information on bodies four and five."

"I know. I should be able to do that for you tomorrow."

"Have you seen the regression?" Maggie asked in a more anxious tone than she had wanted.

"I did, although the first time I tried to, I fell under just like you did! That woman is amazing; her voice sings and weaves into your mind. I have not even smoked since I listened to it."

"Neither have I! Sorry about the restaurant."

"No. Don't be; it was actually really fun to eavesdrop on your date! Years ago, I saw the French revolution in a past life. Maybe you were my teacher!"

Maggie looked doubtful, and she wished that Catalina had mentioned the French Revolution first; then maybe she could believe it was real."So, what did you think of Bill's story?"

"Yes! Some story. It does not match the body count from the archives. But so far, I can say that it somehow matches my psychics."

"Really? Even the body count? How do they do it? Do they use tarot cards? A crystal ball?"

"No, I have never met a clairvoyant with a crystal ball! It would be fun. The method used is called psychometry; the psychics hold an object and tell you what they 'see.' In this case, we have the two watches that were retrieved from the G-AESY in 1939 and sent to my grandmother with my grandfather's belongings. According to four psychics, none of whom have ever met each other, nor have they been given any information about August 15, 1939, the watch not belonging to my grandfather belonged to a tall, slender young man. They all actually said the young man was twenty-five years old and wearing a blue uniform."

"That matches the physique of body number five!"

"Yes, it does; it is the description of the radio operator. I am no mathematician, but what are the odds? They even said he had a mustache."

Maggie nodded and was pensive."The odds? They are probably close to impossible."

"Impossible."

"Didn't you tell me you were in touch with a friend of the radio operator? Did you ask him?"

"No. How could I? I contacted him about seatbelts on the aircraft, and he wrote me a beautiful letter and said that A. S. M. Leigh was his friend, and sure enough, his name was on the list of those who attended Leigh's funeral, Allen Finch."

"He is no longer alive, is he?"

"I don't think so. I believe I read in a newsletter for the Croydon Airport Society or somewhere that he had passed away. I mean, he could be in his 90s, but there really is nothing to ask. Many people do not react well to psychics."

"Yeah, how do you say, 'I heard it from a psychic,' or 'I saw it on my last journey to a past life'?"

The laughter from both sides of the Atlantic was somewhat hollow and perhaps a little bitter.

"And you are young, Maggie. Your generation is so open. Older people tend to be less open-minded. Before all this happened to me, I cannot imagine that I would have believed any of it."

"I grew up with this, all of this. My mum's an avid believer, but if she told me this story, I would not have believed it."

"Well, maybe your generation is not quite that open-minded. So imagine the ninety year olds."

From both sides of the Atlantic, the women laughed, and this time the laughter was full and heartfelt. They were both holding cups of tea. The only smoke came from incense burning in the middle-aged woman's home.

"I have been reading up on Anthony Crossley, and I must tell you, he was very eloquent and could be...how do I say this politely? He was very good at antagonizing his opponents," Maggie said.

"I think so, too, but I don't think it was, maybe even is, unusual for British politicians. There is the booing and cheering and 'here, here'—or is it 'hear, hear'?"

"I don't know. For a backbencher, he is pretty prominent."

"I thought so, too, but he is the only backbencher I have ever researched. He has certainly made me read a lot of books and look up many events. Thanks, Mr.

Crossley." Catalina toasted his picture with her tea and showed the photocopied photograph to Maggie.

"He's quite handsome! He was so opinionated about so many controversial issues. That is the sort of thing that at the very least creates political enemies."

"It does, or worse, and he must have had them."

"Well, I would like to start with a few questions, and the first one is about body number one, your grandfather. Can you find anything that would really point to espionage, other than psychics?"

"Yes, not directly but by personality profile. Here, let me send you a document here via Skype...it scanned as a picture...yes, here it goes. Tell me when you can see it. While you are waiting, I need to make a correction to body number one. I do not have the list on hand yet, but before he worked in the oil industry, Mr. Castillo worked in other fields as a biochemical engineer. I'll send it to you when I get it." "Thanks, oh here it is. Let me see what you sent."

Maggie opened the document and read.

Hitler's Spies by David Kahn

Pages 85–86, Standard Oil of New Jersey.

Pages 99–100, recruitment in Latin America.

Pages 160–161, press and Latin America.

Page 242, Hamburg/networks in Latin America.

Page 279, Latin America.

Pages 287–288, Latin American agents.

Page 296, money paid to Latin American agents.

Page 317, Mexican agents.

Page 318–328, Latin Agents, general information.

A Man Called Intrepid by William Stevenson

Page 7, Mexico.

Page 19, American intelligence/Rockefeller Foundation.

Page 33, "I know too much about war to glory in it. But wars are made by politicians who neglect to prepare for it." Donovan.

Page 35, 1938/Scandinavia.

Page 36–38, Munich Pact.

Pages 41–58, chapter 6, 7, 8, various covert activities in 1938–39.

Pages 59–62, chapter 9, Scandinavia.

Page 63, "Better lose a battle than lose a source of secret intelligence." Stephenson's advice to Churchill.

Page 65, Norway (heavy water).

Page 81–86, chapter 13, intrigues behind Chamberlain's back.

Page 107–108, oil, Latin America.

Pages 280–298, Standard Oil and Mexico.

Pages 345–346, American spies recruited by British.

Pages 439–440, focus group.

IBM and the Holocaust by Edwin Black Page 254,
Standard Oil.

Page 337–338, Standard Oil.

The Irregulars by Jennet Conant

Page 204, Standard Oil.

Maggie printed the document, and each woman held a copy as they looked at each other through their webcams.

"I know this author, David Kahn. My dad read a book on codes."

"*The Code breakers.*"

"Yes, he is a respected historian."

"I have tried to find as many files of respected historians as possible, as well as any traditional well-respected sources, to balance out the un-orthodox, unconventional, by some standards, most questionable list of my other sources, in the last book I mention--the one by Jennet Conant, *The Irregulars*--in the same page I refer to there is a very interesting quote to show how people could be recruited through their vulnerabilities, and I believe that my grandfather fits that profile. With his lifestyle, he could have easily been blackmailed into the world of espionage. That book deals with aspects of espionage after 1939, but Rome was not built in a day. I am sure as far back as organized societies have tried to undermine and battle, spies were necessary and probably recruited in larger numbers through blackmail, rather than conviction. Well, there is, of course, the greed factor. But the spies in *The Irregulars* do not seem to be that well paid."

Both women laughed, and Maggie took the conversation back to the subject of psychics.

"Unconventional, but by many standards, they are not unaccepted."

"By most who surround me, they are."

"Well, my mum always says that people need to remember that Mr. Ronald Reagan, whilst President of the USA, sought the guidance of an astrologer. She claims that J.P. Morgan can be quoted as saying that millionaires do not use astrology, but billionaires do."

"According to the History Channel, so did Hitler."

"What a cynic! I am trying to help you understand that unusual and irregular is not synonymous with mistaken."

"Well, it was for Hitler! But as they say, 'Out of the mouths of babes.'"

"I am not that young."

"Young enough to be my daughter. From my perspective, the perfect word to describe you is youth."

"From my perspective, you are cynical! Too cynical to see what is in front of you. Do you think Bill's past-life regression this last time was influenced by the perspective of the hypnotist who guided him through as an observer?"

"I thought that was really clever of her. No, I believe that he would have experienced or seen, if you like, the same thing, simply in a more painful and difficult way."

"I don't know if I like Anthony Crossley's poem; is it about love outlasting death, or is it a suicide pact?"

"Well, the title is 'The Suicide Pact,' but I read the words as love lasting long after the loved one is gone, after anyone you love is gone. That love is a tangible energy that remains even when the people who are loved are dead. I feel that I love my grandfather. I never knew him, and he died before I was born, but I love him nonetheless...not the idea of who he was, which, the deeper I dig, at times is not very likable, but, well, the very essence of his soul."

Catalina held up the books of Crossley's poetry that she had, showing them to Maggie one at a time in the order in which she acquired them. They all were in pristine condition. Each came with a story of which poem was interesting to her and why. She flipped the pages slowly and told Maggie that the cigar smell from a previous owner gave the books a scent not altogether unpleasant. Some had the dust covers, and one had a drawing by Clare Crossley, his wife. She had four.

Tragedy under Lucifer

Prophets, God and Witches

Aucassin and Nicolette and Other Poems

From One Vagabond to Another

"I like the title of the last one. Isn't it cool? It makes you want to wander the world. Part of the book is divided geographically between Palestine and Arabia, Scandinavia, and then Africa."

"There is Palestine again."

"Yes, he apparently traveled far and wide, and as I guess he was deeply religious, he converted to Catholicism, so his religion was not an obligation of birth but rather an adult choice. So trips to Palestine are an obvious choice, as the Christian Holy Land is there."

"Yes, but politically, he really gets involved in the Arab perspective."

"He does, deeply. I wonder if the Arab and the Christian perspective were linked. Ironically, one of the first books I found Anthony Crossley's name in insinuates that he is a Zionist."

"Really?"

"The author is some notorious Holocaust denier, a Mr. David Irving. That even landed him in jail some years ago. Here, let me see, he has Anthony Crossley on pages 117, 144, and 603. The book is called *Churchill's War*. On page 117, he writes "to one MP hovering on the threshold of the Focus," and he endnotes it as Winston Spencer Churchill to A. Crossley, July 4 (1938), Gilbert V 953208. On page 144, he calls him 'Anthony Crossley, a young MP who had teetered on the brink of the Focus,' which he goes on to insinuate is a Zionist group, but I have found other sources that describe the Focus as a very different type of group."

"I wonder where he got his information."

"I contacted him, and he said he got it at the Churchill Library at Cambridge. It was an odd e-mail; it made me feel uncomfortable. This is the same David Irving who wrote or spoke about H. W. Wicks, according to various sources online."

"Not that man again; he was the red herring in the story."

"More like the wild goose chase."

"But Winston Churchill, a Zionist?"

"Oh, that part is well documented by several sources; here's one book that is dedicated entirely to that subject, and the author does not mention the Focus group—not once: *Churchill's Promised Land: Zionism and Statecraft* by Michael Makovsky. It is very detailed. It came out in 2007, but I do not think that's the reason--"

Unfortunately Maggie interrupted; she could have learned so much more."So maybe Anthony Crossley was teetering on the brink of the Focus."

"If the Focus was the group that David Irving describes, then it is seriously doubtful. If, however, it is the anti-Nazi organization that attracted people from different political backgrounds, then perhaps he was."

"Can you send that to me, too? I am knackered! Can we talk tomorrow? When can I have the info on bodies four and five?"

"I'll do my best. Keep your video recorder handy for Bill's next session. Sweet dreams,

Maggie."

"You too, Catalina."

End of video call. Click.

And with that, the two women on each side of the Atlantic were about to open the last can of worms.

CHAPTER THIRTY-EIGHT – BODIES FOUR AND FIVE

FROM: SecretsoftheG-AESY@hotmail.net.fla.us

TO: Maggiestrylleri@hotmail.net.uk

RE: Body No. 4, Samuel J. Simonton, and Body No. 5, A. S. M. Leigh

Samuel J. Simonton

American passport number 24956.

Issued December 18, 1935, in Washington, DC. Born on March 13, 1902 Height: 1.75 meters.

Weight: (Maggie, I have looked everywhere in my files, drawer-by-drawer, binder-by-binder, and I cannot find Mr. Simonton's weight. I never realized that was missing.)

With regard to body number four, here is the thing that bothers me. He is not described as a heavy man (as you may recall, Herr Beuss is), but if you look at the morgue photos and even the head shot from the BAL archives, he looks, if not fat, swollen. He was swollen in a manner that I would have thought A. S. M. Leigh's body would have swollen after so many hours underwater, but that body shows slender, clearly defined muscles. So there is that, and of course, the last two are described as the most severely burned.

The translated entries from the death certificate are as follows:

7) Mortal accident.
8) Wounds from second and third degree burning on face, body, scrotum, and extremities, and red livid spots.
9) Burning by carbon-oxygen poisoning.
10) Death stiffness and livid spots.
11) No.

Additional Remarks

The body was brought up by the diver together with three others, eight hours after accident. Clothes were nearly all destroyed by fire. Extremities in "fencing position."

From the files in Vordingborg that I was allowed to work with but not photocopy, the very rough translation is as follows.

Simonton

At the autopsy, widespread second degree burns, almost all over the body, have been established, and furthermore, third degree burns have been found on the head and starting carbonization (I am not sure I found the right word). Soot particles have been found in the airways. No signs of violence have been found. No enlargements or fluid overflowing of the lungs have been established, and at the coroner's inquest, no foam around the mouth was found. It must be remarked that the body is in a state of beginning "decay;" thus the importance of the lung findings will be somewhat uncertain.

Personal Note

The pathologist who answered my questions could not tell me what was unusual without closely looking at everything, which I was not able to provide for him. He did say, however, that a body with more severe superficial wounds could very well decay at a faster rate than the others.

Also consider the report from the Legal Medical Institute in Copenhagen, dated August 30, 1939, addressed to the Chief of Police, Nykøbing Falster. On page two it states, "None of the persons have been poisoned by carbon monoxide." The report goes on to name each man, one by one: Alfred Stanley Mardsin Leigh, Anthony Crommelin Crossley, Erich Bruno Wilhelm Beuss and Cesar Agustin Castillo. Each name is underlined the cause of death is claimed to be due to a combination between the drowning and the burns, something to the effect of the shock caused by the burns- keep in mind that the nature of the burns on each body was vastly different. I find it surprising that the four were described in the same manner. The report continues describing the Medical Institute's findings in the matter of Mr. Samuel James Simonton. In what I find a very curious choice of word, it is stated that it "may be regarded as probable" that this death was due to the "shock-condition" alone—As you may recall the burns in this body were brutal, and, of course, as there was no fluid in his lungs, all that in the few minutes before the G-AESY went down, so many questions... I mean how did it decompose quicker than the others?.

Another thing about Simonton, which may or may not matter, I mean, as the plane sunk there was sure to be movement of anything or anyone inside, but it could be interesting to take into account that in as much as the fire and everything that happened is on the left side of the plane, Mr. Simonton, who had the most burnt body, was found under a seat on the right side of the plane. It is one of those things that keeps me thinking at night, which brings me to my what ifs...

You requested personal comments and observations, but I must warn you that this is sheer fantasy, and no psychic or anyone else has suggested it. I just feel that it would make for a great spy novel ...

Well, have you ever read a book from 1953 called *The Man Who Never Was* by Ewen Montagu? Mr. Montagu was a British counterintelligence agent. (I recommend the 1955 movie; it's really good.) It is a true story, respected as one of World War II's most daring operations. So, if I were to tell the story from a completely outrageously fictional point of view, this body would be a man who never was, and Samuel J. Simonton would ride off into the sunset to fight through the OSS for his country.

The obituary in *The New York Times*--it is actually odd as it is on the front page--in the report titled "Two Standard Oil Men Killed in Plane Crash; British MP Also Is a Victim," so it was short.

My grandfather's bio was not included, but as the newspaper's in those days were full of Mexico and oil in a manner in which was not popular, an employee who had served them internationally was perhaps better downplayed, so with his name misspelled, all it said was "a Mexican." There was an article on that very page! But this is about body number four, and he was granted twenty front page lines from which I learned the following about him:

- Lubrication coordinator for the Petroleum Association, parent company of many subsidiaries in Europe, Asia, and South America.

- Native of Allentown, Pennsylvania. (This is also easily found on Ancestry.com U.S. Census.)

- Graduated from West Point and the Army Air Corps.

- Worked for Standard Oil of Louisiana in the aviation section. (As a pilot, maybe?)

- Since 1936, has traveled "widely."

- From the BAL files, we know his wife was at the airport to see him off since she saw Mr. Castillo give someone instructions.

From Ancestry.com, I found the following entries:

- Marriage to Kathleen Stoecklein October 13, 1933 (if this is not again a case of the wrong Wright).

- 1920 Census: Fort Crockett, Galveston, Texas.

- 1930 Census: Allentown, Lehigh, Pennsylvania.

- Ship manifest January 14, 1937, from Southampton, England, to New York, New York, USA. Here the address is c/o L. K. Blood, 30 Rockefeller Plaza. I have several pieces of correspondence from L. K. Blood, as he was also my grandfather's boss.

- Ship manifest September 1, 1939, from Southampton to New York City. When you open to the page in the original manifest, his name is crossed out by a line and has a note from the purser, which says, "Samuel James Simonton, cancelled, did not sail." There are, however, two Kathleen Simonton's (mother and child) on board.

- Another entry from 1927 has his address listed as Brooks Field (US Army), San Antonio, Texas.

I found passport applications with photos from other Intava Employees. I could not find one for Mr. Simonton. I don't think that Samuel J. Simonton had a passport before the 1930s, (we know through the records collected when he died that he did have one issued in Washington, D.C. in 1935) and those records are still unavailable! Pity, it would have been nice to put a live face to him as I have for Anthony Crossley and my grandfather, and to see how much Mr. Beuss' grandson looks like him.

As you well know, in the BAL archives, it is assumed that he was running to the front to try to fly the plane, but he apparently had been in the back where a post card to his brother was found. In the census of 1910 on Ancestry.com, I saw an entry for a brother, Frederick. I contacted many Simonton families in Allentown several years ago, and all were very nice, but none were related to him. I believe it is safe to guess that Samuel James Simonton could possibly have been not just a pilot, but also a very good, experienced pilot. I found newspaper articles from 1939 in *The Galveston Daily News*, where he is listed as one of the reserve officers participating in an "annual gunnery practice."

Alfred Stanley Mardsin Leigh

British Passport number 111037.

Issued in London July 27, 1938.

Born on July 1, 1914.

Height: 1.80 meters.

Weight: 72 kilograms.

I do not have a copy of A. S. M. Leigh's death certificate. I believe if I had not seen one in Vordingborg, I would have made a note of that, so we can assume that there is one there. Just in case, I just checked and unless *lijsynsattes* is another word for death certificate in Danish, I don't see in my list of documents from Vordingborg any death certificates. Anyhow, I cannot imagine that it would be any different from the others. I saw a request for it from the Radio Officer's Union, so one has to assume it was delivered to them.

I have the English translation, which was in every archive, (as you saw at the British Airways archives) like the four previous ones. It states the following:

7.   Mortal accident.

8. Wounds from burning (second degree) on face and burning of hands and forearms. Dried foam around mouth, light red livid spots on dead body.

9. Drowning. Burning. Poisoning by carbon-oxygen (carbon monoxide).

10. Death stiffness and livid spots.

11. No. (No reason.)

Additional Remarks

The body was lifted like the last of those killed in the accident at 6 a.m. Limbs are in the position of fencing (i.e. usual in sudden death by burning). I need to add here that in the recorded diver's statement from my visit to Vordingborg in 2000, the entry on Leigh's body is gruesome. He had been told that there should be a body number five, but he couldn't locate it...The 16th of August at approximately 6:00 a.m., he went down again and saw immediately. It was sitting on the edge of the left chair with the right hand on the shorter of the two handles. It was in the front of the Captain's chair in the cockpit. The body was sitting straight up.

"First, he tried to enter through the radio-room, but he could not fit the diver's helmet through. Then he tried from the outside through the broken window, but also here, he was unable to get through. Again, he went into the cabin, and with one leg, he pushed the body towards the window, where after trying and trying, he got the body out."

This is from a recorded file read by one of the diver's daughter's and then roughly translated by my Danish friend. The thing is with all that pulling and tugging, one would think that body would have shown far more signs of trauma. What do you think? And how long does rigor mortis last? A full day later--should he have been as similar as the other four bodies? Anyhow, maybe you can decide with what I write below.

The entries from the autopsy reports that we took notes from in Vordingborg were roughly translated as follows.

Leigh: exterior, there is only rather small rigor mortis in the muscles. [Early stages of rigor mortis?] No blood, right ear. Some blood, left ear, but difficult to determine whether this blood originates from the inside or outside.

At the autopsy, a number of second degree burns in the face, the back the hands, and the underarms have been established. Soot particles in the airways have been established. On the legs, some minor superficial skinscrabes [I think my friend who translated meant to write scabs] have been established. Besides this, no other signs of violence have been found.

An enlargement of the lungs has been established. The lungs are filled with foaming liquid; likewise, foam is found in upper airways. Furthermore, both lungs contain a substantial amount of fluid. These findings are of such a nature as those typically found in drowning. No signs of illness have been found.

According to the BAL papers, he was buried on August 22, 1939, and that is the day that the body arrived in England on the SS Margrethe. According to the same record at Forest Hill Old Cemetery, various members of BAL attended his funeral. (Also according to that paper, Clifford Wright was not there, yet he was back in England.) Among the names is Finch.

I corresponded with Mr. Allen Finch in 2002. In his first letter, he seemed somewhat unaware of which flight I referred to, so he wrote, "My records say that Lockheed 10a GARSY crashed 15.8.39. It left Hamburg and then apparently caught fire and crashed into the sea. Was this when your Grandfather died, or did he fall ill in the air? I did not know, or, at least, remember J. H. Willans."

In a letter on October 3, 2002, he sent me a wonderful, detailed account of how communications were made in Morse code and what the staff of the aircraft consisted of in 1939. He then wrote the following:

I knew the operator of the aircraft that sadly crashed when your father was killed. An old colleague of mine has written to say that the R/O was called Leigh, whom I knew quite well. On the flight leaving Hamburg, a fire started in the cabin, and Leigh was down to see what it was about, and the Captain started to land the aircraft in the sea. This killed everyone except himself (just accidental, of course).

I sent another letter, all of this, of course, through snail mail, asking if he could describe A. S. M. Leigh to me, but I never heard back.

Mr. Finch's address started with Sparrow's Nest, which I had to say because it is funny for a man named Finch to reside in a sparrow's nest.

According to the records at Camberwell Old Cemetery, Alfred Stanley Mardsin Leatherbarrow Leigh was buried there on August 19, 1939. They would not believe me that his body arrived on the twenty-second, but as you may recall, there was some correspondence or entry in the BAL papers that it was expected on the nineteenth. Anyhow, they also included the names of two other people buried in 1897 and 1906 who "shared" the grave. I am not familiar with graves in any country.

As a point of interest, they added that Mr. Leigh was aged twenty-five and must have been a large man, because an entry in their records was found that stated "extra-large coffin." I guess he was tall for the people of that generation.

On Ancestry.com, I found an entry for the probate of his estate in 1940 and what was left to his mother. Mrs. Leatherbarrow was also mentioned by that name in the BAL papers.

I am still waiting to see if I can get more information about my grandfather. I still look from time to time at Ancestry.com and recently found an entry on Simonton—nothing special, a registration of his death in foreign soil. Maybe I should look up all the others again?

Please do realize that I am not a historian, professional researcher, doctor, engineer, psychic, nor writer. And, as such, my information should be taken into account as very amateurish in nature. I am indeed embarrassed to admit that I am a college dropout. Who just happens to have acquired a strong degree of fluency in four languages: Spanish, English, French, and Swedish.

I learned more through the school of life, mistakes, and hard work than through academia. I was too foolish to appreciate what my parents tried to offer me when I was young, and through no one's fault but my own, if I majored in anything, it was in having a very good time. So when all of this started in the 1990s, I even had to look up the Munich Pact.

Please keep that in mind, Maggie.

C.

P.S. I've attached some telegrams from Standard Oil (INTAVA) and my grandmother that you may find of interest.

COMPANIA TELEGRAFICA MEXICANA

WESTERN UNION

CLASE DE SERVICIO

Este es un mensaje de tarifa íntegra, a no ser alguna de las indicaciones que se expresan en el cuadro de la derecha.

INDICACIONES

DL	Carta Diurna
NM	Mensaje Nocturno
NL	Carta Nocturna
DLT	Diferido
LC	Carta Cablegráfica
CDE	Code

15 AGO 1939

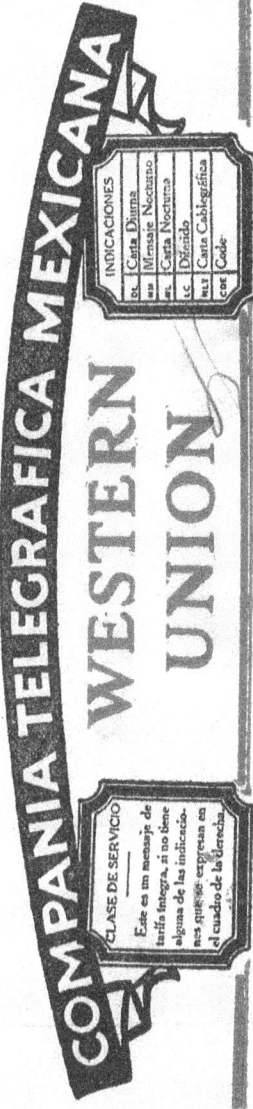

CD114 27 NEWYORK 15 1205P

MRS FLAVIA G DE CASTILLO

CALLE GUANAJUATO 100 MEXCTY

DEEPLY REGRET TO INFORM YOU CESAR WAS KILLED TODAY

IN AN AEROPLANE CRASH AT COPENHAGEN PLEASE ADVISE

WHAT ARRANGEMENT YOU WISH US TO MAKE MY SINCEREST

SYMPATHY

L K BLOOD

RE 1122AM

COMPAÑIA TELEGRAFICA MEXICANA

CLASE DE SERVICIO

Este es un mensaje de tarifa integra, si no tiene alguna de las indicaciones que se expresan en el cuadro de la derecha

INDICACIONES

DL — Carta Diurna
NM — Mensaje Nocturno
NL — Carta Nocturna
LC — Diferido
CLT — Carta Cablegráfica
Ship Code

WESTERN UNION

17 AGO 1939

CD143 22 NEWYORK 17 207P

MRS FLAVIA G DECASTILLO
CALLE GUANAJUATO 100 MEXICOCITY

CREMATION CESAR REMAINS WILL TAKE PLACE COPENHAGEN

AUGUST 19TH PLEASE ADVISE ME WHETHER YOU WISH ANY

RELIGIOUS SERVICE HELD THERE OR LONDON

L K BLOOD

JU120PM

CORREOS Y TELÉGRAFOS

RADIOMEX

Servicio Radiotelegráfico a todo el Mundo en conexión con las
Estaciones RCA-New York, TRANSRADIO-Berlin, TRANSRADIO-Madrid,
Chapultepec-Habana, etc

SELLO
DE LA OFICINA

MX 133 FLAVIA PGE 2/48

HONOUR STOP SPECIFICALLY I WOULD LIKE TO KNOW IF YOU DESIRE A RELIGIOUS

SERVICE EITHER IN LONDON OR AT COPENHAGEN AND IF SO WHAT DENOMINATION

STOP CREMATION IS TENTATIVELY ARRANGED FOR SATURDAY MORNING AT COPENH-

AGUEN STOP ALSO KINDLY EXTEND MY SYMPATHIES TO CESARS FATHER AND FAMILY

NORTON GRUBB

USE USTED ESTA VIA PARA SU CONTESTACION

TODO TELEGRAMA DEBE LLEVAR EL SELLO DE LA OFICINA

LEA USTED EL REVERSO

IOSH

ERICSSON: { 2-47-47
             3-31-61

MEXICANA: { L-73-00
            2-47

EXTENSION:

349

COMPAÑIA TELEGRAFICA MEXICANA

WESTERN UNION

CLASE DE SERVICIO DESEADO

INMEDIATO	
CARTA DIURNA	DIFERIDO
CARTA NOCTURNO	CARTA CABLE-GRÁFICA
CARTA NOCTURNA	

El remitente autoriza al expresado la clase de servicio deseado, DE OTRO MODO SE TASARA A TARIFA INTEGRA.

NUM.	CARGOS
	PALABRAS
	DEL.
	PAGAR.

OFICINA PRINCIPAL:
Esq. San Juan de Letrán e Independencia, México, D. F.

MEXICO CITY AUGUST 17TH. 1939.

GRUBBSTOIL
LONDON

PLEASE HAVE A CATHOLIC MASS SAID IN COPENHAGEN

SATURDAY WITH CESAR REMAINS PRESENT BEFORE

CREMATION STOP APPRECIATE YOUR KIDNESS

FLAVIA

Sírvase transmitir el precedente mensaje con sujeción a las condiciones al reverso las cuales quedan aceptadas.

FIRMA Flavia G. de Castillo   DOMICILIO. Reforma #72.

COMPANIA TELEGRAFICA MEXICANA

WESTERN UNION

CLASE DE SERVICIO DESEADO

INMEDIATO

CARTA DIURNA	DIFERIDO
NOCTURNO	CARTA CABLE GRÁFICA
CARTA NOCTURNA	

El remitente marcará X oprimiendo la clase de servicio deseado, DE OTRO MODO SE TRAMARA A TARIFA INTEGRA.

NUM.	CARGOS
PALABRAS	
MIN.	
HORA	

OFICINA PRINCIPAL:
Esq. San Juan de Letrán e Independencia, México, D. F.

MEXICO CITY AUGUST 21th 1939.

GRUBBSTOIL
LONDON

ONLY CREMATED REMAINS CAN ENTER MEXICO STOP MR HELEV

AUTHORIZED RECIVE REMALES AND BELONGINGS CESAR STOP

MASS WILL CELEBRATE HERE

FLAVIA

Sírvase transmitir el precedente mensaje con sujeción a las condiciones al reverso las cuales quedan aceptadas.

FIRMA _____ DOMICILIO _____

351

COMPANIA TELEGRAFICA MEXICANA

WESTERN UNION

CLASE DE SERVICIO

Este es un mensaje de tarifa integra, si no tiene alguna de las indicaciones que se expresan en el cuadro de la derecha.

INDICACIONES

D.	Carta Diurna
...	Mensaje Nocturno
...	Carta Nocturna
...	Diferido
...	Carta Cablegrafica
...	Code

21 AGO 1939

CD 5   CABLE 55 1/45 LONDON 21 1038A

LC MRS FLAVIA CASTILLO CALLE GUANAJUATO

100 MEXICO

CATHOLIC BISHOP COPENHAGEN REFUSES MASS BECAUSE OF CREMA-

TION STOP AM I CORRECT IN ASSUMING THAT REMAINS CAN

ENTER MEXICO ONLY AFTER CREMATION AND THAT YOU HAVE DE-

VELOPED MATTER WITH CHURCH MEXICOCITY STOP PLEASE ADVI-

SE ME URGENTLY AS

7 11 AM V C

COMPANIA TELEGRAFICA MEXICANA

WESTERN UNION

CLASE DE SERVICIO

Este es un mensaje de
tarifa íntegra, si no tiene
alguna de las indicacio-
nes que se expresan en
el cuadro de la derecha.

INDICACIONES

DL	Carta Diurna
NM	Mensaje Nocturno
NL	Carta Nocturna
LC	Diferido
NLT	Carta Cablegráfica
CPR	Code

21 AGO 1939

2 CD 5   LC MRS FLAVIA 20

CREMATION BEING HELD UP PENDING RECEIPT YOUR FINAL WI-

SHES STOP IN MEANTIME WE ENDEAVOURING OBTAIN RULING FROM

ROME

NORTON GRUBB

7 1 1 AM C

353

CHAPTER THIRTY-NINE – THE TRUTH IS LIBERATING

Maggie felt that she could no longer lie to Bill. His reaction was surprising. He explained to Maggie that he knew the information needed to be shared, that his guides had told him to do so on the first regression. He simply requested anonymity; if the information was ever used, he wanted to be kept out of it.

After a long conversation between Maggie, Bill, and Catalina on Skype, and with the approval of the hypnotherapist, it was agreed that Catalina could be present via Skype for the last session. All arrangements were made to have a laptop at the therapist's office.

It was snowing in London, and the silence of the building gave them the perfect peaceful setting for the third and last regression. Catalina drank a double espresso; Maggie had a strong cup of tea. The sounds of the computer on the London side were muted to avoid disrupting the process, but in Florida, Catalina could hear loud and clearly.

The therapist's melodious voice took Bill to the usual forest, helped him relax into the past. He was given careful directions to detach and see the images as an observer who could stop at any moment if he so desired.

Bill's voice came out in very much the same way it had in previous sessions, with the odd accent and tone, dissimilar from his American accent. He began to recount the story from the London takeoff in the same detail as he had the last time; everyone listened attentively. Then he began to describe what happened when Clifford left the cockpit to look at the commotion in the passenger cabin.

"The copilot is still in the back talking to a man; I ordered the copilot to return to the front. Another man is shouting and telling me to keep quiet and go fly the plane. Everyone is shouting except for one man; I think he's asleep."

Bill's breathing got heavier, and he paused. The hypnotist asked if he could continue, and he nodded, lightly. After a few deep breaths, he continued, and tears could be seen escaping from behind his eyelids.

"He is not asleep; he has blood on his neck and head. There is something very wrong here. One of the men is shouting at me to get back in the cockpit and fly the plane. I start to shout that this man is hurt. We need to help this man, and I order the copilot to use the radio and explain what has happened. He refuses. I go back in the cockpit and continue to fly to my destination. I am shaking; I am very nervous. I smell smoke. The copilot comes into the cockpit, and he goes out again. I get up; I try to force him to stay. We are fighting. He hits me. I kick him with my legs. He's on the floor, and he is looking for something on the floor; I am trying to fly. I see water, and I see land. I start descending; I can hear the passengers trying to fight off the fire. I am going to land in the water.

"Maybe that can put the fire out. The copilot is still looking for something on the floor near the first passenger seat. We hit the water. We hit it hard. He is still looking for something in the same place. It's sinking fast. I get out; I get out by the top. I swim around; I try to open the main door, but I can't. I am swimming. The water is salty and cold, and I am swimming, and I am scared. Someone else has to get out. Someone else has to get out and corroborate what happened. I'm swimming to shore."

"Are you alright?" The hypnotist's voice was softer than ever.

"Yes. I am in a hospital. I am safe. Three men are talking to me. I tell them what happened. That is not the story I am allowed to tell. I am forced to sign a piece of paper; I am doing this because my wife and my livelihood are at stake."

Bill was breathing softly, and the hypnotist guided him to another level. She carefully asked if he had anything to say. Bill explained that Clifford felt a heavy burden and sorrow. He felt that it had been his duty to protect the men on his plane, and that he had somehow failed. The hypnotist explained to him how to let go of the guilt. He had fixed it now. He had told the story. He never needed to remember Clifford again.

She continued with the softest, kindest voice to guide him and explain that his lungs were clean and healthy. That he deserved to live a full and good life in which he would breathe happy, clean air, full of healthy, clean energy. She helped Bill out of the hypnotic trance and guided him to awaken, remembering everything and feeling fully refreshed.

Bill got up and went to the bathroom. The sound in the London office computer was switched back on. Bill returned to the room, and Maggie was the first one to speak.

"Catalina, does this coincide with what the psychometry from the watches revealed?"

"Very much so. It's uncanny; it was reported by *The Daily Telegraph* that he 'repeatedly asked' how the passengers were. Which, knowing he had tried and failed to open the door, is odd."

Maggie was about to say something, but Bill interrupted. The difference in tone and accent from the Bill under hypnosis and the Bill who now spoke was very clear.

"There are some serious discrepancies between what I saw and what we read in the files. I just clearly saw that I got out from the top of the aircraft, I saw and felt very clearly how I opened the top hatch, and the records state that I got out by the window."

Catalina turned the computer around to show him a photo of the G-AESY that was hanging very large on the wall of her office. It was a picture with the plane in pristine condition at an airport. The propellers were in movement. Three men were talking nearby, and another man was standing very close to the airplane. The legs of another man could be seen underneath the plane.

"I visited a museum in Windsor Locks, Connecticut, where a man assembled a Lockheed Electra 10A. The window measures 19 by 13 inches; it would not be that easy for a grown man to exit that way. The pilot was a slender man, but he does not look like a small man. There is another smaller pane in front of that one. I know that each Lockheed Electra was made to order. But when I look at the photos of the G-AESY from around 1937 and enlarge them, it looks like the windows match the windows on the airplane I visited in Connecticut, and those were movable. All anyone had to do was slide the window for air, the small one and the side one; the only fixed window is what I like to call the windshield window...the front, you know? And how did he break the glass with his elbow?"

Bill looked pensive. The other two women sat by and listened.

"I saw him get out the top. I saw him swim to shore, afraid he would not make it there."

"That, too, is a discrepancy, and in one of the files, I saw a report of the pilot's personal effects found on the shore...beach...whatever they called it. It was driving me nuts. How did they float there? Including his cigarettes, a comb, gum...I cannot recall what else. It was one of the files I was not allowed to copy. There are strange documents in the files. For example, the Danish Air Ministry 'final report,' is from September 1939. Yet in October of 1939, the pilot's license was still being requested from the Danish authorities, and as late as December 17, 1939, Major Fill was corresponding with Mr. Eskildsen with information that the chemists in London had not found any combustibles in the linoleum. What has always bothered me is how Mr. Stocks was never interviewed; a painter only mentions the people who pulled the pilot out of the water in reference. There is only one interview with a painter who worked for a company called Alb, N.Hansen & S. Dyrup. The painter claims to have thrown a redningskrans--a life–preserver--and the pilot held on to it and was then rescued by people on a boat. That is something that I hand-copied and roughly translated from file E in the Vordingborg Archives. Don't you think that he should have been a pivotal witness for the final inquest? Witness! What about the witnesses who agreed the plane went down in about four minutes? Why were those well documented? Why aren't they being interviewed in the local Danish papers? Maybe in 1939, that was not the way things were reported? I do not know--as far as I could read, all that is on 'the witnesses.' Where is the testimony from the at least two other divers that went down to the G-AESY? Isn't dykkerne, the plural of dykker? It does not make sense that one local carpenter and self-taught diver was asked to pull out all the bodies when there were divers that were employees of a salvage company available."

"That is very odd!" Maggie sounded indignant, every ounce of her Danish blood on the offence."As a half-Dane I think it is very fair to say that Scandinavians are by nature far more practical than that! And far more brave! Danes were 'The Vikings,' the brave and aggressive ones!"

Bill's expression was full of certainty and relief. Bill knew he would never have to relive the salty waters; for him, it was over. His tone was determined."I am very clear that the pilot swam to shore. I am very clear that the pilot got out through the top. I have never seen anything different, not in my regressions, nor in my nightmares."

Catalina flipped the pages of several large binders full of documents as she spoke and gave the dates of what she explained. They talked about what they knew to be the differences found on the bodies, and through Skype, Catalina showed them the photos of the corpses at the morgue from the Danish archives in Copenhagen. Then Maggie, looking very thoughtful, brought up the subject of psychics again.

"You said the information you got from the psychics was very similar to what Bill has been experiencing. I think all of us want to know everything you know."

Catalina took another file; this one was in a purple, plastic, thick file pouch. She pulled out several manila folders and other materials. She shared how several psychics had described the same man while holding the watches. They all described a tall, slender young man (had even said he was twenty-five years old) with a mustache. They had all said that he knew the plane was going to burn; it was amazing that it matched the past-life regression. She also noted that in the autopsies, there were only "signs of violence reported on the body of the tall, slender young man with a mustache."

"No, you are wrong," Maggie remembered.

"The German had some 'other signs of violence,' as well."

"You are right. On the skull, I believe."

Maggie and Bill agreed on everything else Catalina said. They had carefully read everything before agreeing to another regression. The hypnotist observed and did not ask any questions; her job was to help Bill to separate who he was today from who he had been in a past life. And she was very happy to notice that he was beginning to refer to the events in the third person; he was successfully detaching from his past.

"He did not go the radio operator's funeral, and there were quite a few employees from BAL there."

Catalina opened another folder from the same purple file. She explained that this man who had helped her had asked to be known only as Nan Siente Papa. That she had no contact with him today, but that, on several occasions, he had held the two watches as well as anything else she had found from that era.

"It is written in Spanish, so bear with me, as I will read and translate simultaneously.

"It is dated notes from Thursday, November 13, 1997. He said to call him Nan Siente Papa. He said he was a spiritual healer and was only going to help me with this because it explained the roots of war. That all this related to the origins of war. While holding my grandfather's watch with his eyes closed, he told me basically the same story Bill has just experienced but from the perspective of the back row.

"He also told me that there was a man, an American with a military haircut, who was holding a gun in his hand. That the Englishman, Anthony, had the ability with just a few words to put people in their place."

Maggie had to interrupt. "I read many of Anthony Crossley's speeches online, and he liked to argue--he liked to win. I would agree with that."

"I know; I read them as well. But this man, the Peruvian shaman, had never read any speeches on Hansard, nor had he seen the diary entry in which another MP describes how Crossley put him in his place about 'the Hun.'

"This Peruvian shaman was just holding a watch, saying what he saw. Anyhow, let me see the paper. Okay, so according to the shaman, Anthony Crossley said something that infuriated the American, and the American holding the gun fired and shot him in the head on the side toward the back. He pointed to this part of his head."

She put her finger on her head, not quite all the way back. "I have been told the same thing by two other psychics. The shaman also said that as Anthony left his body, he was a man who felt disappointed and betrayed--that the men on board were trying to have a meeting to prevent war.

"He said he saw weapons that looked like rockets. That he saw Winston Churchill sitting at a desk, holding his head, sad, and another man with little round glasses, a man whom he had never seen in history books.

"The shaman said that all of the men on board that plane were there to attend a meeting. That the meeting was an international effort to try to prevent war. Oh, yes, I said that already, didn't I? I guess I wrote it twice. Anyhow.

"That part of the effort to prevent war included sharing information about weapons. The weapons looked like rockets. There were weapons that looked like rockets in 1939, and here and there I believe you'll find entries that link Anthony Crossley to weapons. If the link between my grandfather's family and Krupp can be made, then there, too, you could find something relevant to weapons in 1939. He talked about Paris and Churchill, and here I have to tell you that I saw a book of love letters from Churchill to his wife, Clementine. There is a letter addressed to her on August 14, 1939, from the Ritz in Paris, so he was in Paris in August of 1939 in that very letter he explains to his wife that the Germans are bound to attack Poland by early to mid-September, to 'avoid the mud season!' War strategies-- don't get me started on my opinion! I believe that same book was one of the sources that documented his return to England on the 23rd of August 1939.He told me I was looking for a flag with a lot of blue, I won't go into the list of the countries he mentioned, because frankly I still do not understand that; I need to do more research. But the technology of rockets in 1939 did exist. The entries in Hansard match things that he said."

She looked at the paper again. "He said to look for a man named Williams; I have always assumed this is Willans. He said that Willans was old but alive, and that he wanted to tell the story, to hurry up before he died. He mentioned Paris again twice; once to say that there is another man in Paris, that the name of that man was something like Muller, that this man was very healthy and would live to be very old.

"He mentioned Paris again and said that it had a connection with a woman from Panama, that he saw the name Madeleine and a boy about eight years old. He went on to suggest sources like the Red Cross to look for her. I've never tried.

"He was adamant that he was a spiritual healer and not a psychic, and that the only reason it was appropriate for him to use energy this way was because this story was ultimately about the manipulations that the powerful and governments used to begin wars. I found him recently on the Internet; he runs a meditation and peace center out West. He is referred to as a Peruvian shaman and a Lakota healer; I guess he never became Nan Siente Papa."

Everyone looked and stared. The hypnotist spoke."How are you going to tell the story?"

Catalina answered. "I think it was Jean-Jacques Rousseau who said something like, 'The world of reality has its limits, but the world of imagination is boundless.' So I'll tell the story the only way I know how. I'll call it fiction, and then I'll bless myself, go to confession, and say I lied."

Both sides of the Atlantic heard laughter. Maggie took Bill's hand; Bill kissed Maggie, who added, "Voltaire said 'History is the lie commonly agreed upon' or words to that effect, so fiction is a great choice."

Finally exhibiting some human curiosity, the hypnotherapist said, "I know one of the men was your grandfather, but you never met him. What made you so passionate and determined to go after this story?"

Catalina shrugged."When I was ten years old, I lived with my grandmother and her second husband, also an Intava man, who was in London in 1939, Louis F. Cuilty."

She held up a photograph for them to see of two men walking in a snowfall across a bridge somewhere in New York City. They were her two grandfathers, the one she never knew, who died in cold Danish waters, and the one she wasn't related to by blood (Tio Luis), but certainly by the bond of great childhood memories, a bond forged in the love and respect that every good grandfather deserves.

"Tio Luis and I would talk--perhaps a better word is argue--all the time about politics. It was an election year in America in 1968, and I knew whom I liked for president, and Tio Luis disagreed. He was seventy and very sweet and patient with me, but one day he got fed up and raised his voice to say, 'You are just like Victor Manuel Castillo! I hope you grow up to be the great lawyer he was so you can argue for a living. And the way you are learning English, also reminds me of Cesar Agustin Castillo; you'll probably grow up to speak five languages like he did.'

"Four years later, I discovered a poem. It was the most beautiful thing I had ever read. I repeated it nonstop to no one in particular, and when my mother heard the words and realized what I was repeating, she handed me this book."

She held up a leather bound book, and in London they read on the screen: *Longfellow's Poems*.

"My mother then opened the book to this page, the one marked in blue ink. She told me that her father never got his last wish, the wish to have the words to that very poem, 'A Psalm of Life: What the Heart of the Young Man Said to the Psalmist,' inscribed on his tombstone.

"I guess that my obsession with this story was triggered by the need to follow the footprints, the footprints my grandfather and the rest of the men aboard the G-AESY left behind in the sands of time."

Everyone nodded, and the conversation turned to small talk. After the usual niceties were exchanged, the four people said good-bye. Maggie and Catalina clicked for the second-to-last time the same button on Skype.

End of video call.

CHAPTER FORTY – THE FINAL CALL

Several weeks later, Maggie's beautiful smiling eyes were brighter than ever. She was glowing. Catalina had missed their conversations and was very happy to see her.

"From your e-mails, I get the impression that you're not very happy at your new job. I hope the package I sent you made you happy. It has everything we found, through any type of source, because unlike you, I am not a snob about the types of sources my information comes from. It seems so silly that you want some sort of a degree next to the name of a source...whether you realize it or not, you are an academic snob."

"An academic snob without the academic background! You are right, and your package arrived. Thank you; it made me so happy. I quit my job and have given myself six months to write a book about everything I found."

"That must mean you liked the files that Bill and I found at Kew?"

"There were many interesting ones. Thank you again! I had never seen file number 406/406/22, the Italy file, and the one with correspondence from the British Legation at the Holy See. That was very interesting. What did you and Bill make of it?"

"Bill and I agreed that it certainly shows a possibility that Mr. Anthony Crossley could have tried to seek out 'International Peace Groups,' and that as long as he did not officially attend as a representative of His Majesty's government, it was something that the British government could have encouraged. We think that it is very possible that if the meeting on the G-AESY was real, it could have begun with that or something like it. You said the meeting had to do with sharing information on weapons so no one would have an advantage, and I found an reference to a note written by a Sir Basil Liddell Hart discussing the production of anti-aircraft guns in 1938. We also looked up your shaman from Peru; he sounds like a very reliable source to me. We think he was right."

"I prefer spiritual healer to shaman. He was a man who spoke in Spanish with great eloquence. I think you might find academic background there."

"Bill also asked me to make perfectly sure that you will respect his wishes for anonymity."

"Absolutely. I understand, and I will respect his wishes. You almost sound like an old married couple, Maggie."

"Well, you may as well know that we are not old, but we are pregnant and married—not exactly in that order, but we are."

No wonder she was glowing and prettier than ever. Congratulations were given and the due date was discussed; many smiles were exchanged.

There was still a file or two to discuss, and they did that one by one until there was only one more file to talk about.

"Bill and I, however, cannot understand the importance of the Foreign Office letter from Rab Butler, the file FO 371/23250."

"Really? The importance is that in June of 1939, the gist of that letter was probably not common knowledge or accepted knowledge as such. Anthony Crossley liked to win every argument, and he seemed to have an extraordinary knowledge about anything that he found important."

"Yeah, and when I Googled Rab Butler, I read that he almost become prime minister."

"Oh, yes; he has an incredible historical record, that one. Let me see."

Catalina got up and pulled out a thick book from her shelf. On the cover it said, *The Oxford Companion to Twentieth-Century British Politics.*

"Here we go. On page 84, it says that Richard Austen Butler was born 1902, a year before Anthony Crossley, and died in 1982. He was nicknamed Rab, and when people talked about him or quoted him, they used the word 'Rabisms'. He was Home Secretary, Leader of the House, his party's leader, and was likely to succeed Anthony Eden as the prime minister, but that did not happen. He was big in the Suez Canal thing. Wow! Look, he wrote a book in 1971 called *The Art of the Possible.* Do you think he is the man with the round glasses?"

"No, I do not. He has a very distinctive, easy to describe face; little round glasses are for the face of a man who looks like any other man. You know that Henry Channon 'Chips' with quotes all over the Internet? In his diary entry of February 26, 1938, he writes that Rab Butler had become "Under-Secretary of the State for Foreign Affairs" and goes on to describe him as "...a scholarly dry-stick but an extremely able, cautious, canny man..." He goes on and on with the compliments, and then states his plans to "cultivate" Mr. Butler. Which when you look up Mr. Channon's bio on Wikipedia, you can tell he did indeed cultivate Mr. Butler, as he became R. A. Butler's Parliamentary Private Secretary."

"Let me see that."

Maggie, with the dexterity and knowledge of her generation, was immediately on a split screen, looking at the entry in Spartacus.

"Look further down September 9, 1938, to the end of the second paragraph--where he describes the League of Nations building 'full of Russians and Jews,' and he seems to accuse them and a certain unnamed journalist as instigators of war, or at the very least, very keen on it. He refers to the League of Nations as the 'anti-dictator' club. But he obviously admires the Prime Minister very much and knows that Neville Chamberlain will stop."

Simultaneously, from both sides of the Atlantic, both women said in rather loud voices, "The Munich Pact!"

"Look, Maggie; look at the next paragraph. This Chips guy is brutal! The one describing a dinner at Plat d'Argent, the silver plate for the non-polyglots ..."

"Snob!"

"I am, I am! But look at what it says! 'Rab almost embarrassed us once or twice with his high staccato laugh.' He is so critical! But gives Rab credit for charming and being charmed by Duff Cooper's beautiful wife Diana."

"And why does that name sound so familiar?" Maggie asked.

"Because of the Munich crisis--his name is prominent. You know, I read somewhere that Duff Cooper started his political career with the Oldham seat, just like Winston Churchill and Anthony Crossley."

"Do you think they were friends?"

"I don't know. Maybe work friends. Anthony Crossley seems to have led a very different social life from many of those who surrounded him. I think that he was more involved with his wife, three kids, and his other interests and obligations. That being said, these other men, like Henry Channon, have some diary entries where they sound so cruel and full of prejudice-- very superficial--and other entries where they show deep sentiment. Like all human kind! Like all of us--very complicated"

"Really? I cannot imagine Chips sounding deep!"

"No, really, there is sadness and depth when war arrives in 1939, and there are others. The saddest I thought was from December of 1942, where he speaks of 'the extermination of the Jews in East Europe, as cynical and as hung up on social standing as he was."

"Perhaps, but why are Anthony Crossley's historical assertions of any relevance to the Foreign Office? Why would Rab Butler ask around about the Hittite and the Tartar tribes?"

"Because they were European tribes that converted to Judaism in the eighth or ninth

Century, as the letter says."

"So what?"

Catalina answered. "Today, it is 'so what' mainly because last year a book written by Shlomo Sand, *The Invention of the Jewish People*, received a lot of attention. Today, thanks to that work, it is common knowledge that European Jewish people descended from those tribes and then converted to Judaism. However, in 1939, one argument for the Jewish right to Palestine was bloodline...the descendants of Abraham, the ones to whom God had promised the land in religious texts. Anthony Crossley explained in 1939 that the European Jewish people were not descendants of Abraham, but rather, descendants of the European tribes that had converted. Anthony Crossley was himself a convert, from the Church of England to Catholicism; as such, you can only imagine how good he would have been to argue that point. It impacted Rab Butler enough to inquire and agree with him when he heard Anthony Crossley's speech on Monday, May 22."

Maggie, with her youthful exuberance, said, "Sounds like Anthony Crossley had found an 'Excalibur' for the Arab cause he seemed so taken by. An argument that could have perhaps changed the course of history."

"I don't think so. Not at all. I think it was just an argument, caused some ripples. Look at the letter. Rab Butler went around asking other sources to confirm what Anthony Crossley had said; he was not the only man holding that knowledge. It caused ripples but was not a game changer."

"I could not find the speech on TheyWorkForYou.com."

"I have found that many online databases do not have all of the entries. There is another Hansard site that is complete. Let me see what I have directly from the Parliament library."

Catalina took out another large green binder with lettering on the side that read "HANSARD," to look for May 22, 1939.

"Here we go. It was a day for a heated and long discussion. Here it is in Hansard: it is volume 347, page 1968. He did make a long, very strong public statement.

You should make an appointment in the reading room at the Parliament library. It is a much cooler way to see history."

"Like the archives at British Airways; that place is such an interesting hidden museum."

Catalina pulled out two books from her shelf and showed them to Maggie. "If Anthony Crossley's knowledge could have had an impact, I think it would have already found its way into history books such as these, *One Palestine Complete* or *Churchill's Promised Land: Zionism and Statecraft*. I think historians like these must have found Anthony Crossley's speeches and correspondence. Sir Martin Gilbert worked directly with his papers, and if this had any bearing, historians would have included this in their books. The letter that Rab Butler wrote to Crossley that we found at Kew was not available to the public until later, but Hansard was, and the Churchill book was not published until 2007. Things like these don't fall through the cracks of history. I'm sure that there are many more speeches in Hansard that are not relevant enough for historians to take notice; there is one in 1936 in which Anthony Crossley is very prominent and makes a statement that a few years later is used against him as abusive, and I hate to say it, but rightfully so.

"There are several speeches by Anthony Crossley on Palestine in the Hansard files you went through online. But as you may recall, he was involved with many causes and was the secretary to the Minister of Transportation. He traveled to Spain and talked to Generalissimo Franco and had a strong involvement with the League of Nations. He had an incredible voice and passion for the cotton industry in his district. In one of his poetry books, Anthony Crossley has a little story to explain how he was inspired to write one of his poems; it involves a walk with a friend, a Mr. Awad. His interest in the Arab cause could be as simple as a friendship."

"I found a horrible website where Crossley's defense of the Arab people is linked to his death."

"I've seen things like that as well. I believe that they are ridiculous and venomous. It is true that in any organized group, one can always find rogue and bad groups. That does not make an organization or a community bad as a whole. There were certain groups of rogue, aggressive Zionists, such as the *Irgun Zwei Leuimi* and the Stern gang. There are records of violent acts committed by the few, and if you want any information about any of them, the best websites are Israeli. That was the first place I looked when I came across Churchill's War. By reputation, I do not feel comfortable with that author as a source, and there are so many questionable sources out there.

"The reason I researched this so much was because Israel was one of the countries that the spiritual healer mentioned when he told me to look for a flag full of blue. I am still looking into the other countries he mentioned. Another psychic told me to look for a man named Abraham, and one of the rogue violent groups, the Stern gang, was led by an Avraham, and from what I read, he was also roaming around Paris in 1939. Mr. Stern was shot dead by the British in 1942; some say trying to escape, some, in cold blood (to any story you can, of course, find two sides). But there are crimes accredited to the Stern gang even long after Avraham Stern's death.

"I think that the healer was simply channeling many of the causes that Anthony Crossley was involved with before he died. I think that I was not supposed to find any one cause in particular but learn about all of them in general."

Maggie looked pensive."Well, it sounds very much like today. There are many millions of Muslims who are very nice people, but there are groups that are dangerous and violent. So it makes it so confusing and scary for those of us who watch the news. It's so sad and it's probably doubly horrible for the nice Muslims who are treated badly, because people look at them and wonder if they should be scared or afraid."

"Yes, I agree. Just read the ridiculous language in Hansard that the politicians used in 1939. It was absolutely acceptable to speak of people of different races or countries in such deprecating terms! And that is just from the few speeches I read. It was a disgrace, and Germany was even worse! Imagine the average person who did not know any better, swayed by those in power to hate entire groups of people. Look at the images of any war, but in particular, look at all of the horrible images of World War II, and especially the Holocaust. And look into the horrors of what happened in the Pacific at the same time. I heard a historian describe things that were done over there, during World War II. I had to pull over and stop the car; I felt nauseous. How can we, as people, do such things to each other? Anyhow, because of violent groups, it does become easy to negatively judge groups of people as a whole by the acts of a few. I can't remember who said this, but I know it to be true: it is never too late to give up our prejudices."

"Really? It was an American, Henry David Thoreau, who said that! So much for my lack of knowledge and the grassy knoll! And I agree, it is never too late to give up your prejudices, and I believe everyone has them. It's just so easy to follow the crowd into the path of fear and hatred."

"I know it is. In my life experience of a little more than half a century, I have found that in all of the countries I have lived in and in all of the groups of people I have known, there are many more good people than bad people anywhere and everywhere. But prejudice does exist everywhere, and people so often do not realize it."

"I think so too. I think people in general are good people, and I am sure that in the world there are many more substantially good people than there are bad people. I also think that the younger people with global communication and so much more travel are less intolerant. I believe that my generation and the ones that follow are capable—world wide—of being more peaceful. Look how the entire world wants to help and is helping Haiti! We are capable of being a peaceful planet. I have to believe that."

The two women spoke, as women do, in detail about all of the wonderful, generous people they had encountered in their travels, in their experiences, in the news of the world. They felt so full of hope for humankind. Eventually they had to discuss their own futures.

"My mum's Sunday afternoon ritual involves an internet radio show. It's from somewhere in America. On it, a woman channels messages from 'Masters of Wisdom.' We asked the 'Masters' last week about past lives. The answer loud and clear was that we are here to work and focus on this life, and that this life is the one that counts."

Catalina knew where this was leading. Although it was not as she would have wished, it was not her place to decide for Maggie. "Those sound like very sensible words; I cannot imagine that a soul could bear the constant burden of where it has been."

"Right, and like I told you, Bill wants assurances that he will always remain anonymous, completely anonymous, so he can enjoy being Bill, being Maggie's husband, being Maggie's baby's father, and being a successfully logical numbers man!"

"As well he should be!"

With a deep, long sigh, the voice from Florida said the inevitable; there was no sense in making Maggie say it.

"I am going to miss you both very much, but especially you, Maggie. Thank you for helping me find the answers to the story. You have left a real footprint on my soul."

"You're welcome. You have, too. So, this is it then; we say a final good-bye—not so long, but a final and definite good-bye."

"Yes. A final goodbye. Shall we click 'end of call' at the count of three?"

Maggie nodded and they counted, "1, 2, click."

The screen went back to the Skype logo, a nice light blue. Maggie and Bill walked off into the sunset of their happily-ever-after. The next time you're in London, and you see a happy young couple in love with each other and their baby, pushing a pram, you might get a glimpse of Bill and Maggie. But don't stare; they want to remain anonymous.

In Florida, the middle-aged woman picked up her fountain pen, her five-dollar Pilot Varsity disposable fountain pen. It wrote so smoothly and effortlessly, but someday, when she sold her first book, she would use a Mont Blanc. She took out a new, fresh yellow legal pad and began to write.

The Bridge of Secrets

(By M. C. V. Egan)

As naturally as espionage came to him, in the end it killed him. The slim trail of evidence he left behind was hard to follow. (But today I finally succeeded.) It was 1939, and the international mood was explosive ...

EPILOUGUE LONDON ~ SUMMER 2012

Raining again--bloody June and it is raining again--we will probably have the worst weather for the Olympics. Next week is Ascot, and I need a hat, where the hell is she? It was her idea that we meet here at Foyles where Maggie met Bill. Same star patterns as two and a half years ago or some other such silly astro mumbo-Jumbo, and if it worked for Maggie, maybe the place could have a bit of magic for me as well....

"Hullo? I thought you were only smoking when you drank these days?"

"I am, but I had to wait for you, didn't...Is that a hatbox? You bought a hat for Ascot without me? You bitch!"

"Erica, you are going to feel like such an ass...I bought *you* the hat you liked. You know the one. We saw it on the window in that little shop..."

"Oh Jennifer! I don't feel that bad; you owed me a good gift."

Erica and Jennifer hugged and laughed. They were Maggie's friends, and now that Maggie was so busy playing mum and wife, they had become best friends.

They were both about to celebrate their 30th birthday on June 30, 2012; they referred to each other as the birthday twins from the moment they met at primary school.

That was the extent of their similarity; Jennifer was always the giver and Erica, the taker. The former always saw the world as full of light with bits of darkness whilst the latter saw the world as darkness with bits of light. Somehow their friendship worked well, and they often found time for each other.

"Off to Foyles then. Or should we repeat the magic and first go into the sex shop across the street?"

"What?"

"Don't you remember? Maggie was at the sex shop buying strange condoms and silly sex toys for a bridal shower. What was her coworker's name?

"I don't remember her name but she was the one with the horrid cranberry-red bridesmaid dresses. Awful photos she posted on Facebook; and Maggie used the very kinky condoms that were for decorative purposes only and managed to get pregnant that very night."

As Erica's mocking laughter subsided, she went on to say. "I'd rather go to Foyles, and have a look at my hat than go to the Sex Shop, isn't the café on the first floor?"

"I've no idea."

"I still don't see why you think we could meet the loves of our lives here? Just because Maggie stalked a bloke from America with an identity crises here as she was carrying a bag full of novelty condoms, doesn't mean we'll get lucky. Anyhow everyone knows the glow in the dark condoms always rip if you are really having fun."

"Not everyone Erica, you would know but not everyone."

"I don't shag every bloke I meet; contrary to what you may think."

"Oh you've missed a few?"

"Oh sod off, it's not like you are the Holy Virgin, Jennifer."

"I don't think there is a Virgin Jennifer…"

The outburst of laughter attracted as much attention to the exotic, pretty young women as did the hatbox. Jennifer's good looks had always been easy to enhance with a bit of make-up, and Erica oozed sexuality and adventure with a few key piercings. Erica attributed her sexiness to the fact that she very much enjoyed sex. That day looking for love, both were particularly attractive.

"Did you know that this store came about because two brothers failed their Civil Service exams and sold their books second hand then realized there was a great market...I really believe this place has a sort of magical energy; I believe this to be a place where dreams come true by mere fluke."

"What? You've been Googling and Wikipedia-ing to no end again?"

"No, actually I found the info on the Foyles website; this was created by a miracle of failure; it is a really nice story."

Erica opened the hatbox and it was the perfect hat, even better than the one they had seen together on the window display.

"It is a different color from the one we spotted on the window when the shop was closed, but I thought this..."

"I love it! It suits me much better. So what are we supposed to do? I am happy just staying here at the café. I am not going to seek out men in the re-incarnation section."

"Astrologically, it is a good two and a half years since Maggie and Bill met here, and I made an Astrology chart, and today this place is full of Magic."

"Really? That mumbo-jumbo again? Oh, yes! You had dinner with Maggie's mum a few days ago; how's the old girl adapting to being a nan?"

"She's thrilled as any first-time nan would be. Astrology has been mostly respected and used by many for centuries; it is simply misunderstood because those who generalize it abuse it. If you plot an actual chart of a person or place, it is quite a different story."

"Well, if I am going to find love, you need to find the section with the *Kama Sutra* or books of that sort because I am not bloody interested in re-incarnation or astrology."

"And with your flexibility, Erica, I am sure you can get into every odd position in the *Kama Sutra.*"

"That I can! Thanks to the compulsory ballet lessons my parents inflicted on me as a child, but the *Kama Sutra* is a very misunderstood and very spiritual book, I'll have you know."

"You are serious? You have actually tried the positions?"

"Absolutely! With no regrets, I might add. And to tell you the truth, it was the bar stretching exercises and the splits make me far more make me sexually flexible than any other absurd moves with names I hardly remember from those horrid ballet lessons."

Jennifer's expression of utter disbelief was replaced by a beaming smile; Erica did not see the very handsome blokes approaching them.

"Excuse me? Do you mind if we sit here? There don't seem to be any other tables"

*Not too bright, it is raining outside. Of course the place is...*Erica's thoughts were interrupted by Jennifer's welcoming voice.

"Are you Americans?"

The men answered simultaneously

"No, we are Canadians."

Jennifer was surprised to be the lead on their part of the conversation but she continued" You look very much alike; are you twins or just brothers?"

One of the handsome blokes answered as the other smiled and nodded.

"Brothers. We are brothers this is Gil, and I am Will."

"That is quite funny; the original creators of Foyles were brothers, and their names were William and Gilbert. Please join us. I'm Jennifer, and this is my friend Erica. What brings two Canadians to Foyles?"

"Gil stands for Giles, and Will stands for Wilbur. Mom read a book about a bookstore in Charing Cross Road and she wanted us to post a picture for her on Facebook. It started to rain like hell, so we came in. We came to London early to train for the Olympics--to get used to the weather and the terrain. We live in Florida, where it is hot and flat, and we wanted a real chance to compete."

Erica had finally caught her breath and gotten past the absurd thoughts...of possible magic, the thought of two brothers and the possibility of re-incarnation. Her sharp tongue however could not help but mock the Canadian's name.

Who on their right mind names a son Wilbur; they are easy on the eyes...

"Let me guess: mum also liked Charlotte's Web"

Once again in unison the two Canadians answered. "She loves E.B. White!"

"Is your family joining you for the Olympics?"

"No, they have to watch on TV."

"Your wives too."

"No we have no wives, no girlfriends; just our bicycles, and we are ready to compete."

Erica found her sexy back and switched it on to its maximum. When men were that handsome and that available, Wilbur could be a perfectly acceptable name.

"I know two perfectly happy, single tour guides to make sure you can post great photos for your mum."

APPENDIX A ~ Store, keep or sell?

Aster, Sidney. 1939: *The Making of The Second World War.* New York: Simon and Schuster, 1973.

This book is very clear and easy to understand. It explains the political comings and goings of 1939. They do not mention Anthony Crommelin Crossley by name, but they do go into detail as to the matters he worked with in Parliament. Look at underlined pages...

It could go in the box.

Black, Edwin. *IBM and the Holocaust.* New York: Three Rivers Press, 2001–2002.

This book's mention on page 175 of the Scandinavian countries could prove to be useful.

Page 179: is important to read every time I need to remember the horrors of war.

Page 254: mentions Standard Oil and is footnoted 111(found on page 489).

Page 337: Standard Oil of New Jersey. Footnote 8 (found on page 502).

Standard Oil of New Jersey; 30 Rockefeller Plaza. Her grandfather had only been transferred to the European branch two weeks before he died. Most data she found on him had his personal address on Riverside Drive or the 30 Rockefeller plaza address c/o a Mr. K. Blood. This book stayed on the shelf.

Catton, Bruce. *The War Lords of Washington.* New York: Harcourt, Brace and Company, 1948.

There were no notes on this one. In the box.

Charmley, John. *Chamberlain and the Lost Peace.* Chicago: Ivan R. Dee, 1989.

The author mentions ACC on pages 58, 117, 128, 150; trouble with constancy, 146.

On page 150, the book explains how the various MPs who opposed the Munich Pact fared politically. The information on ACC is wrong. He had not "lost his seat" in 1945; he had died with her grandfather in 1939. My copy, bought secondhand, is old; look up to see if this was revised or retracted.

(On the shelf.)

Charmley, John. *Churchill: The End of Glory: A Political Biography.* London: Hodder and Stoughton, 1993.

Page 334: ACC mentioned as one of the "motley crew" of "non-Churchillian" abstainers in the matter of the Munich Pact.

Page 350: ACC's contact with Churchill and Eden. I read this at the New York Library in the Martin Gilbert books about Churchill.

Page 355, ACC among others, on probation. Footnoted page 678 from Amery diary.

Page 364: "The Focus" and Sir Henry Strakosch. Contacted author on this entry but received no reply. Only other source on Strakosch I could find is David Irving, and he has a bad reputation. The Focus is mentioned by many other authors but not in the same way. An endnote on page 680 states the source as Gilbert's Churchill V, companion vol. 3. I have not been able to find a copy.

(Back on the shelf.)

Charmley, John. *Churchill's Grand Alliance*. New York: Harcourt Brace, 1995.

In the box. She had looked at this one but found several far easier to read.

Coffey, Thomas M. *Lion by the Tail*. New York: Viking, 1974.

Look up Abyssinia and ACC on Hansard.

Abyssinia was not an important part of her search. The world in the 1930s often felt as complicated as the world in 2010. In the box.

Coit, Margaret L. *Mr. Baruch*. Boston: Houghton Miffl in, 1957.

Page 672: But it was 1939, and the door was very soon slammed. Footnoted on page 765.

Davies, R. E. G. *British Airways: An Airline and Its Aircraft.* Volume I: 1919–1939. McLean, VA: Paladwr, 2005.

Deborin, G. *Secrets of the Second World War.* Moscow: Progress, 1971.

A Russian perspective on the instigation of war. A thorough reader who carefully marked with pencil a comment or two had obviously owned this old copy. Box.

Farago, Ladislas. *The Game of the Foxes.* New York: David McKay, 1971.

About spies; outdated by information that has since become available. But chapter 5 is particularly interesting. It mentions Panama.

Standard Oil had moved her grandfather to Panama in the mid-1930s. So if there were spies in Panama, this book could be useful. Box. No, not box. Shelf.

Fish, Hamilton. *Tragic Deception: FDR and America's Involvement in World War II.* Old Greenwich, CT: Devin-Adair, 1983.

This is an easy, short read, and it made her think. Page 74 was of particular interest for discussing behind the scenes or, should one dare say it, secret meetings in August of '39.

Shelf.

Gilbert, Martin. *Churchill: A Life*. New York: Henry Holt, 1991.

Mr. Gilbert had been so kind to answer her letter. This book was marked in various places, and although he did not mention her ACC by name as he did in his large volumes, it had confirmed certain pieces of information she had received from her "dubious" sources. Shelf.

Haines, C. Grove, and Ross J. S. Hoffman. *The Origins and Background of the Second World War*. New York: Oxford UP, 1943.

This red hardcover is unusual, as it was published prior to the end of World War II. It is surprisingly informative and accurate, considering how so much of the documentation for other books was not available in 1943.

The introduction presents what I need: "It was a period of broadcasting and espionage."

Many other pages had been carefully marked and studied about ten years before. This one she liked by her nightstand, just in case she wanted to reread a page or two.

Hearn, Chester G. *Spies and Espionage: A Directory*. San Diego, CA: Thunder Bay, 2006.

Light blue tabs marked a number of the spies in this book's pages. She wondered if any...was she just grasping at straws? Her favorite was marked, not because he had been a spy, but because he was one of her favorite authors: William Somerset Maugham. Shelf. Irving, David. *Churchill's War*. New York: Avon Books, 1987.

Too many pages and too many notes.

This book was dodgy. She had not realized this when she first stumbled across it in the cooking section in Books-A-Million. As she always did, and still does, she looked at the back for Anthony Crossley's name. There it was in the index, several times.

She knew so little at the time that she felt a rush finding a book that boasted being an "explosive" international bestseller. As she found other books that were very different, she looked directly into Hansard and contacted various historians.

If David Irving had not described the Focus as he did and placed Anthony Crossley "as teetering on the brink of the Focus," she would have neglected to research as much as she had. If John Charmley had not used David Irving as a source, she would have also probably stopped looking for information with regard to the Focus. She contacted both of them with the same question: what was the source? John Charmley

29 Irving, Churchill's War, page 54.

30 Charmley, The End of Glory. See bibliography page 706 (D. Irving, Churchill's War: The Struggle for Power, 1987). See also the endnote from page 336 ("Cads Like Apostles" or "Cavemen"?) on page 677, number 40, page 104.

31 These were the only sources the author found that never answered. Frankly, she wished neither had Irving, as his answer was full of prejudice.

Years later, she came across Mr. Irving again; this time, the subject was Mr. H. W. Wicks. She contacted him again but again felt uncomfortable corresponding with him. Mr. Irving must have also felt uncomfortable, because he wrote that she was "somewhat rude."

This book had served its purpose. Box.

Jenkins, Roy. *Churchill: A Biography.* New York: Penguin, 2001.

Here was another well-marked book. This one marked the important pages with little metal pointers from Levenger. She looked at the index and got the feeling that this historian was a good source. Shelf.

Jones, R. V. *Most Secret War.* London: Hodder and Stoughton, 1979.

The work before September 1939 was interesting in this one. Shelf.

The spine of this book showed great wear, as she had marked and underlined many of its pages. Standard Oil of New Jersey and some of its subsidiaries were mentioned very prominently; also mentioned was how common the recruitment of Latin American and Mexican spies was in that era.

This author would have loved her grandfather's CV and his family background with the stories of the Baron Krupp. This book certainly belonged on the nightstand.

Kater, Michael, H. *Hitler Youth*. Cambridge, MA: Harvard UP, 2004.

It was interesting to try to understand the German correspondence in the British Airways file, but not as interesting to her as Nora Wahl's book...Box.

Liddell Hart, B. H. *History of the Second World War*. New York: G. P. Putnam's Sons, 1970.

APPENDIX B ~ *THE LONDON TIMES* ANTHONY CROSSLEY

1932

-February 17; tariffs; page 17f.

This one is funny, because I do not know if I mentioned that Anthony Crossley's wife was an artist--a painter. So he is speaking on behalf of artists and trying to get some sort of tax-exemption for them, at least the ones who paint in other countries--something to do with the weather.

-April 15; cotton trade; page 7e.

Advice on how to make it more profitable. I never took the time to look at it, but in the New York Library, there was some cotton report baring his name; he really took that industry seriously.

-October 20; Ottawa Agreements; page 7c.

Workers affected by the Ottawa agreements, weavers.

-November 15; means test; page 8a.

He likes this bill, as it is something that will help the area he represents.

-December 20; unemployment; page 7f.

How to help the unemployed without turning them into charities. Isn't it amazing how many of these discussions could be from today?

1933

- March 3; unemployment; page 7e.

Here I know I came across a book that misused this and tried to name ACC as an admirer of Germany. Anthony Crossley does explain that the German Minister of Labor invited him, that because of this invitation, he has the opportunity to notice in several "labour exchanges." I think it means factories, but I am not sure because in the same breath he mentions the unemployed. At any rate, he feels that things of this sort could be implemented in England to help people with lower incomes be able to eat at very reasonable prices.

-March 16; rural industries; page 8a.

-June 17; unemployment insurance; page 6c.

-November 24; Japanese competition; page 8b.

1934

-February 2; unemployment insurance; page 7d.

-February 20; unemployment insurance; page 7c.

-April 21; water supply; page 15e.

One of his funny quips like the funny poems. You know the kind that got him into books in the first place?

-April 24; unemployment insurance; page 8a.

-June 21; newspapers and first offenders; page 7e.

Anthony Crossley feels that the press could harm people who make a mistake but are not "truly criminal." Talks about young student at Oxford who stole books.

-June 28; unemployment; page 9c.

Conservatives were losing supporters, the youth to the socialists, because they (conservatives) could not put before them a picture of where the country should be in a few years.

-December 4; depressed areas; page 7e.

Angry about this bill; feels it does not really help; plaster on a sore. (Band-Aid on a wound?)

-December 7; depressed areas; page 8a.

How to secure money for depressed areas and agricultural industry.

-December 19; cotton trade; page 10c.

Letter to editor on why it is important to finance cotton trade.

-December 22; financial policy; page 5d.

About financing cotton industry; important for Oldham.

1935

-March 8, 9a; March 13, 8a; March 15, 9e.

All about the housing bill.

-April 30; appointment; page 8g.

Austin Hudson, MP, Parliamentary Secretary to the Ministry of Transport, has appointed Mr. A. C. Crossley as his parliamentary private secretary. I believe this is quite a big deal, and that it is doubly impressive that he received this appointment twice.

-May 18; aeroplanes over London; page 10b.

Letter to the editor, complaining about noise.

-May 21; holiday resorts; page 9c.

Something really pissed him off. 'Blood boils' when he sees that the amendments say that one woman should be in this committee or that. I think he means that any spot should be acquired because people are capable and not because a 'minority' is needed to show balance.

-May 21; housing bill; page 9b.

Trying to defend non-provided schools? (Whatever that means).

-June 29; Council of Action for Peace and Reconstruction; page 14d.

Crossley seems to be against Lloyd George and his manifesto.

-July 2; Council of Action; page 18c.

Anthony Crossley says something to the effect that he is the first speaker of fighting age, and that the others are "old men"; he does not totally oppose the manifesto but finds certain particulars not to be of his thinking.

-July 12; foreign policy; page 8f.

Last entry where he represents Oldham. He is pretty tough on Lloyd George; he accuses Lloyd George, (this guy was Prime Minister from 1916-1922) of making speeches that "confuse public thought," and apparently Anthony Crossley feels that Lloyd George in doing this is harming "peace and collective security." Lloyd George was a Liberal, and Anthony Crossley was a Conservative, so I guess the tone is understandable.

-November 16; general election; page 8f. Stretford, Crossley wins.

-December 11; trade agreement; page 8d.

1936

-March 13; air defense; page 8e.

-March 19; hours of work; page 7f.

Here he seems to want to help the worker; funny, he often seems to want to do that, and in American Politics today, the Conservatives are not usually on the side of the worker. I wonder if this was typical of a Conservative in England in the 1930s?

-March 25; Palestine, legislative council; page 8a.

Here Anthony Crossley starts out by defending the Palestinians by making it a point that he chooses to call them Palestinians and not Arabs. He goes on to explain that they have lived in 'that country,' (I do not understand why it isn't that colony) for 1,400 years. There is a mandate being discussed--I am guessing the mandate he claims that the British government is tied to the Balfour Declaration, because every time I look any of this stuff up, it comes up.

So he gives his point of view: that if the future could have been foreseen and how the contradictions of trying to help two peoples were not going to work. His words are, of course, far more elegant than mine. I learned a beautiful word from that entry axiom something that self-evident, that there is no need to prove it. That's how sure he was that the issue of Palestine as the Balfour Declaration had created it and had "no real chance of cooperation for an indefinitely long period".

-May 27; education bill; page 8d.

-May 28; school leaving age; page 8e.

-May 29; Hackney Marshes; page 15d.

Letter to the editor.

-May 30; unemployment benefits regulations; page 7b.

-July 9; malnutrition; page 9d.

Mr. Crossley suggests feeding the hungry with surplus agricultural products.

-November 10; new industries; page 8f.

-November 21; divorce; page 17e.

Anthony Crossley says he is not sure if he is the only Catholic and gives the Catholic point of view.

-December 9; divorce; page 4e.

Here he wants the word "persistent" added before the word "adultery." (I guess a quick slip is okay, but if it happens often, you are out.)

-December 21; Spain; page 12b.

An article about a visit to Spain by a group of conservative British politicians, among whom is Crossley.

-December 30; Spain; page 16.

Letter to the editor of *The London Times*. Observations from his recent trip. His opinions are critical of others and pretty strong.

1937

-January 20; Spain; page 8f.

Here he explains what he saw in Spain and discusses his conversation with General Franco. (This one is worth reading in full). A note of interest: he points out that the most coveted weapon is a Czechoslovakian rifle, which anybody could get; it is regarded as the most perfect rifle ever handled. It says that, of course, Germany wanted to get something out of their intervention, but he (General Franco as explained by A. Crossley) did not believe it was territory. Spain was one of the great sources of raw material in the world, and she (Spain) was geographically so placed as to be in an extremely useful position for a refueling station for the German navy. In addition, there was always the possibility of an alliance.

-February 23; Spain; page 8a.

Letter to the editor, disputing a letter written by a Lord Cecil. Letter signed by Anthony Crossley and Robert T. Bower, House of Commons, February 15, 1937.

-February 23; Palestine, page 9d.

Arabs and British troops. Crossley here again shows an interest in Arab causes Arabs and British troops. He describes a story (you might want to read this one, Maggie). Here a man named Gallagher agrees with him. But a Colonel Wedgwood (Newcastle-under-Lyme, Lab.) questions Anthony Crossley's opinion in regard to the Arabs and their respect of the British Army. Anthony Crossley goes on to rebut that "Prussian methods" do not gain anyone's respect.

-March 25; armaments profiteering; page 8c.

A discussion on how to avoid people making great profits in lieu of helping the government in the necessary manufacture of weapons. Crossley cites that it is to be avoided, as it did occur in the last war.

-April 10; animals in films; page 8b.

This is to pass a bill to protect animals, specifically in films. Here Mr. Crossley cites *Ben Hur* as a film that most likely caused great harm to horses in the chariot races. He points out that the bill should not apply to films that have already been made, as "a retrospective legislation was almost always unfair."

-April 15, Spain, page 8d.

Discusses the Central European problem. Here he is very adamant about nonintervention. He commends the government for its policy thus far but warns against getting involved. On the opposite side of the opinion is, again, Colonel Wedgwood (Newcastle-under-Lyme, Lab.) and Emrys-Evans (Derbyshire, S., U.).

-April 17; divorce; page 8b.

-May 27; arms trade; page 9d.

-May 29; divorce; page 7e.

Mr. Crossley is adamantly opposed to a bill. He is, it seems, very Catholic, and the "forever and ever" commitment sticks. He mentions various reasons why marriages can end, from adultery to insane partners, but seems basically to say, "You made your oath, and you stay with your partner." (Maggie, on a very personal and totally unrelated note, I cannot imagine how miserable my life would have been had I not chosen divorce.)

-June 24; hours of work; page 9a.

Talked about how many hours the workweek should be. Mr. Crossley's point is to make sure this does not cause an imbalance with international labor or endanger industrial relations. (His family had a company called Crossley motors. A lot of older British people I met in the 1990s [most are dead now] explained that at one point, it seemed that all the lorries in England were Crossley motors).

-June 30; public works; page 12d.

Letter to the editor. I think he cleverly swings the topic to rearmament and socks it to Lloyd George, with whom he seems to disagree.

-July 15; Palestine; page 8e.

The partition of Palestine...Mr. Crossley appealed to all interested in the Arab cause to turn their practical attention to the details of the scheme and particularly to the protection of minorities.

-July 22; Palestine; page 8f.

Troubles with terrorism. He proposes that to get a full picture, two Arabs should address the House and give their side of the story.

-July 24; divorce; page 7b.

Back to his Catholic opinion on the bill that is about to be passed.

August 19; hares at airdromes, page 8f.

This one is cute, a short notice from the Strand Hotel in Stockholm.

-November 9; Spain; Page 11b.

This is a really large discussion about Spain and General Franco. Anthony Crossley's opinion differs with Anthony Eden's. (They are pals during the Munich thing later on, and this is often found in history books.)

-November 26; air raid precautions; page 8a.

Basic planning for protection of the people during air raids. Crossley's input was that those chosen to volunteer had to be people who would be there in case of an emergency and not off fighting a war.

-December 3; unemployment insurance; page 8b.

This is interesting because a man (name not given) was very aggressive after Mr. Crossley and others spoke and was taken away. This man called the members of the House "lunatics and corrupters of the Labour party". (Imagine today! It would have been on every little news clip online.)

-December 17; Anglo-American relations; page 8g.

Attitude of the USA under an insult. This particular entry is about the United States 'isolationist' policies. How America knows that it will not be directly physically affected by the impending war and how something 'blatant'--a deliberate attack like "the sinking of the Panay"--would end the isolationist view of the American public. There is an amazing book called *The Irregulars* by Jennet Conant, which explains to what great lengths your country went through to end the 'Isolationism'. Anyhow here he disputes that those who believe America is willing to lend a hand are not forming their opinions based on "the facts"

-December 31; Anglo-American relations; page 14d.

Mr. Crossley seems more prudent in his opinion this time.

1938

-February 3; Anthony Eden; page 9b.

Here Anthony Crossley gives quite a speech in regard to Anthony Eden and discusses how right Eden was during the Munich Pact, and how internationally the perception was that Anthony Eden had been "dismissed." In any book I have ever read, he resigned, as I understand it as a protest to the Munich Pact (but don't forget that half of the stuff I read in those history books is not clear to me). I believe that I told you--when he agreed with Eden, he was the kind to go out on a limb. He is also in the most famous book about Churchill by Sir Martin Gilbert (of course, mentioned in a footnote here and there), but in that, he also shows a

willingness to go out on a limb for Churchill. I wrote to
Mr. Gilbert to see if there was a possibility of accessing
the papers he had used. On December 19, 2002, he
wrote me back, saying, "I am afraid that I was given the
Anthony Crossley material by Crossley's widow some
thirty years ago, and I do not know where the papers
are now." He went on to suggest the Churchill Library
at Cambridge, I think.

I have to tell you that he was one of the few historians
who answered me, and he is the most published and
busiest of anyone I approached. Anyhow, when I met
Anthony Crossley's granddaughter, she suggested that
on another visit we could go to her sister's house and
spend some time looking at bits that may prove to be
interesting. The few visits I made to England after that
never coincided with her schedule; for several years we
corresponded, but slowly after time, we stopped keeping
in touch.

-March 5; conical action; page 8f.

Letter to the editor expressing anger about a test ballot,
defending Anthony Eden, and pretty much showing he
is not very fond of Lloyd George.

-March 9; Palestine; page 7e.

Here he talks about how the mandate for the protection
of holy places should be larger, not smaller. He also

states that the loyalty shown to the Jewish people was not balanced with the loyalty shown to the Arabs, who were potentially just as loyal and devoted. He also goes as far as to say that the Jewish people in Palestine had not displayed anything like sufficient gratitude to the government for all that had been done for them. The House discusses funds.

-March 11; council of faction; page 10b.

Fiery letter to the editor; here's a snip: "...when did Mr. Eden 'demand' the reestablishment of peace and security...?" I feel that he is quite unhappy and is defensive about either Anthony Eden or the League of Nations, or both. I think Anthony Eden really liked him. In a book called *The Reckoning,* he writes that Anthony Crossley and Ronald Cartland's deaths were "to the impoverishment of their country's leadership."

-March 17; Spain; page 9c.

French arms for Spain. Discussion of the types of weapons being used in Spain: many French, some Russian, and it was stated that the eighty-four American-designed ones were probably made in Russia.

-April 2; army alignment; page 7c.

Age and such of enlisted men (kids); Mr. Crossley argued to the benefit of parents of underage, enlisted kids who lasted a short time. Apparently, there was some sort of fine.

-May 18; lack of skilled labor; page 8e.

Discussion on the lack of skilled labor in which Mr. Crossley stated that he was personally affected by this as he was "the Director of an Engineering Firm between Nottingham and Derby." (I have never been able to find said firm unless of course he refers to Crossley Motors.) The firm in question had apparently had a problem finding or replacing workers with particular skills. He explained that the firm was a good place to work that they are "model employers."

This could also help explain some of the data acquired through psychics.

-July 27; League of Nations. Page 8e

Anthony Crossley, until recently, was a co-opted member of the League of Nations. You might want to read this one. On a personal observation, there is very little on Anthony Crossley during the Munich Pact, yet this is the subject on which you are likely to find him mentioned in history books.

-November 7; sea trout; page 8e.

About fishing. Did I tell you I bought a fishing book by Crossley, and that in it was a letter with the embossing of the House of Commons? It was pretty cool. It is actually a good book; I never imagined I could enjoy a fishing book. The people he mentions in his book are interesting in and of themselves. I find a lot of his poetry very difficult to understand or simply not to my taste, but this fishing book is really fun to read!

-December 16; export trade; page 8d.

Crossley is quoted under the liberal view that welcomes the government to protect the export trade and standard of living. Interesting; you might want to read it.

-December 20; meetings with constituents; page 6e.

You might really want to read this; he got grilled, and he was in trouble, I am assuming, for all his views during the Munich Pact. It said they (General Council of the Conservative and Unionist Association at Urmston) kept him in a closed meeting for three hours! Anyhow, no decision was to be made for three months.

1939

-February 14; Czech frontiers; page 8e.

While discussing Czechoslovakia He mentioned the Munich Pact; and the opposition cheers…something about an 'optant clause' that he said "was not a vague expression of hope." He went on sadly to talk about terrible things that had been taking place. As I am sure you recall Anthony Crossley is in every book on the Munich Pact as one of the Anti-Appeasers.

-February 28; national service rearmament; page 9b.

-May 12; conscription; page 8a.

-May 23; Palestine; page 10d.

In this entry, he was so vocal that he actually landed in the New York Times. He said something to the effect that the Arabs had a friend in the House. You might want to read this one in full online in Hansard.

-June 28; finance bill; (I cannot find the page number). Claims of motorcyclists; taxes on new cars. Crossley's opinion was that the ones not purchasing new cars should get some benefit.

-July 15; export credits; page 7c.

Crossley said that the government had a belated realization that they must equip their allies in order to be effective.

-August 1; foreign policy; page 8e.

The last time *The London Times* quotes him alive, he had strong words. You might want to read it. In reference to the Munich Pact, he said, "Did we not take responsibility last autumn for certain changes for the benefit of Germany?" You really should read it, Maggie.

-August 16; death; pages 10c and 12c.

There were no reports on the day his body arrived to England, August 22, 1939 (or none that I found).

BIBLIOGRAPHY

Allen, Oliver E. *The Airline Builders (Epic of Flight)*. Des Moines, IA: Time Life Books, 1981.

Aster, Sidney. 1939: *The Making of the Second World War*. New York: Simon and Schuster, 1973.

Bernstein, Morey (with new material by William J. Barker). *The Search for Bridey Murphy*. 1956. Reprint, New York: Doubleday, 1989.

Best, William Newton. *Burning Liquid Fuel*. New York: UPC Book Company, 1922.

Berry, Michael F., C. M. Floyd, and Anthony Crommelin Crossley. *A History of the Eton College Hunt*. London: Collins, 1968.

Black, Edwin. *IBM and the Holocaust*. New York: Three Rivers Press, 2001–2002.

Bornwell, John. *Hitler's Scientists*. New York: Penguin, 2003.

Bourdillon, F. W. (translated by). *Aucassin & Nicolette*. London: The Folio Society, 1947.

Calvocoressi, Peter and Guy Wint. *Total War: The Story of World War II*. New York: Pantheon Books, 1972.

Catton, Bruce. *The War Lords of Washington*. New York: Harcourt, Brace and Company, 1948.

Charmley, John. *Chamberlain and the Lost Peace*. Chicago: Ivan R. Dee, 1989.

Charmley, John. *Churchill: The End of Glory: A Political Biography.* London: Hodder and Stoughton, 1993.

Charmley, John. *Churchill's Grand Alliance: The Anglo-American Special Relationship 1940– 57.* New York: Harcourt Brace, 1995.

Churchill, Winston S. *The Second World War, Volume I; The Gathering Storm.* Boston: Houghton Mifflin Company, The Riverside Press Cambridge, 1948.

Coffey, Thomas M. *Lion by the Tail.* New York: Viking, 1974.

Coit, Margaret L. *Mr. Baruch.* Boston: Houghton Mifflin, 1957.

Conant, Jennet. *The Irregulars; Roal Dahl and the British Spy Ring in Wartime Washington.* New York: Simon & Schuster, 2008.

Crossley, Anthony. *From One Vagabond to Another.* London: Christopher's, 1935.

Crossley, Anthony. *Aucassin and Nicolette and Other Poems.* London: Christopher's, 1925.

Crossley, Anthony. *Prophets, Gods and Witches.* London: Christopher's, 1927.

Crossley, Anthony. *The Floating Line for Salmon and Sea Trout.* London: Methuen, 1939.

Crossley, Anthony. *Tragedy under Lucifer: A Pastoral Poem with a Prose Poem Epilogue with a Defense of Modern Poetry.* London: Christopher's, 1931.

Davies, R. E. G. *British Airways: An Airline and Its Aircraft.* Volume 1: 1919–1939. McLean, VA: Paladwr, 2005.

Davies, R. E. G. *Lufthansa: An Airline and Its Aircraft.* McLean, VA: Paladwr, 1991.

Deborin, G. *Secrets of the Second World War.* Moscow: Progress, 1971.

Dominguez Castillo, Ruben. *Los Recuerdos... Quien te los quita?* Tuxtla Gutierrez, Chiapas. Mexico: 2003.

Earle, Hubert P. *Blackout: The Human Side of Europe's March to War.* Philadelphia: J. B. Lippincott, 1939.

Eden, Anthony. *The Eden Memoirs: the Reckoning.* London: Casell, 1965.

Elliott, William Yandell and H. Duncan Hall, eds. *The British Commonwealth at War.* New York: Alfred A. Knopf, 1943.

Ellisen, Stanley, A. *Who Owns the Land?* Portland, OR: Multnomah, 1991.

Evans, Richard J. *The Third Reich in Power.* London: Penguin, 2005.

Farago, Ladislas. *The Game of the Foxes.* New York: David McKay, 1971.

Fish, Hamilton. *Tragic Deception: FDR and America's Involvement in World War II.* Old Greenwich, CT: Devin-Adair, 1983.

Gellately, Robert. *Backing Hitler.* New York: Oxford UP, 2001.

Gilbert, Martin. *Churchill: A Life.* New York: Henry Holt, 1991.

Graber, G. S. *History of the SS.* 1978. Reprint, London: Robert Hale, 1982.

Haines, C. Grove, and Ross J. S. Hoffman. *The Origins and Background of the Second World War*. New York: Oxford UP, 1943.

Hearn, Chester G. *Spies and Espionage: A Directory*. San Diego, CA: Thunder Bay, 2006.

Henderson, Sir Nevile. *Failure of a Mission: Berlin 1937–1939*. New York: G.P. Putnam's Sons, 1940.

Higgins, Jack. *The Eagle Has Landed*. London: Pan, 1976.

Irving, David. *Churchill's War*. New York: Avon, 1987.

James, Robert Rhodes. (Edited) *Chips: The Diaries of Sir Henry Channon*. Harmondsworth, Middlesex. UK: Penguin: 1970.

James, Robert Rhodes. *Churchill: A Study in Failure*. Cleveland, OH: World Publishing, 1970.

Jenkins, Roy. *Churchill: A Biography*. New York: Penguin, 2001.

Jones, R. V. *Most Secret War*. London: Hodder and Stoughton, 1979.

Kahn, David. *Hitler's Spies: German Military Intelligence In World War II*. Cambridge, MA: Da Capo Press, 1978.

Kater, Michael, H. *Hitler Youth*. Cambridge, MA: Harvard UP, 2004.

Keegan, John. *The Second World War*. New York: Penguin, 1989.

Klein, Alexander. *The Counterfeit Traitor*. New York: Pocket Books, 1958.

Klemperer, Victor. *I Will Bear Witness [Ich will Zeiugnis ablegen bis zum letzten: Tagebücher 1933–1945 von Vitor Klemperer]*. Berlin: Random House, 1995.

Liddell Hart, B. H. *History of the Second World War*. New York: G. P. Putnam's Sons, 1970.

Longfellow, Henry Wadsworth. *The Poems of Henry Wadsworth Longfellow with Biographical Sketch by Nathan Haskell Dole*. New York: Thomas Y. Corwell Company, 1901.

Lukacs, John. *A Thread of Years*. New Haven: Yale UP, 1998.

MacMillan, Harold. *The Blast of War: 1939–1945*. New York: Harper & Row, 1968.

Makovsky, Michael. *Churchill's Promised Land: Zionism and Statecraft*. New Haven, Yale UP, 2007.

Manchester, William. *The Last Lion: Winston Spencer Churchill, Alone 1932–1940*. Boston: Little, Brown and Company, 1988.

Marson, Peter J. *The Lockheed Twins*. Tonbridge, Kent: Air Britain Historians, 2001.

Martin Moreno, Francisco. *Mexico Secreto*. Mexico: Joaquin Mortiz. Mexico D. F.. Editorial Planeta, 2002.

Masterman, J. C. *The Double-Cross System in the War of 1939 to 1945*. New Haven: Yale UP, 1972.

Maugham, W. Somerset. *Ashenden or The British Agent*. New York: Doubleday, 1941.

McCartney, Laton. *The Teapot Dome Scandal*. New York: Random House, 2008.

McGovern, James. *Crossbow and Overcast*. New York: William Morrow, 1964.

Montagu, Ewen. *Beyond Top Secret Ultra*. New York: Coward, McCann & Geoghegan, 1978.

Montagu, Ewen. *The Man Who Never Was*. 1953. Reprint, Annapolis, MD: Naval Institute Press, 1996.

Morrison, David. *Heroes, Antiheroes and The Holocaust: American Jewry and Historical Choice*. Jerusalem: Milah, 1995.

Mosley, Leonard. *On Borrowed Time: How World War II Began*. New York: Random House, 1969.

Nicolson, Nigel. *The Harold Nicolson Diaries 1907–1963*. London: Orion, 2004.

O'Donnell, Patrick K. *Operatives, Spies, and Saboteurs*. New York: Kensington, 2004.

Overy, Richard. *1939 Countdown to War*. New York: Viking/ Penguin Group, 2010.

Oxford UP. *The Oxford Dictionary of Quotations, Third Edition*. Oxford: 1979.

Pool, James, and Suzanne Pool. *Who Financed Hitler: The Secret Funding of Hitler's Rise to Power, 1919–1933*. New York: Dial, 1978.

Ramsden, John, ed. *The Oxford Companion to Twentieth-Century British Politics*. Oxford: Oxford UP, 2002.

Record, Jeffrey. *The Specter of Munich: Reconsidering the Lessons of Appeasing Hitler*. Dulles, VA, Potomac Books, 2007.

Sand, Shlomo. *The Invention of the Jewish People*. London: Verso, 2009.

Segev, Tom. *One Palestine Complete*. New York: Henry Holt, 1999.

Shakespeare, William. *William Shakespeare: The Complete Works*. New York: Dorset, 1988.

Shermer, Michael and Alex Grobman. *Denying History*. Berkeley, CA: University of California Press, 2000.

Sherwood, Tim. *Coming in to Land: A Short History of Hounslow, Hanworth and Heston Aerodromes 1911-1946*. Hounslow, UK: Hounslow Library, Heritage Publications, 1999.

Smith, Herschel. *A History of Aircraft Piston Engines*. Manhattan, KS: Sunflower UP, 1981.

Soames, Mary. *Winston and Clementine; the Personal letters of the Churchills*. Boston and New York: [a Mariner Book] Houghton Mifflin Company; 2001.

Stevenson, William. *A Man Called Intrepid*. New York: The Lyons, 2000.

Taylor, A. J. P. *The Origins of The Second World War*. New York: Athenaeum, 1961.

Thompson, Inspector Walter Henry. *Assignment: Churchill*. New York: Farrar, Strauss and Young, 1955.

Verney, John. *Going to the Wars*. London: Collins & the Book Society, 1955.

Vincent, Isabel. *Hitler's Silent Partners*. New York: William Morrow, 1997.

Waln, Nora. *The Approaching Storm*. 1939. Reprint, London: The Atlantic Monthly/Little Brown and Co., 1967.

Watt, Donald Cameron. *How War Came: The Immediate Origins of the Second World War, 1938–1939*. New York: Pantheon, 1989.

Weinberg, Gerhard L. *World in the Balance: Behind the Scenes of World War II*. Hanover: University Press of New England, 1981.

Weir, L. Macneill. *The Tragedy of Ramsay MacDonald: A Political Biography*. London: Secker & Warburg, 1938.

Weiss, Brian. *Same Soul, Many Bodies*. New York: Free Press, 2004.

Weiss, Brian. *Many Lives, Many Masters*. New York: Fireside, 1988.

Wicks, H. W. *The Prisoner Speaks*. London: Jarrolds, 1938.

Woolger, Roger J. *Other Lives, Other Selves*. New York: Bantam, 1987.

Wright, Peter, with Paul Greengrass. *Spycatcher: The Candid Autobiography of a Senior Intelligence Officer*. New York: Viking Penguin, 1987.

Young, Brigadier Peter. *The World Almanac Book of World War II*. Upper Saddle River, NJ: Prentice Hall, 1981.

Other Sources

Langham, Rob. "Is the reluctance of aircraft manufacturers to implement changes in their designs a major cause of airliner accidents? A discussion." Aviation Honours Project, London Metropolitan University.

Films

Amelia. A Mira Nair Film. Fox Searchlight Pictures and Avalon Pictures; 2009.

Dead Again. A Kenneth Branagh film. Paramount Pictures; 1991.

The Man Who Never Was. Andre Hachim Director. Twentieth Century fox; 1955.

Newspaper and Magazine Sources

The London Times (London)

The Daily Telegraph

Daily Mirror

Urmston Western Telegraph

Stretford Borough News

The Chronicle (Oldham)

Manchester Guardian

Lancaster Observer and Morecambe

Chronicle

(Lancaster, Lancashire, England)

Lancaster Guardian and *General Adv. Of North Counties*

(Lancaster, Lancashire, England)

All of the following Danish or German Newspapers were used from August 15, 1939 (evening editions) until August 18, 1939. As the world began to face World War II, the G-AESY became old news fast.

Praesto Avis

Fredericksborg Amts Avis

Politiken

Amstidende

Vordingborg Dagblad; Folkeblad for Vordingborgegnen

Berlinske Tidende

Lollands Falster Folketidende

Nordsjellands Vensteblad Social-Demokraten

Braunschweiger Tageblatt Braunschweiger Anzeiger

Storstomsbroen 50 Ar (Special edition commemorating 50 years of the Bridge with a two page story on August 15, 1939 including four photographs).

Flyvehistorisk Tidsskrift (Dansk Flyvehistorisk Forening) 1-88 February.

Pages 17-21 and 23

The New York Times

FlyPast

National Geographic

Planes and Pilot

Flight Magazine

Flight Magazine (Flight Global Archives)

April 8, 1937, page 348, "Wrightways Go Ahead."

December 9, 1937, page 584, "Accident Investigations."

April 27, 1939, page 439, "Intava LTD."

June 15, 1939, page 616, "Airline Fleet Maintenance."

August 24, 1939, page 186, "Another British Airways Loss."

June 23, 1949, page 745, "Operating Factors and Design."

June 6, 1952, page 679, "Advice from Experience."

March 25, 1955, page 383, "Maintenance of Helicopters."

May 13, 1960, page 657, "Plant Representative."

INTERNET SOURCES

Search Engines

Yahoo UK and Ireland

Yahoo Deutschland

Yahoo Danmark

Other Internet Sources

Please note that to access some of the sites included, one must first go to a search engine for the specific country where the site is found.

www.TheyWorkForYou.com

Keeping tabs on the UK's parliaments & assemblies.

www.hansard.millbanksystems.com UK Parliament

www.ajjcollection.co.uk

This photographic collection is where I found photos of the G-AESY from around 1939, ready to leave, we believe, from Croydon Airport.

www.flightsafety.org

Aviation safety Network; detailed information on the G-AESY.

www.criticalpast.com

There are several videos of interest, and still photos can be purchased. The stills can also be published; the author was informed on April 5, 2011, by Critical Past at (800)249-4430 or (302)742-4153. This book used specifically the video clips numbered 65675035704, 65675035705, 65675035706 and

65675035711; Neville Chamberlain walks past the G-AESY on his way to Munich.

www.kcl.ac.uk

Note by Liddell Hart on discussions with Anthony Crossley, MP, about the production of antiaircraft guns.

www.history.co.uk

Biographies of all political figures mentioned.

www.isracast.com

Isracast is a multimedia broadcast and distribution network through which I searched for Avraham Stern and the Irgun Zwei Leuimi.

www.mtholyoke.edu

This is the site where the memorandum for the "Attorney General Relative to a Request for Grand Jury Authorization to Investigate the International Oil Cartel," June 24, 1952, is found. (Intava) www.parliament.uk

All groups, places, and individuals mentioned in the book were researched on this site.

English, Danish and German Wikipedia.

en.wikipedia.org

da.wikipedia.org

de.wikipedia.org

All historical British personalities and events mentioned in the book were researched on this site.

www.spartacus.schoolnet.co.uk

I searched for airplane engineers, Lockheed Electra, and Intava on this site.

www.Flightglobal.com

I searched for the Irgun or Zwei Leumi as well as the Stern Gang and the Munich Pact on this site.

www.jewishvirtuallibrary.org

I searched for all individuals from the G-AESY and those who investigated it on this site.

www.ancestry.com

Key Publishing is Europe's leading aviation publisher, according to their website.

KeyPublishing.com

National Archives UK. Although I visited them on several occasions, some of the files used for the book were purchased from them online.

www.nationalarchives.gov.uk

I searched for information on Rockefeller and Standard Oil on this site.

www.reformation.org

Chapter 4, Standard Oil Fuels WWII.

http://www.reformed-theology.org/html/books/wall_street/chapter_11.htm

AirAccUK.htm (local)

History of Air Accidents Investigation Branch, UK.

www.lockheedelectra10a.com

www.wonderful_denmark.com

www.vikingdenmark.com

ARCHIVES

The National Archives UK

Kew, Surrey TW9 4DU, UK www.nationalarchives.gov.uk

British Airways Heritage Center

Heathrow Airport

Hounslow, Middlesex

Greater London TW6 2JA, UK www.bamuseum.com

Rigsarkivet

The Danish National Archives

Rigsdagsgaarden 9 DK-1218 Copenhagen, DK www.sa.dk

The box file I was allowed to work with at the police station in Nykøbing Falster is an archive that needs to be requested through the Danish police.

Author Biography

M. C. V. Egan lives in South Florida. She is fluent in four languages; English, Spanish, French, and Swedish. From a young age, she became determined to solve the mystery of her grandfather's death. She has researched this story for almost two decades. The story has taken her to Denmark, England, and the unconventional world of psychics and past lives.

VISIT HER WEBSITE

http://thebridgeofdeaths.com/